1803

To
Rich Edsall,
with appreciation and
best wishes,
Charles

Liberty and Morality

American University Studies

Series IX
History
Vol. 162

PETER LANG
New York • Washington, D.C./Baltimore • San Francisco
Bern • Frankfurt am Main • Berlin • Vienna • Paris

Charles W. Snyder

Liberty and Morality

A Political Biography of Edward Bulwer-Lytton

PETER LANG
New York • Washington, D.C./Baltimore • San Francisco
Bern • Frankfurt am Main • Berlin • Vienna • Paris

Library of Congress Cataloging-in-Publication Data

Snyder, Charles W. (Charles William).
    Liberty and morality: a political biography of Edward Bulwer-Lytton /
Charles W. Snyder.
        p.   cm. — (American university studies. Series IX, History;
vol. 162)
    Includes bibliographical references and index.
    1. Lytton, Edward Bulwer Lytton, Baron, 1803–1873—Political and
social views. 2. Politics and literature—Great Britain—History—
19th century. 3. Great Britain—Politics and government—1837–1901.
4. Novelists, English—19th century—Biography. 5. Politicians—Great
Britain—Biography. I. Title. II. Series.
PR4931.S6   823'.8—dc20   [B]   94-900
ISBN 0-8204-2471-4
ISSN 0740-0426

Die Deutsche Bibliothek-CIP-Einheitsaufnahme

Snyder, Charles W.:
Liberty and morality: a political biography of Edward Bulwer-Lytton /
Charles W. Snyder - New York; Washington D.C./Baltimore; San Francisco;
Bern; Frankfurt am Main; Berlin; Vienna; Paris: Lang
    (American university studies: Ser. 9, History; Vol. 162)
    ISBN 0-8204-2471-4
NE: American university studies / 09

The paper in this book meets the guidelines for permanence and durability of
the Committee on Production Guidelines for Book Longevity of the
Council on Library Resources.

Printed in the United States of America.

For My Parents

Beneath the rule of men entirely great
The pen is mightier than the sword.

Edward Bulwer-Lytton

TABLE OF CONTENTS

PREFACE

I would like to begin by expressing my debt of gratitude to Professor Nicholas C. Edsall, who directed the dissertation on which this biography is based. After each of my many conversations with Professor Edsall, I left feeling that the task before me was somehow simpler and easier than it had seemed before. His deep reserves of learning and sagacity were invaluable resources for me in this undertaking.

I would also like to thank Professor Martin J. Havran for his many helpful comments and suggestions about this biography, and for the wise counsel from which I have gained so much over the course of many years.

I am obliged to the staffs of numerous libraries and archives: those of the Firestone Library at Princeton, the Huntington Library, the Boston Public Library, and the National Trust at Hughenden, among others. In particular, I would like to thank Mr. Peter Walne and his staff at the Hertfordshire County Record Office, where I did the greater part of my research, for their help and cooperation.

I wish to express my thanks to Lord Cobbold for giving me permission to quote from the Lytton Papers.

I also want to thank Dennis Frampton and Rachelle Cummings for all their work in preparing the manuscript.

I also want to acknowledge my debt of gratitude to the late Frances Lackey for her many helpful editorial comments. I only wish she were here to see the final product.

Finally, I want to express my gratitude to my parents, Benjamin and Fay Snyder, for all they have done, and for all that they are to me.

Edw Lytton Bulwer

INTRODUCTION

This book is about the political life of the Victorian novelist, Edward Bulwer-Lytton. Once renowned, now nearly forgotten, Bulwer-Lytton captured the spirit of his times as well as any of the more celebrated authors of the era. Notwithstanding posterity's unflattering opinion of his talents, the exceptional popularity he enjoyed in his own day highlights his stature as a spokesman for an age. His books were best sellers precisely because of his instinctive understanding of the moods and aspirations, the hopes and the fears, the tastes and the prejudices of Victorian Britain. To help understand that time and place, this study focuses on Bulwer-Lytton, not as a writer, but as a public figure who eloquently expressed thoughtful opinions on the controversies of the day.

Bulwer-Lytton had a long and active political career. He won his first election to the House of Commons in 1831; he did not finally leave that body until 1866, when he was elevated to the House of Lords. He witnessed, and participated in, the transformation of Britain from oligarchy to democracy. Indeed, his political career spanned the era of Parliamentary Reform that began with the Reform Act of 1832 and culminated in the Reform Act of 1867.

When Bulwer-Lytton first sought a seat in the Commons in the early 1830's, he had to concern himself not with winning the votes of the masses but with gaining the favor of the few who exercised influence in Parliamentary boroughs. Most boroughs were controlled by powerful magnates or by corrupt coteries of voters. Because the electoral map had remained unchanged for centuries, some uninhabited places remained Parliamentary boroughs, while many a rising metropolis sent no representatives at all to Westminster. The 1832 Reform Act gave the vote to owners or tenants who occupied premises with a clear yearly value of ten pounds. The effect of this franchise varied, just as property values varied, from place to place. But the common oversimplification that the Reform Act enfranchised the middle class, but not the working class, has a substantial measure of truth. Still, the Act set in motion the march of democracy and foreshadowed far greater extensions of the franchise in the future. These portents of popular government would preoccupy Bulwer-Lytton, and many of his contempories, for decades to come.

The fact that the Victorian Age witnessed the progress of political liberty is overshadowed by its reputation as a time of repression. The image of an era of stifling moralism, while not without basis, amounts to a caricature of a complex period of history. Despite its celebrated excesses, Victorian sensibility also fostered a collective social conscience mindful of the obligations the rich owed to the poor. It was a time when popular conventions derived from experience, not experimentation. The tension between the expansion of liberty and a transcendent public morality gave the Victorian Age its unique character.

Because he was for so many years active both as a writer of popular novels and as a participant in politics, Bulwer-Lytton gave special attention to this relationship between liberty and morality. With his distinctive eloquence in addressing, as author and Parliamentarian, the subjects of liberty, morality, and order, he spoke, not only for his era, but to posterity as well. This is the reason that warrants the present reconsideration of his political career.

CHAPTER ONE

INORDINATELY AMBITIOUS

All his life, Edward Bulwer-Lytton pursued two careers: one in literature, the other in politics. In both, he set his sights for the summit of achievement, and as a novelist at least he seemed to have succeeded. For consistent popularity, his books outstripped those of all the other authors of his generation, even Charles Dickens. Bulwer-Lytton could never have suspected, of course, that after his death a critical reaction would deprive him of his standing among the masters of English letters. He thus died confident of literary immortality.[1]

But Bulwer-Lytton never did so well in his political career, and the wonder was that he did not abandon politics altogether, considering how much better he was faring as a novelist; this would have suited his proud, self-conscious, hypersensitive personality. The fact that he did persevere in politics suggests a compulsion: as if his two careers reflected two distinct sides of his personality. Much as he loved literature, literary success failed to satisfy all his ambition. He needed to be a man of action as well.

The name "Bulwer-Lytton" itself symbolizes this duality of character.[2] "Bulwer" was his father's family name and "Lytton" his mother's. At the risk of falling into the fashion of attributing every dichotomy in any individual's character to conflicting maternal/paternal strains, one can suggest that Bulwer-Lytton derived his political ambition through the influence of his father, and his literary taste from his mother. Aptly then should these two surnames stand on either side of the hyphen — the punctuation mark that suggests both conflict and combination — in the name of the scion of these two ill-matched clans.

Actually "Bulwer-Lytton" was only one of several surnames the subject of this biography bore; many contemporary critics ridiculed his apparent affectation of changing his name.[3] In retrospect, these changes seem symbolic. In his early life, when he went by "Bulwer", his ambition for a political career loomed the larger, and he viewed his literary talent as a tool to further his advancement in politics. By middle age, however, he was clearly doing better as a novelist; and his writing began to matter as much or more to him than politics. At this stage he was calling himself "Bulwer-Lytton." In old age, upon his elevation to the peerage, he chose the title "Lord Lytton of Knebworth." The years that followed he devoted to his literary interests. Never did he speak in the House of Lords. To all practical purposes, his political ambition had vanished, as had the "Bulwer" from his name.[4]

I have said that Bulwer-Lytton derived his political ambition from the example of his father, although his father had not himself been a politician, but a soldier. Nonetheless, General William Bulwer served as a model of worldly ambition for his son, for, while Bulwer-Lytton never really knew his father (who died when he was only four years old), he inherited many of his father's characteristics. For a time he even planned to become a soldier, too, but instead channeled this drive into politics.

General Bulwer himself had by no means been insignificant. During the Napoleonic War he commanded one of the four military districts into which Britain had been divided under the plan for resisting the expected French invasion. The invasion never came, and General Bulwer, as if frustrated at being deprived of his chance at martial glory, devoted his remaining years to another sort of campaign, attaining recognition for his services through a peerage. He had in mind for himself the grandiloquent if unwieldy title, "Lord South Erpingham." Unexpectedly, however, he died, his ambition still unfulfilled, but left as a legacy to his son.[5]

Bulwer-Lytton did inherit this ambition, and resembled his father in other ways as well. General Bulwer's personality combined the qualities of a provincial squire and a military despot, at once proud and petty, imperious and impatient. Bulwer-Lytton would grow up equally proud, equally quick to quarrel. And in no way did father and son more resemble each other than in their conduct as husbands. General Bulwer wrecked his marriage by treating his wife cruelly, and Bulwer-Lytton, the child of that failed marriage, caused his own to fail by doing just the same.[6]

It is especially odd that Bulwer-Lytton should have taken after his father as much as he did, since, from his birth, he was emphatically his mother's son. He was all she had. By the time Edward was born, Elizabeth Lytton Bulwer no longer loved her husband. She no longer had control of her first two sons, for the eldest, William, had gone to Norfolk to be the heir to General Bulwer's estate there, and the second son, Henry, virtually snatched away from his mother, had gone into the care of his maternal grandmother, destined to be her heir. For Elizabeth, only Edward remained. Upon him she concentrated all her hitherto suppressed affection.[7]

Edward Bulwer grew up, then, practically an only child. He had his mother's love, but no satisfactory family life. His father had disliked him. So also did the only other male authority figure (after the General's death) he knew: his maternal grandfather, Richard Warburton Lytton.[8] Nonetheless, Richard Warburton Lytton — albeit unknowingly — potently influenced his grandson's development. Scholarly and devoid of personal ambition, he represented the antithesis of General Bulwer, thus serving as Edward Bulwer's model of the purely literary man. Richard Warburton Lytton was indeed a great scholar. He belonged to that peculiar breed whose mother tongue, one could fairly say, was Latin. He had mastered several other dead languages as well, and even wrote a full length play in Hebrew, purely as an intellectual exercise. No wonder Bulwer-Lytton would write that his grandfather "loved learning for learning's self. He disentangled himself from the world, from pleasure, from ambition. . . ."[9]

The Lytton influence accounted for Edward Bulwer's intellectual precocity. He was fortunate to have as a mother a woman as cultured and intelligent as one would expect the daughter of so scholarly a man to be. And Edward's childish imagination joyously comprehended the spirit of "Lyttonism." He would always remember how, as a child, he roamed among the books in his grandfather's voluminous library:

> Where I found a book in English it sufficed for me, no matter how dry and how far above my reason; I still looked and lingered — read and wondered. All variety of dim ideas thus met and mingled in my brain. Many an atom of knowledge, chipped off from the block and stored up unconsciously in the mind, was whirled into movement in later years . . . .[10]

In his novels, Bulwer-Lytton frequently described reclusive scholars resembling his grandfather. In one of the earliest of his novels, *Pelham* (1828), such a character appears: "Clutterbuck." From his description of this character, we may gauge Bulwer's attitude at that point toward the type of life his grandfather had lived:

The mere man of languages and learning—the machine of a memory heavily but unprofitably employed. . . —for him there is no daydream of the future, no grasp at the immortality of fame. Beyond the walls of his narrow room he knows no object; beyond the elucidation of a dead tongue he indulges no ambition; his life is one long school-day of lexicons and grammars . . . elaborately useless, ingeniously unprofitable; and leaving at the moment it melts away, not a single trace of the space it occupied, or the labor it cost.[11]

This, to reiterate, was written in his youth, when Bulwer himself was unabashedly "grasping at the immortality of fame." By middle age, his attitude had altered, as we can see from his novel *The Caxtons* (1849) in which another character based on Richard Warburton Lytton appears: "Austin Caxton," an utterly unworldly scholar, habitually absorbed in his obscure researches to the extent that he cannot concentrate on even the most pressing matters of business. He is nonetheless a lovable character, sympathetic, warm, and wise. And, significantly, "Austin Caxton" has a brother, a military man, "Captain Roland de Caxton," (the nobiliary particle insisted upon), a bluff, simple man, to whom honor is the guiding principle for all that is worthwhile in mankind. At one time, "Austin" and "Roland" had not gotten on, for, among other reasons, they had squabbled over whether they could claim descent from William Caxton, the first English printer (as "Austin" proudly maintained), or from a knight of the same name who had fought at Bosworth Field for Richard III (as "Roland" insisted). But in the course of the book, the brothers grew to understand each other. Even the question of descent became a moot point, as, for affection's sake, each would take the other's side.[12] We must conclude that just as "Austin" represents Richard Warburton Lytton, so "Roland" is an idealized portrait of General William Bulwer; that the brothers' former antagonism stands for the conflict within Bulwer-Lytton himself, between the two contradictory elements in his own nature; and that the reconciliation of the two "Caxtons" suggests that at the time he wrote this book Bulwer-Lytton had at last succeeded in reconciling the two sides of his own personality.

This point (at length) made, let us commence an account of the young Edward Bulwer's development. For reasons we have seen, he grew up under the protection of his mother, apart from the rest of his family. He got used to passing his time alone. Isolation led to introversion, and introversion to introspection. But an excess of that last characteristic hastened the end of his safe if over-sanitized childhood idyll. When only eight, he approached his mother with the following question:

"Pray, mama, are you not sometimes overcome by the sense of your own identity?"

Mrs. Bulwer decided then the time had come for her son to go to school.[13]

Bulwer's schooldays marked the first contact between this fastidious, sensitive boy and the insensitive world. At none of the schools he attended did Bulwer ever fit in (and, not fitting in, he went to many schools). If he could not belong, at least he could lead. That he would try to do when he grew older, but at his first school, when so small and so inexperienced, he could do nothing except be miserable. He never forgot what happened:

> Oh, that first night, when my mother was gone, the last kiss given, the door closed, and I alone with the little mocking fiends to whom my anguish was such glee! I was an especial and singular diversion to them, not having been brought up with other boys. My utter ignorance of their low, gross slang, the disgust with which their language, their habits, their very looks, inspired me — all this was excellent sport for them.[14]

There followed, inevitably, beatings at the hands of bullies, and these led him in due course to a determined study of the art of boxing. If he could not make himself liked, he would make himself feared. After a few years at school, Bulwer would recall, he "became . . . fond of athletic pursuits, and was esteemed the best pugilist of the school."[15]

At school, skill in sports usually brings popularity as a matter of course. Bulwer, however, remained too much "overcome with the sense of his own identity"; he never did learn to submerge his individuality so to become merely one member of a group. In a quasi-autobiographical novel, *The Disowned*, he recalled this difficulty under the guise of describing the book's leading character, "Algernon Mordaunt":

> Truth obliges us to state, despite our partiality to Mordaunt, that when he left his school, after a residence of six years, it was with the bitter distinction of having been the most unpopular boy in it. His ill health, his long residence at home, his unfriended and almost orphan situation, his early habits of solitude and reserve, all these . . . made him, on his entrance at school, if not unsocial, appear so: this was the primary

reason of his unpopularity; the second was that . . . he was sensitive
. . . to the . . . misfortune of his manner, and in his wish to rectify it,
it became doubly unprepossessing; to reserve, it now added
embarrassment, to coldness, gloom; and the pain he felt in addressing
or being addressed by another, was naturally and necessarily
reciprocal. . . .[16]

With popularity impossible, only ambition remained: Bulwer's dream
that he might outstrip his fellows and command their esteem. And his
pride, fostered since childhood by a mother who regarded her family as
among the most aristocratic in England, grew proportionately with his
loneliness. What did it matter if others failed to appreciate him; better to
consider this their failing rather than his own, and still more proof of his
superiority to the "herd."

In his unfinished novel *Lionel Hastings,* Bulwer drew a portrait of
himself as a schoolboy, in the form of a letter from a fictional
schoolmaster to "Lionel Hastings'" mother:

The quality most pronounced in him is energy and his worst fault, as
a schoolboy, is his impatience of routine and discipline . . . . He is not
exactly quarrelsome, but he is terribly fond of fighting . . . . He is
very fearless, and on the point of honor, only too Quixotic. But . . .
there is another side to the medal. Your son is not an amiable boy. He
seems to have little or no tenderness in his nature. He forms no
friendships with his school-fellows; which I think a bad sign both of
temper and disposition. He is inordinately ambitious (sleeps with
"Plutarch's Lives" under his pillow), has much too high an opinion of
himself; and in word, does not seem to me likely . . . to be popular in
domestic life; nor yet to stoop to that subordination, or manifest that
respect for others . . . necessary to the conduct of any young man who
would rise in public life.[17]

The outstanding point in this passage concerns the youth's "quixotic"
obsession with "honor"; this ideal, which he associated in his mind with
his father,[18] remained with him through life and frequently clouded his
judgment.

When Bulwer's "impatience of . . . discipline" caused his expulsion
from one school,[19] he was removed to a private school at Ealing, where
the able tutoring of the Reverend Charles Wallington at last readied him
for the University, and for life. Bulwer liked and admired the Rev.
Wallington, whom he pointedly remembered as "a very handsome man,

with an air more martial than priestly." The Rev. Wallington taught more than the classics; he often read to his students from the "Parliamentary Debates," and Bulwer would remember how this "infected" him with "the passion for public affairs." The Rev. Wallington also encouraged students to make speeches of their own, and Bulwer "caught from this practice quite an oratorical mania," and he "mouthed out declamations with the enthusiasm of an embryo Gracchus."[20]

At Ealing, Bulwer laid the intellectual foundations of a lifetime. He voraciously read both popular works and classics, and especially immersed himself in poetry. As always with him, books were "incentives to action."[21] Impatient to make a name for himself, Bulwer spent much of his spare time composing verses, very much in the Byronic vogue. Whatever their real merit, these juvenile poems impressed the Rev. Wallington, who decided they merited publication; and he managed to persuade Mrs. Bulwer, who had her doubts, to permit committing these verses to print. Bulwer himself also wrote home to explain why he wanted to publish so early in life:

> I certainly intend publishing at some period of my life . . . . But it will be far more advantageous for me to publish now . . . [as] any faults . . . committed, would [later in life] be noted and criticized; now, however, they would be overlooked. My Youth, like the shield of Ajax, will ward off those darts which, at a later age, can meet no considerable resistance or obstacle . . . . In the law, or any other profession I may embrace, or even at College, it will be of the greatest assistance to me. It will give me a passport, not only to the best company (to which, independently of that, your connections and my rank would entitle me), but what is far more rare, and to me more valuable, the first literary society.[22]

One should note three points in this letter: how Bulwer already regarded literary success as a "passport" to greater things; how he proclaimed himself a born aristocrat entitled by "rank" to the best society;[23] and his sensitivity to criticism, even before the dawn of his literary career. His hypersensitivity would eventually become notorious. But it was assumed that the incessant ridicule *Fraser's* magazine and other publications heaped upon him and his early novels made him that way.[24] Instead, Bulwer's early home environment and school experiences bequeathed to him his thin skin, just as they accounted for his ambition, pride, and friendlessness.

Bulwer's little book of verse, *Ismael, an Oriental Tale*, duly appeared in 1820. Few read it, of course, but those few thought the author a prodigy. It was a wonderful experience for a youngster of seventeen; but it would not be for *Ismael* that Bulwer would remember Ealing: for it was at Ealing that he first fell in love.

He met a village girl, and soon they felt for one another "a pure and passionate" attachment. Then, tragically, she stopped coming to their rendezvous by the river; her father, Bulwer would learn, had forced her to marry; and, within a few years, presumably pining away for her true love, she died. From her deathbed she had written Bulwer, requesting he visit her grave. He did so, passing at that spot a night of stormy emotions; he left at dawn, feeling "as if rebaptized or re-born."[25]

Bulwer-Lytton frequently drew upon this experience in his literary work, notably *Kenelm Chillingly* (1873) the last of his novels. Thus, it would seem, he felt the loss of his first love to the end of his days. But then, one also feels, had such a tragedy as this never occurred, Bulwer would have invented one. He had need of darkness in his past; for, at Ealing, he fell under an influence which profoundly affected his outlook, and which he never fully shook off: the Byron mania.

True, "Byronism" affected an entire generation, and many otherwise well-adjusted youths were acting it up as melancholy corsairs. But Bulwer was particularly affected, — so much so that some of his friends began addressing him as "Childe Harold."[26] For him, Byron was more than a poet, more even than an idol: he was an inspiration, a heroic model who enlarged for him the horizons of future possibility. Bulwer would recall how Byron had nourished his

> craving for adventure and wild incident which the habit of watching for many years the events of a portentous War, and the meteoric career of the modern Alexander, naturally engendered. . . .

And, Bulwer recalled, too, the devastating impact of Byron's death:

> Never shall I forget the singular, the stunning sensation, which the intelligence produced. I was exactly at that age, half man and half boy, in which the poetical sympathies are most keen. . . . We could not believe the bright race was run. So much of us died with him, that the notion of his death had something of the unnatural, of the impossible. It was as if a part of the mechanism of the very world stood still. . . ,

and all our worship of his genius was not so strongly felt as our love for himself.[27]

A poet and a man of action, Byron had appealed to both sides of Bulwer's personality. Thus we see the influence of Byron not only in the style of his verses, but in the growth of his ambition. At this time, he wrote frankly enough to one of his school-mates:

I intend to have my letters published after my death, like every other great man. And I hope therefore you will take the hint and not destroy either by fire or sword my epistles.[28]

Another of his schoolboy letters gives us our first hint about his political opinions, fired by the Rev. Wallington:

The Ropers are . . . extremely rich . . . . Their only son is just of age, and, *mirabile dictu*, without a foot of land in the county has set up for a candidate at St. Albans. What venal, what infamous elections are those of boroughs! They are bought and sold like cattle, and the Guardian of our laws, the Rectifier of the mistakes of the nation, the Representative of the Majesty of the People, is placed in our senate, either as a Tool to be employed by those who obtain him the office, or by an abominable pecuniary contract enters (himself in either way a mercenary and base character) to that *sanctum sanctorum* of Britain, her Parliament.[29]

This incipient radicalism, of course, foreshadows Bulwer's advocacy of the Parliamentary Reform Act of 1832. But more interesting is the aristocratic premise that led him to his radical conclusion. The spectacle of interlopers elbowing aside the landed class, buying their way into Parliament, — this stirs his indignation; instinctively he stands for the principle of deference and for the traditional social cohesion now undermined by low greed and tainted money. It would be thirty years before Bulwer-Lytton actually associated himself with Tory Radicalism; but this letter shows how early on his thinking already tended in that direction.

We have abundant information about Bulwer's political opinions from 1820 on; for in that year he entered Cambridge University, where he devoted much of his time to debating at the Union. There, Bulwer took the liberal side on nearly every issue. He supported, for instance, a resolution stating that "a systematic opposition to the measures of the [Tory] Administration [is] conducive to the happiness of the people"; he also argued that the suspension of the Habeas Corpus Act in 1794 was not justified; and that the reign of George III had not favored the liberties of the subject. On the other hand, when the Union debated the relative merits of the British versus the American Constitution, Bulwer's aristocratic bias led him to prefer the British.[30]

At these debates, Bulwer had the chance to match wits with many of the most brilliant of his contemporaries. An able debater, Bulwer nonetheless made a very slight impression compared to such rivals as Thomas Babington Macaulay or Winthrop Mackworth Praed. Another Cambridge man of the period remembered that young Bulwer "was always heard with lively interest, for he had studied his subject, and my impression was that, to some extent at least, he had prepared his speech."[31] Here was a left-handed compliment indeed, — considering the premium debaters placed on sounding fresh and spontaneous.

Bulwer needed elaborate preparation; without it, he would lose his nerve. Despite his egotism, he remained unsure of himself when appearing before others. For example, in July 1825, when he won the much coveted gold medal for English poetry (for a poem called "Sculpture"), he wrote the following letter to his speech teacher:

> Will you now favor one by a line to say whether I can attend your instructions tomorrow, and if so what hour will be convenient . . . . I have obtained a prize at the University for a poem which I shall have to recite. I read so excessively ill that I look forward to this recitation much more as a painful ordeal than an honorable exhibition and I wish therefore to avail myself of what benefit I can derive from your lessons during the week.[32]

Bulwer would labor for years to improve as a speaker, but improvement, when it came, came slowly. Bulwer knew he had to master the arts of articulation before he could hope to master the House of Commons. In that era, the power of speech governed men as never before or since. Bulwer had a long way to go at this stage, but he was doing his best to get ready.

After finishing his studies at Cambridge, Bulwer embarked on a tour of England, and then on a "grand tour" of France. The latter was almost mandatory for young men of his class, but the former was decidedly unusual, and therefore more important. It gave him special insight into his country and his countrymen. Dressing himself so as not to attract notice, he mingled with the poorest classes. He observed everything with the discerning eye of an incipient novelist; and how well he learned the habits and even the slang of paupers and highwaymen is evident from *Paul Clifford* and other books. The tour also affected his political outlook. He saw how poverty and crime went together, and how the brutality of the law achieved nothing except further to demoralize the people. His observations, as well as his studies, made him a radical reformer.

At the same time, his experiences caused him to take a jaundiced view of extreme reformers. Prominent among the latter was Robert Owen, the Utopian Socialist, whom Bulwer visited when his tour took him to Scotland. When Owen poured forth his theories on how to regenerate mankind, Bulwer listened in admiration; when Owen showed off his school—full of well disciplined, well educated children—Bulwer was again impressed. But he had second thoughts later, after conversing with an old woman of the neighborhood. She astonished Bulwer by telling him Owen's students "turned out vera ill!" When Bulwer asked why, she explained:

> "They have never been taught this," and she laid her locked hands on the Bible. "They have no religion, and what is to support them . . . when they go into the world?"[33]

Ever afterward, Bulwer would emphasize the importance of religion and morality in education. He regarded these influences, and not repressive laws, as the true antidote to crime and social unrest. In time, he would come to perceive an interconnection, indeed, a mutual interdependence, among three ideals: morality, liberty, and order. That is to say, — liberty can flourish only in a society whose moral principles gird it against excesses that would otherwise undermine the social order. In this basic idea we find the essence of Bulwer's political philosophy.

In the fall of 1825, Bulwer sailed for France. The spirit of his grand tour we can today divine from the delightful pages of *Pelham*: bouts of drinking and gambling, indulgence in French cuisine and Latin puns, affairs of honor and affairs of love. Here was Bulwer the dandy *par excellence*, whose *sang-froid* imperfectly disguised emotions that seethed underneath the surface. An acquaintance of his Paris days, a Miss Cunningham, remembered him thus:

He was at that time particularly sensitive to the praise or blame of the world. He adopted a style of dress and manner different to that of other people, and he liked to be noted for it. My mother often laughed at him for his vanity, and his "beautiful curls" were a standing joke amongst his friends.[34]

At school, Bulwer had been chagrined to find himself set apart from his peers, unable to mix with or share the feelings of others. Now, he accepted, even relished that state of affairs. He wanted to stand out; hence, his dandyism.

But it would be wrong to believe Bulwer was at any time a mere fop. He had too much ambition for that; even his dandyism served his ambition, because it attracted notice. Moreover, even during his stay in France, he kept his essential seriousness. Miss Cunningham also observed that, to Bulwer

prolonged dissipation was distasteful, and from this life of excitement he would often retire to Versailles, wandering there for weeks about the then deserted palace . . . . No doubt . . . one [other] motive for his frequent, often prolonged, and generally sudden, disappearances from the society of his friends, was his love of reading; which was even then, remarkable . . . . [35]

This impression is confirmed by notes Bulwer made during this tour, — accounts of visits to observatories, libraries, hospitals, churches, — all in an effort to understand the various levels of society and the social questions of the day.[36]

Even so light-hearted a book as *Pelham* would reveal the broadening of Bulwer's interests; amid its general frivolity he managed to denounce the severity of the game laws and the ineffectuality of English education.[37] Utilitarianism was becoming his passion, and Jeremy Bentham had succeeded Byron as the object of his admiration. And he wrote of the intellectual excitement he experienced on discovering his new philosophy:

. . . I was quite astonished at the new light which had gleamed upon me. I felt like Sinbad, the sailor, when, in wandering through the caverns in which he had been buried alive, he caught the first glimpse of the bright day. . . . I had no prejudices to contend with; no obscure notions gleaned from the past . . . . Every thing was placed before me as before a wholly impartial inquirer — freed from all the decorations and delusions of sects and parties . . . . We went over the whole . . .

Encyclopedia, over the more popular works of Bentham, and thence
we plunged into the recesses of political economy. I know not why
this study has been termed uninteresting. No sooner had I entered
upon its consideration, than I could scarcely tear myself from it . . . . [38]

These studies gave him a new sense of purpose. By the time of his
French tour, if not considerably earlier, Bulwer had decided to go into
politics. Not that he had discounted other possible careers; as with all
ambitious men, an element of opportunism affected his thinking. He was
determined to make his mark; it did not so much matter how. Politics was
one possibility, literature another; but it may well have been that a third
was the nearest to his heart's desire: the army and the chance for martial
glory.

It was not remarkable he should feel that way. Bulwer had before
him not only the example of his father, but of the men the age most
admired: Napoleon and Wellington; and even Byron had died a soldier.
As a schoolboy, Bulwer had seriously contemplated going off to the army
instead of to Cambridge, but did not for reasons plain enough from the
following letter, which he received from a friend of his mother's:

I am glad you do not follow the drum, both because it would have
pained the best of mothers, and because your head is fit for greater
things. I think you wrong yourself by saying you are not submissive,
and therefore unfit for the Army, where subordination is required.[39]

Strange he should have reconsidered this decision at age
twenty-three, when he had other fair prospects before him. Was this a
subconscious desire to emulate his father? One can only speculate. But
we do know that he became an officer in the British army in 1826,
purchasing for 450 pounds an unattached Ensigncy. However, he was not
appointed to a regiment, and following the success of his novel *Pelham*
a few years later, he sold the commission. It was only then his dreams of
military glory came to an end.[40]

That drive he would sublimate into politics, already the focus of his
active ambition. As noted, he had decided to try for the House of
Commons even before returning from his French tour. "I had long wished
to represent in Parliament the chief town of my own county,"he wrote in
1826, at the very moment a special election was in fact underway in
Hertford. Too impatient to wait until his return from France to stake his
claim, and confident his mother's connections in Hertford "had secured

its leading influence to the fulfillment of this wish," he mailed certain vital "letters and introductions" to his brother Henry Bulwer (the brothers had gotten to know one another at Cambridge) whom he apparently expected to act as his campaign manager. Henry, however, had loftier ambitions, and he used these very letters to set *himself* up as a candidate at Hertford.[41]

Though miffed, Edward Bulwer took the preemption in his stride, generously concluding that Henry had acted "from want of thought [and] not with any treacherous intention." But it did rankle to be the only non-candidate among the brothers Bulwer. Even William, the eldest and now a generally unambitious Norfolk squire, was standing for the House of Commons. But Edward was watchfully awaiting *his* chance. He even entered into negotiations for another seat, as he wrote to his friend in Paris, Mrs. Cunningham:

> As for myself, I will not spend money upon the very little chance there is (from the King's health) Parliament's lasting a sufficient time to answer to me. I have offered however £800 a year for a seat instead of paying the capital all at once, but I fear the offer will not be accepted — if not, I shall try hard for the next two or three years to acquire a literary reputation and come in with the next Parliament.[42]

Despite a third abortive try to win a seat later in the year — when we find him writing with transient confidence, "I have made myself an opening for the House; in all probability I shall enter it in December"[43] — he adhered to this plan. After all, under the prevailing system of borough mongering, seats cost money, and more of it than he could count on getting from his mother. To succeed in politics, he needed first to succeed in literature, not only for the sake of reputation, but for the sake of a steady income. In September, 1826, he wrote to Rosina Wheeler, setting forth his ambition in plain terms:

> There are two sorts of distinction to be gained-- *power* and *reputation*. Mr. Canning, for instance, has the former; Mr. Moore, the latter. In naming these persons you will see at once that *reputation* is obtained (in the highest degree) by exertion in literature, and power *almost solely* by devotion to politics. Now it is our object to obtain *power* rather than reputation; the latter gratifies *vanity, not pride*; it gives *eclat*, but no real importance. In this servile and aristocratic country we must make to ourselves a more independent and commanding rank.

For myself I should not care a straw about the fame of stringing couplets and making books . . . . Literary honors are not, therefore, so desirable as political rank; but they must not for that reason be despised; they are the great stepping stones to our ultimate object. To get *power* I must be in the House of Commons. To obtain my seat there, I must pay a certain sum of money. I find, however, that it can be done through the ministry for £1,100 a year; and directly I can raise that sum I can enter the House. My mother will pay £600 a year only — the remaining £500 I must, therefore, make up myself. I can spare nothing from my present income [his allowance] and this deficiency I therefore hope to supply by writing. I shall therefore, directly the winter begins, commence *regular author* . . . . If my works succeed, in the course of the winter, I expect before the *end of that* spring to be in the House. Then I consider the road clear.[44]

The recipient of this letter would herself make more difference to Bulwer's future than all these plans he was so confidently concocting. Rosina Wheeler — young, witty, attractive, Irish, and without a trace of respectability in her background — had already become his mistress, and would in less than a year be his wife. As she would profoundly affect Bulwer's political career, it is appropriate here to deal with the origins of their relationship.[45]

Contrary to the usual version of the matter, it seems likely they met just before, rather than after, his tour of France. Rosina, years later, told a confidant she first met Bulwer shortly before her twenty-third birthday; that is, before November 2, 1825. It must be, then, that they met in either September or October of 1825, and that Bulwer left for France a little later that same autumn.[46]

In the brief interval between their first meeting and his departure, they — probably — became lovers. It may well be that Bulwer's unsettled state of mind while in France — his bouts of gloom alternating with bursts of devil-may-care dissipation — resulted from anxiety about his relationship with Rosina. His over-developed sense of honor was troubling him; he considered it his duty to marry her. Although she certainly attracted him, it was his sense of honor, and not love, that was to bring about this ill-fated marriage.

While still in France, he wrote to his friend, Mrs. Cunningham:

I am at this time in a state of great and increasing anxiety. You may form an idea about this when I tell you that in England, to which I go solely by necessity, there is a person to whom I am bound by honor to sacrifice myself . . . . [47]

One might contemplate worse sacrifices than marriage to so beautiful a woman as Rosina Wheeler. Perhaps Bulwer was worrying about his political career. He was counting on his mother's financial backing to enable him to obtain a seat in the House of Commons; yet he knew his mother would oppose his marrying a woman like Rosina, — even to the extent of disowning him if he did so. In regard to his mother's ideas about whom he should marry, he once complained to Mrs. Cunningham:

According to her [i.e. his mother], to her Pedigree there never was a Family like the Lyttons and not above three Lady Maries in the Kingdom fit to marry with the descendant of the Runic Kings and the Norman Plantagenets.[48]

Rosina was no "Lady Mary." But Bulwer still felt obligated to her. Soon after his return to England in the Spring of 1826, he wrote again to Mrs. Cunningham, keeping her informed of his feelings:

I am returned to London. . . . I am still free — at least I may call myself. But do not congratulate me. The thought of it gives me no pleasure. I cannot sufficiently express to you my admiration, my depth of — not love, for it is a nobler, and even tenderer sentiment for — you know whom. And yet I am wretched, and scarcely know what I am writing. . . .[49]

About this time, or soon afterward, he proposed to Rosina, and she accepted him.[50] As expected, his mother bitterly opposed the marriage, and her attitude caused the engagement for a time to be broken off. But, because Bulwer had made Rosina his mistress, he could not abandon her without abandoning too his proud self-image as a "man of honor." Consequently, the engagement was renewed, and the wedding set for August 29, 1827.[51]

When Elizabeth Bulwer-Lytton realized all her blandishments would fail to prevent this marriage, she resorted to the threat of cutting off Edward's allowance, her last hope of changing his mind. To Edward, whose literary powers were as yet unproven, this threat seemed to sound the death knell for his hopes of entering Parliament. Just before the marriage, therefore, he wrote his mother to plead that she not forsake him:

> Put yourself in my place for one moment . . . . Only suppose that I see every hope, every object of ambition, I have cherished for years and years, cut down at one stroke; that this stroke must be dealt by my own hand; that I see myself condemned, in the very spring of my age, with every aspiration restless within me, to a life of seclusion and poverty forever . . . . Recollect my nature — never contented, never at rest — then ask yourself whether I need any aggravation of its miseries by you; and whether it must not be a powerful inducement that can make me confront and endure it. That inducement . . . is the conscientious conviction that I am acting rightly. . . . A man is either the slave of passion or the servant of duty. And in this matter, Heaven knows, I am not Passion's slave.[52]

Of course, Bulwer could not explain to his mother precisely why he believed it his duty to marry Rosina; in any event, this appeal failed, and Bulwer began his married life dependent on his pen to provide him his living.

His first novel, *Falkland* (1827), proved an inauspicious beginning. This morose tale of thwarted love was the final emanation of Bulwer's youthful Byronism, and for its remarkable evocation of that peculiar state of mind, it may interest readers of today. But at the time it fell flat. Nothing has less appeal than a fashion just past. And Bulwer learned he had to change his tack if he were to achieve a popular success.

Luckily, he had exactly the right sort of book ready to hand: *Pelham*, a work as light and sportive as *Falkland* had been dark and gloomy. The demand for books of its type — "Silver Fork Novels" — had already been stimulated by such authors as Plumer Ward and Benjamin Disraeli; and Bulwer capitalized handsomely by appealing to this well established market. Moreover, as every young novelist must, he had chosen a topic he knew thoroughly; ordinary people wanted to know about dandies: their clothes, their manners, their conversation. All this Bulwer could and did tell them in *Pelham*. Thus, Bulwer's extraordinary instinct for knowing just what sort of books people wanted to read, had manifested itself for the first time. That he was never to lose this knack goes far to explain why he would remain all his life so popular a writer; but it may also explain why, for the most part, the appeal of his books has proven ephemeral.[53]

Bulwer's financial worries did not end with the success of *Pelham*. He and Rosina had plunged into London society, and were spending their money as swiftly as he could make it. To support their reckless extravagance, Bulwer wrote ten novels in ten years of married life, all on top of much other literary and political work. The strain these prodigious labors wrought upon his nerves and his health would have dire consequences before long.

But now let us resume our account of Bulwer's early essays into politics, for the success of *Pelham* by no means dimmed his ambition to be a man of action. For instance, in a letter to Mrs. Cunningham in 1828 which he wrote to tell her, "Pelham takes wonderfully," he went on to remark, "People are in a terrible ferment about the administration — would to Heaven, I were in the House — but my time will come."[54]

In 1830 it seemed his time had come. The death of King George IV that year necessitated a general election; and that summer the conflagration of Revolution in France ignited in England the demand for Parliamentary Reform. Bulwer, allying himself with the Reformers, began in earnest the search for a seat.

It did not prove an easy task. During the summer, he journeyed to Cornwall to contest an election in the borough of Penryn. Bulwer half jokingly expressed the hope that "the Land's End does not prove my own," — and indeed he soon withdrew from what had turned out to be a hopeless venture. Then he turned his attention to the borough of Southwark, where an even more frustrating experience awaited him. This campaign looked very promising at first; Dr. John Bowring, a prominent Radical — noted for his popular translation of the "Marseillaise" — was boosting Bulwer's candidacy. Then, some local Radicals put into nomination the name of Lord John Russell, solely in order to pay homage to their leader, for Russell had no intention of accepting election for Southwark. Nonetheless, Bulwer felt obliged to withdraw, for he could afford neither the expenses nor the opprobrium among the Radicals that opposing Russell would entail. And so the search for a seat went on.[55]

It seemed to Bulwer that Hertfordshire would offer him his best prospects. Normally, his mother's influence there should have made his task relatively easy; instead, Mrs. Bulwer-Lytton was acting to block her son's ambitions. His marriage was not the principal cause of this — by 1830 she had reconciled herself to it and relations between mother and son had begun to improve — but rather she deplored his advocacy of Reform. Mrs. Bulwer-Lytton could not help the fact that two of her sons — Edward and Henry — were seeking election to the House of Commons as Radicals; but she did insist that they remain outside her bailiwick while they did so.

Nonetheless, Henry went ahead with his second attempt to win the borough of Hertford. This campaign touched off an incident that would make matters still more difficult for Edward. Henry withdrew from the contest, and went on a diplomatic mission to France; while he was abroad, Lord Glengall, a supporter of one of his opponents, alleged that Henry had accepted a bribe to drop out of the campaign. Edward then made himself the champion of the family honor and challenged Glengall to fight a duel. This threat forced Glengall to apologize, thus vindicating Henry. But this sordid and unpleasant affair annoyed Mrs. Bulwer-Lytton, and strengthened her determination to keep her sons out of Hertfordshire politics.[56]

This would not have mattered so much except that soon afterward Bulwer became interested in standing for the borough of St. Albans, also in Hertfordshire. While he preferred not to destroy in a moment the fruit of years of effort to restore good relations with his mother, he could not bear to waste so promising an opportunity. Thus he wrote at once to re-assure her that "the harassment you had about Hertford would not be repeated in my case." But he could not not limit himself to that dignified appeal; instead he gave vent to his sense of isolation and injured pride, and expansively expressed his life-long conviction that no one appreciated him as well as he deserved:

> I have seen men of my own standing at Cambridge — men not more distinguished than myself — put forward by their relations and friends, and by them returned to Parliament. No such pains having been exerted on my behalf. I have, alone and unaided, tried every place where there was any chance of success. . . . St. Albans[now]. . . is the only town in which. . . I could at once obtain a triumphant support, and in which. . . I could be sure about my expenses. If I do not accept this offer, there is no other place where I can come in, and consequently all hope of entering Parliament must be abandoned. . . .[57]

But Mrs. Bulwer-Lytton remained adamant, and Edward acquiesced to her wishes.

Fortunately, he had overstated the bleakness of his prospects. In the spring of 1831, the Whig Ministry Reform Bill suffered a setback, and the government called for a general election. Demand for Reform was soaring to unprecedented heights. It soon became obvious the Reformers would sweep the country, a fact that would certainly open doors for men like Bulwer. And, indeed, not long after the St. Albans fiasco, he wrote again to his mother, again asking for help, but under very different circumstances:

> I write in very great haste, to beg a very great favor. I am just about to leave town for St. Ives. My election is certain. Will you in this case help me out with the expenses by lending me any sum you conveniently can from £500 to £1000? I will fully and faithfully repay it in less than a year.[58]

At last the result matched the expectations. Bulwer won at St. Ives, and took his seat in the Reform Parliament in June 1831. After all his anxieties, he had reason to regard the future with confidence. In two careers, he had made promising starts. He might now go as far as his abilities could carry him. The time of preparation was past; the time of struggle was to begin.

NOTES

1. Edmund Gosse, *Some Diversions of a Man of Letters* (London: William Hunemann, 1919), 115-137.

2. For the reasons developed in the text, as well as for the sake of tradition, I consider it appropriate to refer to the subject of this biography at each stage of his life by the particular surname he bore at the time; hence,-- for the period 1803 to 1838, I shall call him Bulwer; for the period 1838 to 1866, Bulwer-Lytton; and for 1866 to 1873, Lord Lytton. When speaking of him without reference to any specific period, I shall designate him Bulwer-Lytton.

3. Michael Sadleir, *Bulwer: A Panorama* (Boston: Little, Brown, 1931), 193-195

4. This is not to suggest any connection between his changes of name and his changes of attitude beyond a symbolic one. He had, in fact, practical reasons for making these changes: in 1843, he inherited from his mother the great Lytton estate near Knebworth; accordingly, he thought it proper to add the name "Lytton" to his surname. Likewise, when elevated to the peerage in 1866, he chose the title "Lytton of Knebworth" owing to his ownership of that property.

5. The Earl of Lytton, *The Life of Edward Bulwer, First Lord Lytton* (London: Macmillan and Co., 1913), volume I, 7-10. Henceforth this work will be referred to as "Earl of Lytton."

6. Sadleir, *Bulwer, A Panorama*, 14-18.

7. *Ibid.*, 17-20

8. Earl of Lytton, I, 15.

9. *Ibid.*, 31

10. *Ibid.*, 36

11. Edward Bulwer, *Pelham* (New York: Popular Library), 1974, 254.

12. Edward Bulwer, *The Caxtons* (London: George Rutledge, 1880), *passim.* Also, on Bulwer-Lytton's using Richard Warburton Lytton as the model for "Austin Caxton," see Earl of Lytton, 68.

13. Earl of Lytton, 36.

14. *Ibid.*, 40-41.

15. *Ibid.*, 44.

16. Edward Bulwer, *The Disowned* (London: George Rutledge, 1880).

17. Robert, First Earl of Lytton, *The Life, Letters and Literary Remains of Edward Bulwer, Lord Lytton* (New York: Harper & Brothers, 1884), 165-167. Hereafter called "Owen Meredith," the *nom de plume* he used in his literary career.

18. This is an inference drawn from the supposition that "Roland de Caxton" was based on General William Bulwer.

19. Earl of Lytton, 48-50.

20. *Ibid.*, 51-56.

21. Owen Meredith, 326.

22. Edward Bulwer to His Mother, April 2, 1820. Quoted by Owen Meredith, 133-134.

23. On the impact of his sense of being an aristocrat upon his personality, see Sadleir, *Bulwer: A Panorama*, 3-4.

24. *Ibid.*, 221-224, and 328-331.

25. Earl of Lytton, I, 83.

26. Owen Meredith, 349.

27. [Edward Bulwer], *England and the English* (New York: J & J Harper, 1833, Volume II, 50, 64-65.

28. Edward Bulwer to Drake Garrard, February 21, 1820. In Owen Meredith, 141.

29. Same to same, September 15, 1820. *Ibid.*, 142.

30. *Ibid.*, 217-222.

31. *Ibid.*

32. Edward Bulwer to J. Thelwall, n.d. Parrish Collection, Princeton University.

33. Earl of Lytton, 92-94.

34. Owen Meredith, 348-349.

35. *Ibid.*

36. *Ibid.*, 338

37. Bulwer, *Pelham*, 47, 143, 152, 247, 264.

38. *Ibid.*, 143-145.

39. Mrs. Porter to Edward Bulwer, December 24, 1820. In Owen Meredith, 145.

40. *Ibid.*, 358.

41. Edward Bulwer to Mrs. Cunningham, May 8, 1826. *Ibid.*, 431-433.

42. Same to same, May, 1826. Lytton Papers, Hertfordshire County Record Office, D/EK C26.

43. Same to same, October 25, 1826. Owen Meredith, 442.

44. Edward Bulwer to Rosina Wheeler, September, 1826. In Louisa Devey, ed., *Letters of the late Edward Bulwer, Lord Lytton to His Wife* (New York: G.W. Dillingham, 1889), 63-67.

45. On Rosina's background, see Sadleir, *Bulwer, A Panorama*, 67-83.

46. Devey, *Letters of Bulwer to His Wife*, 21. One should note that Victor, Second Earl of Lytton argued that the first meeting between Edward and Rosina could not have occurred before April, 1826. But his arguments are directed against the opinion of his father (First Earl of Lytton, or "Owen Meredith") that they met in April, 1825. Victor, Lord Lytton's arguments are not persuasive against the possibility that the meeting in fact took place in October, 1825. For instance, Miss Devey in her collection of letters prints a love letter from Edward to Rosina which must have been written after they had known each other for several months; and she dates this letter as "April, 1826." Since Victor, Lord Lytton believed they had only just met that month, he states that Miss Devey must have dated the letter incorrectly. But he gives no evidence to support that assertion. See Devey, 27-32; and Earl of Lytton, I, 155, 169-170.

47. Edward Bulwer to Mrs. Cunningham, n.d. Lytton Papers, Hertfordshire County Records Office, D/EK C26.

48. Same to same, n.d. *Ibid.*

49. Same to same, May 8, 1826. Owen Meredith, 431-433.

50. Devey, *Letters of Bulwer to His Wife*, 27-32; and Louisa Devey, *Life of Rosina, Lady Lytton* (London: Swan Sonnenschein, Lowrey, 1887), 67.

51. See Sadleir, *Bulwer, A Panorama*, 83-97, for details of their engagement and marriage. Also Bulwer later wrote to J.P. Beavan, June 25, 1847: "Lady Bulwer . . . cohabited with me before marriage, --and attests my honor in marrying her at every sacrifice of worldly prospects." Lytton Papers, D/EK C26.

52. Edward Bulwer to His Mother, August 20, 1827, in Owen Meredith, 455-456.

53. An example of the impact of *Pelham* is the fact that its strictures established the fashion of black evening dress for men that has survived to our own day. See Earl of Lytton, *Bulwer-Lytton* (London: Horn & Van Thal, 1948), 40.

54. Edward Bulwer to Mrs. Cunningham, June 20, 1828. Lytton Papers, D/EK C26.

55. Owen Meredith, 592-595.

56. Thomas H. Duncombe, ed., *The Life and Correspondence of Thomas Slingsby Duncombe* (London: Hurst & Blackett, 1868), 139-140.

57. Edward Bulwer to His Mother, March 8, 1831. In Owen Meredith, 600-601.

58. Same to same, April, 1831, *Ibid*.

CHAPTER TWO

A MORAL INFLUENCE

The general elections of 1830-1 made manifest the popular demand for Parliamentary Reform. So completely did this single issue dominate public discussion that voters tended to categorize Parliamentary candidates as either reformers or anti-reformers. In this sense, consequently, these elections marked a significant advance in the transition from factional politics to a two-party system.

In the 1830's, however, a two-party system did not yet exist. Certainly, the Parliamentary following of Lord Grey did not constitute a cohesive political party. Instead, it contained several distinct blocs. Among these, two major forces stood out.

First, there were the Whigs themselves, an exclusive coterie of aristocrats, heirs to the anti-Royalist traditions of the seventeenth century. Bolstered by experienced office-holders, supported by the wealth of great magnates, and fortified by the habit of command, the Whigs dominated the Reform Ministry. And they admitted few outsiders, regardless of abilities or opinions, to their charmed circle.

Uneasily allied to the Whigs were the independent Radicals. Loyal to the Ministry on the Reform Bill, but restless in spirit, the independent Radicals looked forward to striking out on their own. As disparate a group as they no doubt were, they shared one essential purpose, for, unlike so many of the Whigs, the independent Radicals regarded the Reform Bill not as a "final measure," but as an indispensable first step toward the realization of a fundamental reform program. They planned to rationalize and restructure British society. To them, 1832 was the dawn of a new age. They believed they were riding the wave of the future, a wave that they supposed had already submerged the Tories, and which, they hoped would soon sweep the Whigs as well into oblivion.

Edward Lytton Bulwer, as a newly elected M.P. in 1831, was an independent Radical in that he agreed with many of the ideas fashionable among that group. But he subordinated himself to no one, and acknowledged no party discipline. He described his position as follows:

> I know not that party . . . to which I can be said to belong. I am an advocate for a strong government, yet I am not a Tory. I love the people, yet I am not a Radical. I am for a rational compromise between the Past and the Present, yet I am not a Whig . . . . He who advocates the institution of Monarchy and an established church can scarcely in these times please the popular passion. He who traces the evil influences of aristocratic power, can scarcely please the great aristocratic factions. But though he fail in these points, perhaps he may speak the truth![1]

Bulwer's opinions, while fitting no party label, had nonetheless a consistency of their own.

The declaration of political independence just quoted shows that Bulwer did not intend to stake his political future on the gratitude of party leaders. He refused to be merely a faithful follower, preferring to make his way by the force of his talents. Seldom did he underestimate his own abilities. A few years before his election, he had written to Rosina that, once in the House of Commons,

> I consider the road clear. If I have any ability less inconsiderable than another, any one of which I have devoted the most time, labour, thought, patience, any one in which I surmounted the disadvantages of nature, and acquired the powers of art, it is the talent of public speaking. For three years I practiced it constantly, for the greatest part of that time with the most wretched success . . . ; but I did succeed at last, and with such a success as to justify my most sanguine expectations.[2]

But Bulwer had not "acquired the powers of art," but rather an air of artificiality. His gestures became excessively vigorous, but his voice remained weak. He had failed to surmount the "disadvantages of nature." As Benjamin Disraeli, a sharp observer of Parliamentarians in the early 1830's from his perch in the Strangers' Gallery, commented after one debate:

> Bulwer spoke, but he is physically disqualified for an orator, and, in spite of all his exertions, never can succeed.[3]

Bulwer's studied oratorical style and his lingering dandyism made for an odd mixture. Another observer in Parliament did note Bulwer's powerful intellect, but more or less as an afterthought:

> [Bulwer] does not speak often. When he does, his speeches are not only previously turned over with great care in his mind, but are written out at full length, and committed carefully to memory. He is a great patron of the tailor, and he is always dressed in the extreme of fashion. His manner of speaking is extremely affected: the management of his voice is especially so, but for this he would be a pleasant speaker. His voice, though weak, is agreeable . . . . You see at once that he is a person of great intellectual acquirements.[4]

On July 5, 1831, Bulwer delivered his maiden speech in the House of Commons, advocating speedy passage of the Reform Bill. Despite his careful preparation and well thought-out arguments, Bulwer's address was a failure, due to his ineffective presentation.[5] But the failure may not have been entirely his fault. Circumstances were against him. With so many new Members in the House, virtually all of whom supported the Reform Bill, only a brilliant orator could have stood out. Moreover, although the question of the Reform Bill dominated public discussions, the issue had ceased to be in doubt in the House of Commons. Few arguments remained, *pro* or *con*, the Members had not heard before. And while there were indeed important amendments (notably the Chandos clause) the House would consider, no one could doubt the House would pass the Bill in some form once again. The critical test would come in the House of Lords. Bulwer's speech, therefore, could really affect nothing but his personal fortunes. But it did shed light on his political philosophy.

The ideas Bulwer used to buttress his arguments in support of the Reform Bill included at least two major components of that philosophy: his passion for social order; and his admiration for the middle class and for "middle class morality," in the broadest sense of that term.

Like so many of his contemporaries, Bulwer was obsessed with the fear of Revolution.[6] A few months before his maiden speech, Bulwer had written to his mother (who opposed the Reform Bill) that:

> For your own sake, you should not actively oppose the reform. The people are so unanimous and so violent on the measure, right or wrong, that I do not hesitate to say that persons who oppose it will be marked out in case of any disturbance.[7]

Bulwer had good reason to feel as he did. He had seen the destruction wrought by the reform riots in Norfolk,[8] and the July Revolution in France certainly seemed the harbinger of worse things to come. In his maiden speech, he stated that the situation in England had so deteriorated that,

> Authority can longer support itself by the solemn plausibilities and the ceremonial hypocrisies of old, [thus] it is well that a government should be placed upon a solid and sure foundation. In no age of the world, but, least of all in the present, could any system of government long exist which was menaced both by the moral intelligence and the physical force of a country.[9]

Then, addressing himself to the Tories, who had cited the need to secure social order as a reason for opposing the Reform Bill, Bulwer indicated he shared their concern, and then added:

> But so entirely do I agree with the honorable Gentlemen opposite . . . that it is the practical stability, and not the theoretical improvement of the commonwealth, that ought to be our first object—that I would become a willing and cheerful convert to the rest of their sentiments on this great measure, the moment they can show me, amidst the tumults of neighboring nations, and the crash of surrounding thrones, a better security for the institutions of power than the love and confidence of an united and intelligent people.[10]

Many of the "intelligent people" belonged to the largely unenfranchised middle class. To alienate such people by continuing to exclude them from the political nation, Bulwer believed, must lead to instability, even to revolution. On August 25, 1831, Bulwer told the House that,

> In large towns, the more persons excluded from voting, the more enemies the constitution has. Those who are not electors are a disorderly and disaffected rabble; all those who are raised into the ranks of electors are converted into citizens, and interested in the preservation of public safety.[11]

Unlike some other Radicals, Bulwer did not accept it as a general principle that the more people enfranchised, the better. He wanted not so much to expand the electorate as to improve it. Only people of a sound "moral character" could contribute to this improvement. Hence, he argued that the "strong headed and sturdy middle classes," with their "warm and hearty attachment to the security of property," belonged in the political nation. They would strengthen the stability of the state, not undermine it. They were too intelligent to be swayed by revolutionary demagogues. As Bulwer put it,

> The progress of liberal opinions is in exact proportion to the progress of education, and it is impossible to influence such persons without addressing their judgment.[12]

The working classes, he hoped, would look upon the Reform Bill's ten-pound borough franchise as an incentive rather than as a barrier against them. Bulwer wanted to encourage the poor to emulate the admirable middle classes. "The poor," he told the House, "are exempted not only because they are poor, but because they are ignorant also, and subject to the influence of the richer persons about them." They therefore must "exert industry and energy" to raise themselves to the level of electors.[13]

He wished to help them to do so. The stability of national institutions depended, in his view, on the moral character of the people. Sloth, ignorance, and immorality were the seeds of revolution. Thus Bulwer proposed, particularly in his celebrated analysis of the English national character, *England and the English* (1833), that a strong, directing government take steps to effect moral improvement.

To begin with, he called for a national system of education, aimed at inculcating in the laboring masses the virtues of the respectable middle classes. This meant that ideals of religion and self reliance would become integral parts of the curriculum. Unlike many other Radicals, he favored the existing Church schools, and wished to incorporate them into his proposed national system:

> I wished to establish a Universal Education. . . . Let us accomplish our great task of common instruction, not by banishing all religion, but by *procuring* for every pupil instruction in his own. I propose, then, that *the state* shall establish universal education . . . founded on, and combined with, religious instruction.[14]

He stressed, moreover, that it was up to the State to make certain education was universal. "Whatever education be established," he wrote, "the peace and tranquillity of social order require that it should be tolerably equal, and that it should penetrate everywhere." He added, characteristically, "where intelligence is equalized . . . — then demagogues are harmless and theories safe."[15]

Bulwer pointedly described the sort of education that such schools should provide the children of the poor. As he put it in *England and the English*,

> Every boy at the popular schools shall learn the simple elements of agricultural and manual science; that he shall acquire the habit, the love, and the aptitude of work; that the first lesson in his moral code shall be that which teaches him to prize independence, and that he shall practically obey the rule of his catechism, and learn to get his own living.[16]

Toward the same ends, Bulwer advocated reform of the Poor Law. He denounced the existing system as a boon to sloth and sin, because it enabled "sturdy beggars" to live better than the poor who struggled to support themselves. Furthermore, it was, in Bulwer's view,

> equally prejudicial to the sexual moralities. In the rural districts, a peasant-girl has a child first, and a husband afterwards . . . . [The Poor Laws] encourage improvidence, for they provide for its wants; they engender sexual intemperance, for they rear its offspring . . . ; they deaden the social affections for the labourer, for his children become to him a matter of mercantile speculation.[17]

On this point, certainly, Bulwer agreed with the "Philosophical Radicals" who would bear major responsibility for the Poor Law Amendment Act that Parliament was to pass in 1834. Indeed, the previous year, Bulwer had anticipated one of the major features of that Act, when he wrote in *England and the English* that, to promote morality and self reliance among the masses,

> the principal machinery of reform should lie in the discipline of the workhouse. It is a fact at present, that where the comforts at a workhouse exceed those of the independent labourer, pauperism increases; but where the comforts at the workhouse have been reduced below those of the independent labourer, pauperism has invariably and

most rapidly diminished. On this principle all reform must mainly rest.[18]

Bulwer considered it a disgrace for the institutions of the state to undermine, not elevate, the ideals of order and morality. As bad in this regard as the old Poor Law were the prisons. Indeed, the entire system of criminal law he regarded as in dire need of reform.

Bulwer waged his battle for legal reform more in his role of popular novelist than of fledgling politician. The perennial popularity of crime stories--which he was typically quick to take advantage of--enabled him to reach wider audiences than he could have in any other way. Hence he wrote his series of "Newgate Novels," starting with *Paul Clifford* (1830) and ending with *Lucretia* (1846), "to draw attention to two errors in our penal institutions, viz.: — a vicious Prison Discipline and a sanguinary Penal Code."[19]

Bulwer's career as a crime novelist has had extensive treatment elsewhere.[20] For our purposes, a brief description of *Paul Clifford* should suffice. "Paul," a youth of extraordinary precocity, is wrongfully arrested and jailed. In prison, his companions include hardened criminals whose influence later leads him to become a notorious highwayman. In the flippant style-reminiscent of *Pelham* that still characterized his writing, Bulwer commented:

> Young people are apt, erroneously, to believe that it is a bad thing to
> be exceedingly wicked. The House of Correction is so called because
> it is a place where so ridiculous a notion is invariably corrected.[21]

In the end, the law catches up with "Paul." He is tried, convicted, and sentenced to death (though not executed, for reasons that need not detain us). At his trial, "Paul" blames society itself for making him a criminal. Bulwer, rather obtrusively, rejects so extreme an abnegation of individual responsibility, but his treatment of "Paul's" plight is nonetheless sympathetic. In a preface to the novel, he wrote:

> We see masses of our fellow creatures — the victims of circumstances
> over which they had no control — contaminated in fancy by the
> example of parents — their intelligence either . . . stifled in ignorance,
> or perverted to apologies for vice. A child who is cradled in
> ignominy; whose schoolmaster is the felon; whose academy is the
> House of Correction; who breathes an atmosphere in which virtue is
> poisoned, to which religion does not pierce — becomes less a

responsible and reasoning human being than a wild beast which we suffer to range in the wilderness — till it prowls near our homes, and we kill it in self defense.[22]

In his campaign for penal reform, Bulwer used literary means to advance political ends. His literary celebrity gave him an influence far greater than other backbench M.P.'s enjoyed, and, in expressing his ideas, he reached vaster audiences than did most Ministers. Although so long as he had no office, he could do little to effect change, he could at least help prepare the way. Such, at least, was his aim, as he explained in *England and the English*:

> To counteract a bad moral influence . . . you must create a good moral influence. Reformed opinion precedes reformed legislation. Now is the day for writers and advisers; *they* prepare the part for true law givers; they are the pioneers of good; no reform is final, save the reform of the mind.[23]

"To create a good moral influence" Bulwer believed especially important, since he also maintained that "the spirit of the age" inevitably determines the course of events. He made this point repeatedly in his historical novels,[24] and expressed the same idea in Parliament. "The most democratic law," he told the Commons in 1831, "cannot do more than hasten a democracy, which, before that law would be received, must already become inevitable."[25] Thus, as noted above, he cited the prevailing popular mood as a reason for passing the Reform Bill. Similarly, when Parliament debated whether to abolish flogging in the Army, Bulwer supported abolition on the ground that, "no mode of punishment can be long continued if it goes directly in the teeth of popular opinion."[26] And he opposed Sabbatarian legislation because such laws were, he said, "opposed to the spirit of the times"; he added that the existing laws on the subject had become a dead letter because all "laws become impracticable . . . when they are not suited to the spirit of the people."[27]

Bulwer's estimate of the importance of the "spirit of the age" caused him, in the early 1830's, to feel dissatisfied with the Whig Ministers, for he felt they were too slow in satisfying the public demand for various reforms. Later, however, as the national mood was evidently becoming more conservative, Bulwer supported the Whigs' cautious approach, and quarreled with those Radicals who still insisted on forcing the pace of change. Bulwer prided himself on being a pragmatist, and deprecated equally those who ran too far in advance of the "spirit of the age," and those who lagged stubbornly behind it.

While Bulwer would not actually change his political allegiance from Liberal to Conservative until the 1850's, the drift in that direction had already begun in the 1830's. Perhaps his shift was really one from optimist to pessimist. We have already discussed Bulwer's idea that only by instilling the ideals of morality among the masses can a society safely allow free rein to liberty, without risking the excesses of revolution. So long as he took an optimistic view of the moral character of the "spirit of the age," he would remain liberal. By the same token, increasing pessimism would gradually lead him to conservatism. His principles did not change, only his perception of the realities of the time.

Bulwer's perception of the realities of the early 1830's made him, for the time being at least, quite an optimist. This attitude suited the age. As G. Kitson Clark has written of this period,

> Some men were inspired by the revival of religion to accept for themselves a higher standard of morality and to condemn practices which . . . all preceding centuries had accepted without question.[28]

Bulwer recognized this development. "All experience proves," he told the House in 1834, "that the country is progressing in moral and religious, as well as intellectual improvement."[29] He adopted the new tone in his literary work. Gone was the flippancy that had given his Regency novels their distinct flavor. He even went so far as to bowdlerize the new editions of *Pelham*, incising every hint of the impudent or risque. The dandified rebel of Regency silver-forkery had become the quintessence of the Victorian novelist.[30]

It may seem paradoxical that Bulwer was championing freedom of expression at the same time he was bowdlerizing his own books. Yet, in fact, his Parliamentary activities in this period focused on the fight to liberalize the laws affecting the drama and the press. And, according to his own lights, he was being perfectly consistent. He felt obliged to make his own books accord with the moral tone of the age; and the laws that restricted freedom of expression on the stage and in newspapers, he believed, kept those media from attaining the same moral tone. Bulwer was optimist enough to suppose that, just as moral improvement paves the way for liberty and order, so too would freedom from government regulation enable morality to prevail.

On May 31, 1832, Bulwer rose in the House of Commons to move for the appointment of a select committee to inquire into the state of the drama. In so doing, his purpose was to prepare the way for the abolition of the monopoly of the two patent theaters — Drury Lane and Covent Garden — on performing the "national drama" (legitimate theater). There were other theaters, "the minors"; but these could operate only so long as the laws were not strictly enforced. To avoid prosecution by the patent theaters, the minors limited themselves, in Bulwer's words, to performances "of the most mountebank and trumpery description." Meanwhile, the patent theaters, free from competition, failed to foster the national drama. In moving for the committee of inquiry, Bulwer said of the patent theaters:

> When we look round and see the dioramas, and the cosmoramas, and the jugglers, and the horses, and the elephants, and the lions, which have been poured forth upon the stage, we can not but feel that the dignity of the drama has not been preserved, and the object of these patents has not been fulfilled.[31]

Bulwer also called for two further reforms: the abolition of censorship, and the establishment of a dramatic copyright. The absence of the latter obviously inhibited the development of the English drama. "If Shakespeare himself were now living," Bulwer proclaimed, his plays "might bring thousands to actors, and ten thousands to managers — and Shakespeare himself . . . might be starving in a garret."[32] Few could doubt the justice of extending to playwrights the privileges other authors already enjoyed.

But in his opposition to censorship, Bulwer had considerably less support. Still, he made a provocative case. Never in this controversy did Bulwer deny the necessity of preserving the moral tone of theatrical performances. Rather, he maintained that the office of censor was "idle and unnecessary" and "useless so far as morality was concerned," because

> The only true Censor of the age, is the spirit of the age. When indecencies were allowed by the customs of real life, they would be allowed in the representation, and no Censor would forbid them. When the age did not allow them, they would not be performed, and no Censor need expunge them. For instance, while the Licenser at this moment might strike out what lines he pleases in a new play, he has no power by strict law to alter a line in an old play. The most indelicate plays of Beaumont and Fletcher . . . might be acted

unmutilated, without submitting them to the Censor; but they are not acted, because the good taste and refinement of the age would not allow them; because instead of attracting, they would disgust an audience.[33]

Such were the issues that, Bulwer proposed, a Parliamentary committee of inquiry should be established to investigate. And, as it happened, Parliament not only acceded to his motion, but made Bulwer himself the committee's chairman. For the next two months, this committee heard voluminous testimony from playwrights, actors, managers, and all manner of theatrical people. The patent theaters proved to have many defenders; and not a few others expressed genuine concern that, should the monopoly end, unscrupulous entrepreneurs would open theaters in areas where the local residents did not want them. Another dispute concerned whether to provide for the licensing of theaters in the provinces, or to apply the provisions of the Bill only to greater London. Bulwer expressed his viewpoint on these matters in a letter to one of the members of his committee:

> My own wish on any Bill on the dramatic question would be to render it obligatory on the magistrates in their jurisdiction, as it would be on the Chamberlain in his, to license *any* theater for which the majority of resident householders in the town or parish should petition. This will suffice to emancipate the provinces as the metropolis, and mete out justice to both. But there will be great difficulty in this addition, from the opposing view of many of the committee. What has already been won was no easy matter. If I can hope to carry all, I shall try all; if not, I should be unwilling to risk much for the chance of getting more.[34]

Ever the pragmatist in politics, Bulwer wound up disappointing some of his Radical allies by limiting the scope of the Bill he presented to the House, in order to improve its chances of passage. He jettisoned much excess baggage. The Bill for one thing, would apply only within a twenty mile radius of London. It would extend the right to perform the "national drama" only to the licensed theaters, leaving many of the minors still without legal protection. The Bill did contain the provision Bulwer wanted for protecting districts against unwanted theatrical speculations, and it also proposed to give the Lord Chamberlain the sole authority to license plays. As to censorship, much to his regret, Bulwer came to the conclusion that he had to leave that just as it was, if the Bill were to have any chance at all.

Bulwer had nicely calculated the mood of the House. It passed this Dramatic Performances Bill in addition to his other Bill to establish a copyright law for dramatists. The latter Bill, in fact, became law; but anticlimactically, the House of Lords rejected the Dramatic Performances Bill. In spite of Bulwer's prodigious efforts, another decade would pass before Parliament finally did away with the theatrical monopoly.[35]

In the early 1830's, Bulwer took a prominent part in another struggle for freedom of expression: the movement to abolish the stamp duties on newspapers and advertisements, the so-called Taxes on Knowledge. Here too he would find how limited were the opportunities for constructive statesmanship, when unsupported by practical power.

Bulwer made several speeches on this subject. In essence, he argued that, because the Taxes made newspapers too expensive for working class people to afford,[36] the Press failed to contribute to the moral improvement of the people. But there were contraband periodicals, which remained cheap by evading the Taxes, that did circulate among the poor, and,

> The writers in these papers could scarcely be well affected to the law, for they broke the law . . . ; in fact, I have seen many of these publications — nothing could be more inflammatory or dangerous. One paper took a particular fancy to the estates of the Duke of Bedford — another paper has been remarkably anxious for the assassination of the Duke of Wellington.[37]

Thus, ironically, governmental interference with liberty — in the form of the Taxes on Knowledge — favored the forces of revolution. Bulwer argued that if all views had a fair hearing, the result would be the triumph of the rational over the irrational, of morality over vice; and thus would the social order be secure. Or, as Bulwer put it, revolutionary propaganda can be

> easily controverted . . . ; for the English operative would listen to reason . . . ; but the Legislature does not allow them to be controverted . . . . You either forbid to the poor by this tax. . . all political knowledge, or else you give to them . . . doctrines the most dangerous . . . ; to the . . . poor . . . whom you ought to be most careful to soothe, to guide, to enlighten, you give the heated invectives of demagogues and fanatics . . . . Of what greater crime could a

Government be guilty than that of allowing the minds of the poor to be poisoned? than that of pandering to their demoralization?[38]

By using this argument, Bulwer appealed not only to the Radicals who would normally support this sort of libertarian measure, but to conservatives as well, for they would certainly wish to stifle sedition. Thus, he showed sound Parliamentary generalship. But his opponents did not fight him on his chosen ground. The Ministry took the position that it simply could not afford the loss of revenue repealing the Taxes would entail. On this aspect of the matter, Bulwer was less sure of his footing.

In making his first motion to abolish the Taxes on Knowledge (in June, 1832), Bulwer characteristically tried to turn the revenue question into a moral issue. He suggested the loss could be made good by increasing the excise on gin, and ridiculed a system that discouraged learning and encouraged drunkenness, adding: "any tax is better than one which corrupts virtue. . . ."[39] But he was too intelligent to leave the matter at that. Making a comparison with America, where newspapers were cheap, Bulwer calculated the increase in circulation that would result from repealing the Taxes; he concluded that so many additional sheets would be published that the increment to the paper tax (which, of course, he did not propose to repeal) would more than make up for the loss of the stamp duties. Moreover, he proposed the establishment of a committee to inquire into the feasibility of a penny-postage system to facilitate the circulation of newspapers once the stamp duty had been removed. Here he cited the success France had had with such a system, and concluded that the penny postage would bring in as much or more as did the Taxes on Knowledge.[40]

Despite Bulwer's inexperience with financial matters, there was nothing shallow about this speech. Laden with statistics and arithmetic calculations as inevitably it was, it must have put much of the House to sleep; but it made sense.

In answer to Bulwer, Lord Althorp, the Chancellor of the Exchequer, made a debater's reply. He entirely admitted the substance of Bulwer's case against the Taxes; he simply argued that the revenue the stamp duties brought in could not be spared. In answering Bulwer's assertions that this lost revenue could easily be made up, Althorp spoke superficially, but with a sort of calm simplicity that seldom fails to make a good impression. He expressed the opinion that Bulwer must have exaggerated the increase in circulation of newspapers that would follow repeal of the stamp duties; unlike Bulwer, Althorp did not bore the House with a torrent of statistics to back up his opinion; instead, he remarked that such matters were better suited for discussion in the "the closet" than in the House of Commons, no doubt winning the heart of many a weary backbencher. It was enough for Althorp to say Bulwer's arguments had left him unconvinced.[41]

Only on the matter of the penny-postage plan did Althorp say anything which left Bulwer an opening for reply. The Chancellor suggested that delivering the greatly increased volume of newspapers that, according to Bulwer's calculations, would follow repeal of the stamp duty, would multiply the costs of the post office. He also indicated that it would be unfair to the provinces to put so much of the burden upon them for making up the loss in revenue, since London residents would not have to share in the expense of paying postage for their newspapers.[42]

Both of these arguments had plausibility; but both were wrong. For if the circulation of papers increased as much as Bulwer had calculated, the revenue from the paper duty would more than offset both the expenses of the post office and the loss of the stamp duty revenues. As for the unfairness to the provinces, one could hardly consider a penny-postage more burdensome than the four-penny stamp duty Bulwer proposed to abolish.

Bulwer noted the fallacies in Althorp's speech. But he did not reply. He consulted with other Radicals, and among these, Daniel O'Connell, Eliot Warburton, and others urged him not to push the issue to a division, on the grounds that it was too late in the session for a committee to be set up; and, in any event, Althorp had conceded that the Taxes ought, in due course, to be abolished.[43]

Bulwer yielded to their arguments, and withdrew his motion; but not without a pang, for he had deliberately delayed making his proposal until June, on the ground that by then the Budget would have been completed. He consoled himself, however, with the thought that when the Reformed Parliament met in 1833, the atmosphere would be more amenable to measures of this kind.[44]

Events soon disillusioned him on that score. The Whigs remained in control; and their attitude on the Taxes on Knowledge question soon dissipated whatever confidence Bulwer had placed in them. Although Bulwer had pledged he would once again move the abolition of the stamp duties when Parliament re-convened in 1833, he never got the chance to make good that pledge. As he put it, "those incidents which so often and so unexpectedly start up in the way of any independent Member bringing forward a Motion in the House, obliged me to defer the question" until the 1834 session. He then reiterated the same basic arguments he had made two years before, adding only a belated rejoinder to Althorp's criticisms of his penny postal plan, and a pointed reminder that the Chancellor had, two years, before, pledged himself eventually to support repeal.[45]

During this speech, Bulwer evidently had to contend with the institutionalized rudeness that characterizes the atmosphere of the House of Commons, especially when a motion is offered that a large and organized party opposes. In replying this time, Althorp noted Bulwer's complaint of the "apathy" with which the House had listened to him, and inferred from this that the mood of the House was hostile to the motion. He added that he by no means considered himself pledged to support repeal, and then essentially repeated his previous statements to the effect that the government could not afford to lose the revenue the stamp duties brought in.[46] The occasion was not propitious, but Bulwer was determined for once to force the issue to a division. He lost, 90 to 58.[47] The following year, Bulwer had to deal with a new Chancellor of the Exchequer, Sir Thomas Spring-Rice. The debate followed the familiar pattern, but this time, at least, Bulwer elicited from the Chancellor a definite commitment to repeal the Taxes the following year, assuming "the revenue can bear it." In respect of this pledge, Bulwer acceded to Spring-Rice's wish that he withdraw his motion without pressing it to a division.[48]

This strategic retreat provoked a bitter comment from Bulwer's fellow Radical, Joseph Hume, who had earlier seconded his motion.[49] Clearly, as regards the Whigs and the Radicals, Bulwer was falling between two stools. The latter—for the most part—could not abide his pragmatic approach. He was too patient, too willing to compromise, to fit in with a faction to whom ideological purity mattered more than concrete results. In 1836, Bulwer acknowledged his differences with the other Radicals; for that year marked the end at least of this phase of Bulwer's campaign against the Taxes on Knowledge, as Spring-Rice redeemed his pledge by reducing, if not abolishing, the stamp duties. Bulwer supported the Chancellor in this, stating,

I have been much blamed out of the House, and a little in it, for not pressing the House to a division on the last occasion that I had the honor of bringing forward the subject of the stamp duties on newspapers. My decision upon that occasion was founded upon my

42

conviction . . . that my object would be fully satisfied without going
to a division. . . . As to the proposed reduction of the newspaper stamp
duties to ld, I am still distinctly of the opinion that the entire abolition
of this is far more desirable . . . . But I should not think of rejecting
the proposal . . . which I can consider to be the best compromise
which can be offered.[50]

Although, with Spring-Rice's reduction of the duties in 1836, Bulwer
could claim a measure of success, the affair had, on the whole, been a
matter of frustration. The same could truly be said of Bulwer's entire
Parliamentary career to this point. This frustration was reflected by the
fact that he spoke very infrequently in the House of Commons. Since he
had been unable to push through either the repeal of the Taxes on
Knowledge or the abolition of the theatrical monopoly, he was
understandably reluctant to take up other causes. He learned during these
years the inadequacy of political independence, and the importance of
associating himself with an organized political party. But, which party
could he join? In the 1830's, it seemed a choice between the Whigs and
the Radicals; but, as we shall see, neither of these would prove to be the
answer.

NOTES

1. Bulwer, *England and the English*, 1, 7.

2. Bulwer to Rosina Wheeler, Sept. 6, 1826, in Devey, *Letters of Bulwer to His Wife*, 65-
66.

3. Benjamin Disraeli to Sarah Disraeli, February 7, 1833, in W.F. Monypenny, *The Life
of Benjamin Disraeli* (New York): Macmillan Co., Vol. I, 223.

4.I. Grant quoted by Walter Besant, *Fifty Years Ago* (New York: Harper and Brothers,
1890), 148.

5. Rumor had it that he spoke so badly that afterwards his wife ridiculed him (which
would have been characteristic for her) and this precipitated the first of their many
quarrels. See Justin McCarthy, *Portraits of the Sixties* (Freeport N.Y.: Books for Libraries,
1971), 150.

6. On the Victorian fear of Revolution, see Walter Houghton, *The Victorian Frame of
Mind* (New Haven: Yale University Press), 54-57.

7. Edward Bulwer to his mother, April 1831, *Owen Meredith*, 602.

8. *Owen Meredith*, 596-598.

9. *Hansard's Parliamentary Debates* (London; T.C. Hansard, 1832), Third Series, Vol. IV, 756-761. This series will hereafter be referred to as *Hansard*.

10. *Ibid.*

11. *Ibid.*, Vol. VI, 608-610.

12. *Ibid.*

13. *Ibid.*

14. Bulwer, *England and the English*, I, 234-237.

15. *Ibid.*, 193.

16. *Ibid.*, 238.

17. *Ibid.*, 144.

18. *Ibid.*, 147-148.

19. Edward Bulwer, *Paul Clifford* (New York: Hurst, 1880), v.

20. Keith Hollingsworth, *The Newgate Novel 1830-1847* (Detroit: Wayne State, 1963), *passim.*

21. Bulwer, *Paul Clifford*, 76.

22. *Ibid.*, vii.

23. Bulwer, *England and the English*, II, 176-177.

24. In many of these works, the hero fails in the end, despite his virtuous character and great abilities, because he opposes the spirit of the age; thus he is the "last" of his type, be it the *Last of the Barons*, or *Last of the Roman Tribunes*, etc. On this point, see Curtis Dahl, "History on the Hustings: Bulwer-Lytton's Historical Novels of Politics," in Robert C. Rathburn and Martin Steinmann, ed., *From Jane Austen to Joseph Conrad* (Minneapolis: University of Minnesota Press, 1958), 60-71.

25. *Hansard*, IV, 756-761.

26. *Ibid.*, XXXVII, 891-892.

27. *Ibid.*, XXIII, 316-321.

28. G. Kitson Clark, *The Making of Victorian England* (New York: Atheneum, 1969), 40.

29. *Hansard*, XXIII, 321.

30. In Bulwer's most famous novel, *The Last Days of Pompeii*, the destruction of the decadent city of Pompeii by the eruption of Vesuvius, can be taken to symbolize the displacement of the decadent Regency mood by the new Victorian "seriousness." The conversion of the character "Glaucus" to Christianity at the end of the novel is indicative of this parallel.

31. *Hansard*, XIII, 241.

32. *Ibid.*, 247.

33. *Ibid.*, 244-245.

34. Edward Bulwer to Thomas Slingsby Duncombe, October 3, 1832. In Thomas H. Duncombe, ed., *The Life and Correspondence of Thomas Slingsby Duncombe*, II, 29.

35. For an account of this question, see Watson Nicholson, *The Struggle For A Free Stage In London* (New York: Benjamin Bloom, 1966), *passim*.

36. Bulwer, on this point, did not ignore the fact that people might read newspapers, for instance, at coffee houses, without purchasing them; he pointed out, however, that the papers were written to interest the more well to do persons who did pay for them, and thus the papers had little appeal for the working classes. See *Hansard*, XIII, 623.

37. *Ibid.*, XXIII, 1196. This quote is from his 1834 speech on the Taxes on Knowledge; he first made the same point in his original motion in 1832, but, as I consider the latter speech more to the point in its phrasing, I have chosen to quote from it.

38. *Ibid.*, 1196-1197.

39. *Ibid.*, XIII, 629-630.

40. *Ibid.*, 630-632.

41. *Ibid.*, 634-637.

42. *Ibid.*

43. *Ibid.*, 647-648. Also, Edward Bulwer to Albany Fonblanque, n.d. Lytton Papers, D/EK C26.

44. This is inferred from the fact that, earlier, Bulwer had requested Fonblanque's advice whether he should delay his motion until June for this reason. Edward Bulwer to Albany Fonblanque, May 1, [1832], Lytton papers, D/EK C26.

45. *Hansard*, XXIII, 1193-1206.

46. *Ibid.*, 1210-1213.

47. *Ibid.*, 1222.

48. *Ibid.*, XXX, 835-862.

49. *Ibid.*, 862.

50. *Ibid.*, XXXII, 358-359.

CHAPTER THREE

RADICAL OR WHIG?

Bulwer always plumed himself on having a practical approach to politics. Thus, when he considered what party to join, he saw how much he could benefit by attaching himself to the Whigs. After all, they had power; for the moment they had supporters and opponents, but no rival. As Charles Greville put it in 1833, "there exists no *party* but that of the government."[1] To gain their favor would be to take a certain step toward office and honor. Bulwer would hardly have had to make a great sacrifice of principles to enter the Whig camp, for he generally supported them anyway. Such Ministerial measures as the Reform Act of 1832, the Factory Act of 1833,[2] and the New Poor Law of 1834 he regarded as magnificent achievements. It would not have been at all difficult for him to downplay the differences he had with the Whigs, and clearly he would have had much to gain by doing just that.

Yet Bulwer deliberately kept his distance from the Whigs. While the editor of the *New Monthly Magazine*, he responded to certain Radicals who had criticized him as too moderate: "It would almost seem as if they mistook us for Whigs—a bitter suspicion which we are unwilling to believe we can by any possibility have deserved."[3] Such comments can hardly have raised his stock with the party in power.

To understand Bulwer's anti-Whiggism, one must first recall that his attitude antedated his election to Parliament. Even his earliest novels show evidences of it. In *Pelham* he wrote of "the Whig, who says in the Upper House, that whatever may be the distresses of the people, they shall not be gratified at the cost of one of the despotic privileges of the aristocracy."[4] Two years later, he similarly satirized the Whigs in *Paul Clifford*. This so-called "Newgate Novel" was also a political *roman á clef*, in which Bulwer playfully depicted various political personalities as outlaws and highwaymen. The character representing the Whigs,[5] while in jail, continually complained about being placed among ordinary

48

convicts, insisting he is better than his fellows. As a "moderate Whig," he proclaimed that he loved liberty, but hated democracy.[6]

Bulwer clearly regarded the Whigs as irresponsible aristocrats, and accordingly opposed them. He even seemed at this stage an antagonist of aristocracy itself. In *England and the English*, in particular, he denounced aristocratic influence. Venal aristocratic patronage had, he wrote, corrupted the established Church; and the lax morals of titled court wastrels similarly discredited the monarchy. The decline of these institutions tended to undermine social stability and increased the danger of revolution.[7]

What a paradox, to find Bulwer an opponent of aristocracy! Who could have been more aristocratic in outlook and manner than he? Since his childhood, his mother had taught him to believe himself descended from the finest families in England. And, despite Bulwer's early radicalism, one can judge from the names of the heroes of his early novels — *Pelham, Godolphin, Falkland*, and *Devereaux* — how thoroughly he identified himself with the aristocracy.[8]

But the aristocracy did not accept him as one of its own. Despite their ancient pedigrees, neither the Bulwers nor the Lyttons had enjoyed high social standing in recent generations. To contemporary patricians Edward Bulwer was an abrasive upstart who wrote impudent novels for a living, and who frequented the soirees of the demimondaine Lady Blessington. He was "a low fellow," not to be taken seriously.[9]

Thus, Bulwer denounced the aristocrats in part because they had deprived him of the status he regarded as his birthright. For whatever reason, Bulwer focused this resentment against the Whigs. The Tories, with all their faults, at least sometimes "brought forward the man of low or *mediocre* birth," Bulwer observed; "but the Whigs when they came into power, had only their *grand seigneurs* to put into office."[10]

Nor did Bulwer's Norman and Plantagenet blood impress the typical Whig aristocrat, who, as Bulwer put it, "laughs at antiquity; he has no poetry in his nature."[11] And the Whig clique was quintessentially exclusive:

The Whigs are the Hebrews of politics. Regarding themselves as a chosen race, the privileges of their creed are to be inherited at birth, not conceded to proselytes. They court no converts, even amongst those whom they aspire to govern. . . . No Tory from Edom, and no Radical from Moab has a right to claim admission into the sacred tribes . . . .[12]

Certainly Bulwer had once wished to join these "sacred tribes" and he must for a while have had great expectations of doing so. After gaining fame as a novelist, Bulwer found the Whigs easy to get to know, and he no doubt hoped these social contacts would mean a swift rise in the world of politics. But it was not to be. Bulwer later recorded that:

The Whigs have more largely owed their political influence . . . [to] the urbane sagacity which has led them to court social intercourse with all distinction in literature, science, and art . . . . Being most cordial in welcome to every newcomer who has achieved a success, the Whigs have been . . . most exclusive in the appropriation of power. Receiving into their drawing rooms as familiar equals every man who has won a name for himself, it has been only by compulsion, and then with muttered disfavor and more than muttered distrust, that they have received into their cabinets any man whose father had not the name of a Whig.[13]

In a curious way, then, Bulwer in the early 1830's was nurturing a grudge against the Whigs even as he was at least nominally supporting them in Parliament. His anomalous position must have occasioned him a good deal of frustration, which he found it easiest to work off in his fictional writings. In that form he could safely dabble with ideas too dangerous to express any other way.

In the historical novel *Rienzi* (1835), Bulwer bared what may have been his ideal ambition. This work was a fictionalized biography of Cola di Rienzi, the fourteenth-century Roman who succeeded briefly in setting himself up as "Tribune of the People," before meeting a Mussolini-like end. A number of similarities between Bulwer's own circumstances and those of Rienzi suggest themselves. Until the time of Rienzi's uprising, certain aristocratic families had long dominated Rome, just as Whig and Tory oligarchs had ruled in Britain. Rienzi became the champion of the anti-aristocratic forces in society. Even so, as with Bulwer, Rienzi himself was no mere plebeian. As the grandson of a Holy Roman Emperor, Rienzi considered his lineage superior to that of the aristocrats, just as Bulwer prided himself on his Norman/Plantagenet blood.

The Tribune succeeded eventually in arousing the populace, and he briefly broke the power of the oligarchs. Historians, until Bulwer's time, regarded Rienzi as a demagogue and adventurer, who deservedly fell when the Mob turned against him. But Bulwer rejected this conventional wisdom and made the Tribune a hero. He drew from the story of Rienzi the lesson that social stability depended on sturdy national institutions;

and that the security of these institutions fundamentally depended on the moral character of the people. Thus, in his defense of Rienzi, Bulwer concluded:

> The moral of the Tribune's life . . . is not the stale and unprofitable moral that warns against the ambition of an individual . . . . It proclaims that, to be great and free, a People must not trust to individuals but to themselves . . . — that it is to institutions, not to men, that they must look for reforms that last beyond the hour — that their own passions are the real despots they should subdue.

With a calm and noble people, the individual ambition of a citizen can never effect evil.[14]

Bulwer's own ambition was certainly strong, and so palpably did he identify himself with his hero that one contemporary critic contended that *Rienzi* had been written as a forecast of the role its author intended to play in British politics.[15] While Bulwer could never have been a demagogue, the point was well made. At the same time that Bulwer conceived of writing the story of Rienzi, he was also planning to help form a new "national party" that would displace the aristocratic factions. In 1833, he wrote:

> What manner of men will they be who shall compose this national party? — My friends, they cannot be the aristocrats. The aristocracy on either side are pledged to old and acknowledged factions, one part to the Tories, another to the Whigs: the party to which I refer must necessarily consist chiefly of new members, and of men wedded to no hereditary affections.[16]

This meant that Bulwer had to make common cause with the Radicals, even though, with his support for the established Church and the monarchy as props of social stability, he was far more conservative than most of them. Such ideological considerations carried less weight with him than the practical mechanics of attaining power.

His aim, therefore, was to break the power of the Whig oligarchs. On that point, he and more extreme radicals could easily agree; indeed anti-Whiggism was the broadest patch of common ground he had with them. Bulwer accordingly undertook to attack the ministers in a way the radicals could readily applaud; he accused the Whigs of failing to follow up the Reform Act with further necessary constitutional innovations and of exploiting the reform movement to further their own selfish ends. In *England and the English*, Bulwer thus described the typical Whig:

> His father was a Whig before him; and for the last twenty years he has talked about "the spirit of improvement." . . . While he talks of enlightenment, he thinks it the part of a statesman to blind [sic] to everything beyond the Reform Bill. He is for advancement to a certain point — till his party come in; he then becomes a conservative — lest his party go out.[17]

Specifically, Bulwer urged on the Whigs familiar radical demands, such as the ballot and shorter Parliaments.[18] When the Ministers opposed the bill for repealing the Septennial Act (which allowed the government seven years before dissolving Parliament), he accused them of hypocrisy because they had argued for more frequent dissolutions when it suited their purposes during the debates over the Reform Bill.[19] In a similar vein, Bulwer criticized the Whigs for employing policies of repression, even as they posed as the champions of liberalism. His denunciations of the sentence of transportation against the Dorchester laborers exemplified this.[20] Even more tellingly, Bulwer took to task the Ministerial policy toward Ireland, and in particular, the proposal by Edward Stanley, then Chief Secretary for Ireland, to crush by means of Coercion the Irish agitation for repeal of the Act of Union.

As a matter of fact, even some Ministers, notably Lord Durham, opposed Stanley's Coercion Bill. Nonetheless, the Prime Minister, Lord Grey, effectively backed Stanley. With Whig prestige thus attached to so questionable a measure, Bulwer saw a chance to unite the independent members against the Government. He again invoked the spirit of 1832: "Did we not all feel how generously the Irish Members helped us in our Reform," he asked, evidently addressing himself to the independent radicals. "Shall we repay them . . . by a donation of musketry and a Repeal of the Trial by Jury?" He went on to clarify his own position:

> I support the Government, because it has pursued a policy of liberal concession; I oppose the right hon. the Irish Secretary, because he has pursued a policy of arbitrary power . . . . Can it be supposed that the independent Members — the 300 new Representatives allied to no old party — attached to the superstition of no Whig names — can night after night, hear the facts delivered by the Members for Ireland — facts of grievances, answered by demands for soldiery, without dropping off in some defections from the Ministerial majority.[21]

Bulwer's derisive reference to the "superstition of . . . Whig names" gave vent to his resentment against that exclusive faction. At the same time, he pointed out, rather defensively, that he normally supported the Government. Here was no mere rhetorical device intended to underscore the perfidy of the measure he was (unsuccessfully) opposing. Bulwer's attitude toward the Whigs was in fact complex and often contradictory.

Even as he denounced them, Bulwer lacked the sense of purpose — or strength of character — to make a complete break from the Ministers. They had power. There was much he wanted that only they could give: honors, influence, office. Bulwer wanted to lay claim to the gratitude of the Whigs. When he failed to get it he would frequently complain of what he deemed the Whigs' ungrateful response to his loyal support.[22]

Apart from his desire for honors, Bulwer had other, worthier motives for adopting this ambivalent attitude. As already noted, he agreed with the Ministers on many issues. And, perhaps more significantly, he recognized, realist that he was, that the "national party" did not yet exist, and that if the Whigs fell, the hated Tories would succeed.

If Bulwer disliked the Whigs, he despised the Tories. They, in turn, rained torrents of abuse upon him. He would never have done anything he thought might benefit these reactionaries (as he regarded them) and, unlike some other Radicals,[23] Bulwer did not consider that the Reform Act had destroyed the Tories as a political force. He therefore cautioned his fellow Radicals:

> Don't believe the coat-holders, my friends, when they tell you with so assured an air that the Tories, as a party, are extinct. The are *not* extinct; the spirit of Toryism never dies . . . . The Tories in a year or two hence will perhaps be as formidable as ever . . . . They have a majority in the Lords, and in the Commons they are at least three times as numerous as the ultra Radicals . . . . Like the hare, they sleep with their eyes open, and, like the snake, they are hoarding venom.[24]

Bulwer lent what support he could to the more progressive Ministers, as against such conservatives as Stanley. Practically speaking, after all, the liberal Whigs had the best chance to put into effect those reforms the spirit of the age demanded. After the Irish Coercion controversy, therefore, Bulwer took this discriminating view of the Ministry and its prospects:

We see the destruction of the present government — unless removed of some men . . . — as a matter of certainty. . . . The great fault of this year . . . was the fault of the Irish Coercion Bill, the fault of Mr. Stanley. . . . The country and the House of Commons will have to decide *between Mr. Stanley and a fraction of the same Administration* . . . ; on the triumph of either will depend the future fate and destiny of the country . . . . So say we to the Administration, — "You are born of the Reform; it is by the Reform that you must govern." The power of a particular party only lasts so long as they fulfill those wants of the age which called them into power.[25]

He envisaged, then, a coalition between moderate Radicals and liberal Whigs, which the latter would lead. Given the threat the conservative Whigs like Stanley and the Tories posed to the cause of progress, Bulwer believed all reformers had necessarily to stick together. For this reason, paradoxical though it might seem, Bulwer wound up in the position of urging other Radicals to stand by the Whigs. For example, he wrote the following to Benjamin Disraeli, a close friend from the world of literature, who was at the time standing for Parliament in opposition to the Whig Charles Grey (son of the Prime Minister):

Don't abuse Ministers, express privately (so it may come to his ears) sorrow at being obliged to oppose Lord Grey or *any reformer* [emphasis added] — but claim priority of ground and I'll try all I can to prevent opposition, but don't irritate our party or the government — it may hurt and can't serve you.[26]

Bulwer feared that, should the Radicals fail to maintain their alliance with the Whigs, the latter might feel tempted to abandon the reform movement and "gently amalgamate themselves with the Tories in order to stand."[27] To prevent such a catastrophe, Radicals such as himself needed "to drive [the Whigs] strait and right."[28] For this reason, he clung to his credentials as a Ministerial loyalist.

A major political crisis in 1834 gave him a rare opportunity to act effectively along these lines. In November of that year, King William IV dismissed the Whig Ministry and brought the Tories unexpectedly to power. With a general election then imminent, Bulwer promptly wrote a pamphlet, eloquently setting forth the case for the Whigs. Privately, he explained his motives:

> I think that this is a moment in which all men not against us are for us. When all see that at such a crisis even Mr. O'Connell drops the cry of repeal and entreats permission to cooperate with all Reformers of whatever shades of opinion — we must feel the necessity of forgiving all minor offenses and suffering no division in our camp. In the pamphlet I have just published . . . I have buried a thousand public — a thousand private causes of complaint in serving the Whigs — the cause demands it from honest men. . . . [29]

In the pamphlet itself, Bulwer made clear what course he wished to see British politics take in the future. Even while deploring the change in Ministry, he made it clear that he was himself no Whig, nor a hireling of that party:

> I am not writing a panegyric on the Whigs — I leave that to men who wore their uniform and owned their leaders. I have never done so. In the palmiest days of their power, I stooped not the knee to them. By vote, pen and speech, I have humbly but honestly asserted my own independence; and I had my reward in the sarcasms and the depreciation of that party which seemed likely for the next quarter of a century to be the sole dispensers of the ordinary prizes of ambition. [30]

Bulwer then went to make the point that the dismissal of the Ministers might prove a blessing in disguise; thus chastened, the Whigs might realize their dependence on Radical support, and once returned to office, resume direction of the reformist cause. As Bulwer put it:

> If the Whigs return to office, they must be more than Whigs; you are now fighting for things, not men — for the real consequence of your reform. In your last election your gratitude made you fight too much for names; it was enough for your candidate to have served Lord Grey; you must now return those who will serve the people. [31]

Bulwer thus wrote the "Crisis" pamphlet not merely to serve the Whigs, but to help bring into power "a strong, directing government" of the sort he believed the times demanded.

Despite the qualified character of his support for them, Bulwer did the Whigs a real service with his pamphlet. One can only guess how much such writings influence the outcome of elections, but certainly the fact that "The Crisis" sold at such a spectacular rate — thirty thousand copies went in six weeks[32] — suggests that Bulwer did succeed in reviving an enthusiasm for the Whigs that had long lain dormant. He also raised his own stock appreciably, for the power of his pen made him a man to reckon with in politics. In recognition of this new status, after the Whigs returned to office by winning the 1835 elections, their leader, Lord Melbourne, offered Bulwer a junior lordship of the Admiralty.[33]

This gesture may have been well meant, but one could not call it generous. Bulwer might reasonably have expected that his talents and exertions entitled him to a higher office, and, accordingly, he declined the position. It is, therefore, not necessarily logical to conclude that Bulwer's refusal represented a definite decision to abandon politics in favor of literature.[34] At the same time, one must acknowledge that, in the years that followed, the pace of Bulwer's Parliamentary activities slowed significantly. Certainly had Bulwer accepted the junior lordship, he would at least have had a toehold on the ladder to a high office. Accordingly, it is appropriate to consider at this point what other factors might have affected Bulwer's thinking as he contemplated his future.

Bulwer himself later attributed his refusal of office to want of confidence in the Whigs. He had, in his "Crisis" pamphlet, clearly predicated his support for that party on the assumption that, once returned to office, they would vigorously pursue a policy of reform. A number of factors, notably the elevation of Lord John Russell, who had somewhat ambiguously termed the Reform Act of 1832 a "final measure," persuaded Bulwer that the Ministry would not vindicate the reformers' expectations. Lord John Russell was definitely not a man in whom Bulwer could place his confidence.[35]

Bulwer of course had no qualms about discussing publicly how he had sacrificed personal advancement for the sake of political independence. But there was another factor that more strictly constrained his freedom of action, and about which Bulwer had nothing to say except in private: the disastrous failure of his marriage.

This was a story not without elements of tragedy. The early years of Bulwer's marriage had been "the glad, confident morning" of his life. There was something extraordinarily appealing about this talented young couple as they impetuously set off upon their life together, defying parental disapproval and disinheritance, confident that, even lacking any certain means of support, they could take the world by storm. And, against great odds, they succeeded; I say *they* succeeded, for Rosina undoubtedly deserved much of the credit for Bulwer's early social and literary triumphs. For instance, when he began work on the crime novel *Paul Clifford*, she read the entire *Newgate Calendar* in order to be able to provide him with background information.[36] One might reasonably assume, moreover, that the sportive cleverness of Bulwer's early novels owed a good deal to Rosina's mordant sense of humor. Certainly wit was not Bulwer's strong suit, and his later novels would be virtually devoid of it.[37]

During the years of their marriage, Edward and Rosina lived life at a furious pace, and, to their eventual cost, they took on far too much at once. Their extravagant determination to live the lives of social lions inexorably plunged them ever deeper into debt. To meet these demands, Bulwer desperately scribbled out novel after novel, and while he actually managed a best-seller a year, he nonetheless failed to keep pace with their expenses. At the same time, he was vigorously pursuing his political ambitions; and, if that were not enough, from 1831 to 1833, he edited (and wrote copiously for) the *New Monthly Magazine*. The strain on Bulwer to sustain these efforts became unbearable and, in the end, wrecked his health, dissipated his energies, soured his personality, and destroyed his marriage.[38]

In Bulwer's case, the malaise of overwork led to an extreme irritability, a natural outcome, given his deep-seated pride and sensitivity. Rosina, of course, had to bear the brunt of this irritability. And, indeed she put up with it very well, so long as she remained in love with Bulwer. Unfortunately, over a period of years, his abrasiveness wore away even the last vestiges of this affection, until there only remained an extraordinary legacy of bitterness and hate.

By the summer of 1834, matters had gone past the point of no return, as the following incident clearly indicates. As Edward and Rosina were dining one evening, he became irrationally irritated by her failure to respond to some inconsequential remarks of his. Bulwer then, at least according to Rosina's account,

> seizing a carving knife. . . cried, "I'll have you to know that whenever *I* do you the honor of addressing you, it requires an answer!" . . . He then dropped the knife and springing on me, made his great teeth meet in my cheek, and the blood spurted over me. The agony was so great that my screams brought the servants back, and presently Cresson, the cook, seized him by the collar; but he broke from him, and seizing one of the footman's hats in the hall, rushed down Piccadilly.[39]

The danger that such disgraceful outbursts might become known to the public terrified Bulwer. He could not bear the thought of such humiliation. His impulse, therefore, was to withdraw from the public eye, as the following letter of contrition, which he wrote to Rosina soon after his assault upon her, indicates:

> I will only beseech you . . . not to arouse yourself more against me than is necessary. . . . I do not blame you for the publicity which you gave to an affront nothing but frenzy can extenuate . . . which has probably by this time made me the theme for all the malignity of London. . . . I am only fit to live alone. God and Nature afflicted me with unsocial habits, week [sic] nerves and violent passions . . . . Willingly I retire from a struggle with the world, which I have borne so long and with such constitutional disadvantages . . . . I shall retreat then at once from public life, and from the world. I shall go abroad as soon as possible — change a name which is a torment to me, and obtain. . . rest, obscurity, and solitude.
>
> I shall write from the Continent to England after a short time, announcing, from ill health, my retirement from Parliament.[40]

While Bulwer did not resign his seat (perhaps because he found that Rosina had not publicized his actions as he feared she would), he certainly curtailed his activities in Parliament. His anxiety that his failings in private life might surface to humiliate him in his public capacity weighed heavily upon him. Nor did matters improve after his final separation from Rosina in 1836, for Bulwer lived the rest of his life haunted by the hectoring of his once loving wife, who periodically demanded he increase the support he had agreed to pay her. In the years of this squalid sequel to their marriage, Rosina played upon her husband's morbid sensitivity by doing all she could to embarrass him in order to coerce him into concessions concerning their settlement. The conflicts and recriminations that resulted proved a source of irritation and humiliation for him until the end of his days. Thus, in the end, the story of Edward and Rosina became not a tragedy, but a tawdry scandal.[41]

In the mid-1830's, clearly, Bulwer was suffering from severe mental strain and deep depression. Yet, despite what he wrote at the time to Rosina, he did not abandon his political career. He felt compelled to go on, to achieve his ambitions, and as he put it, to gain "a career of some honor and a name that will not die."[42] But he would pursue this ambition less obtrusively and more quietly than he had before. He recognized, as the Ministry of Lord Melbourne failed to live up to the lofty hopes Bulwer had expressed in "The Crisis," that he must attach himself to a new political force. This, however, he would have to do by acting behind the scenes, in fomenting new political alliances, and not in standing out in the public limelight of Parliament. Given the circumstances of his private life at the time, the more circumspect and inconspicuous he could be while pursuing his abiding ambitions, the better he liked it.

It was at this time that he hitched his political hopes to the (seemingly) ascending star of Lord Durham, then a former Minister and the most radical of the Whigs. At last Bulwer had found a man he could wholeheartedly acknowledge as his leader. He had first been introduced to Durham in 1833 by Lady Blessington, whose notorious Gore House soirees both men frequented. Beforehand, Lady Blessington had, wisely, cautioned Bulwer on how to behave:

> You are going to meet Durham and he is prepared to admire and like you. Pray do not be supercilious to him as you are to most people.[43]

Thus chastened, Bulwer reserved all the charm he could muster for Durham, and the meeting proved a success. Politically, they had much in common; indeed, the most radical of the Whigs and the most moderate of the Radicals agreed on all the major questions of the day. Both saw a need for a bold but realistic program of reform. And, on a personal level, they quite hit it off. "I shall not easily forget," Bulwer later wrote Durham, "that of the Whigs, you alone seemed to think favorably of my abilities."[44] Bulwer, for his part, admired Durham, both as a man and as a political phenomenon. While visiting Ireland, he wrote of this to Lady Blessington:

> All here seem as much impressed with the shadowing of Lord Durham's coming premiership as you are in England. . . .Durham has written his horoscope on People's hearts—they only want to tell him of his destiny.[45]

Bulwer thereafter did his best to ingratiate himself with this man of destiny. But if Bulwer believed that by so doing he was assuring himself of a high place in a "coming" Ministry, he was setting himself up for disappointment. The high hopes that so many Radicals had of Durham were to come to nothing. Durham remains an enigmatic figure. He readily aroused enthusiastic followers whom, however, he as readily frustrated with his reluctance to take action to force his way to the top. Bulwer himself came up against a curiously diffident streak in his hero. For a number of years, Bulwer had expected the formation of a new

Radical (or, as he preferred to call it, National) political party. In 1835, he raised the pros and cons with Durham:

> You are probably aware that arrangements are making for the formation of a new party. The Whigs are to form one section of the Liberals — O'Connell and his tail another. And now comes the third, assuming the title of Whig-Radicals. All this your Lordship doubtless is perfectly acquainted with. . . . I see no objection to the party itself, but I see some objections to *my* joining in it. And it is upon this point that I venture to ask your advice which will entirely guide me. I do not call myself a Radical, though I am generally called so. Now nearly all of this party go greater lengths than I do — nearly all are, for instance, for the separation of Church and State . . . .
>
> These, my Lord . . . are my objections not to the party itself but to my joining it. And all these objections would vanish at once if you advocate the purposes of the party, if you think it instrumental to that cause which in my opinion can only in your triumph be thoroughly triumphant, and if on the whole you counsel me to join it, or it have in any way the sanction of your name.[46]

After this quasi-medieval act of fealty, Bulwer must have found Durham's reply — professing ignorance of the proposed Radical party — disappointing. Durham only suggested Bulwer await events; if the Whigs remained "timid," then "the exigencies of the times will call forth such a party as you may fairly and honorably belong to." But, should the Whigs prove progressive, after all, Durham told Bulwer, "you, from your great talents will be better included amongst the practicals than amongst the theorists." While Bulwer indicated, in reply, his surprise at Durham's ignorance of the proposed new party, he did not find advice of that kind difficult to take. "I will leave my vote in your Lordship's hand," he wrote, in the sycophantic tone he used to no one else, "to belong to whatever party is the most identified with you."[47]

Nonetheless, when Durham became Ambassador to Russia, Bulwer remained uncertain what course to follow. He kept up a lively correspondence with the great man, hoping, perhaps, to act as a conduit between Durham and the English Radicals. Continuing to explore the possibility of a new Radical party, Bulwer reestablished his contacts with John Stuart Mill, who was then actively working to organize such a party.

Early in 1835, Mill was pleased to observe that Bulwer "is zealously with us."[48] While never one of Bulwer's admirers, Mill considered him a great catch for the cause, and shamelessly pandered to Bulwer's almost legendary vanity in his efforts to cement the alliance. "Nobody can doubt," Mill wrote Bulwer, "that whenever you do make politics . . . your principal object . . . there is a place reserved for you in the political history of the country which will not be a humble one."[49]

While Bulwer had struck Mill as "zealous" about the idea of a Radical party, his doubts about the project were in fact increasing. Despite all their talk of forming a new party (the scheme Bulwer was involved with was only one of many), the various cliques of radicals remained too attached to their own particular projects and panaceas to coalesce into a unified political force. For this reason, Bulwer, as ever self-consciously the practical politician, tended to deprecate other radicals as impractical ideologues. Even leading figures among the Parliamentary Radicals with whom he had been closely associated, as George Grote and Noah Warburton, he readily dismissed as not "very accurate . . . [nor] practical judges of mankind." As Bulwer reported to Durham,

At present we look anything but united; and I own I think that before two years are out the Radicals will fly off in solitary particles from the Whigs as they did before, not choosing either to unite themselves or unite with others. I am persuaded that each positive party in the House requires a leader, and the Radicals are all leaders.[50]

Bulwer expressed similar reservations to Mill, indicating also that, ideologically, he considered himself far more moderate than the others likely to join the proposed party. Mill did his best to answer these objections; he argued that while he and Bulwer differed on various issues, their agreement on tactics — on the need for an organized, pragmatic amalgamation of Radicals to press for necessary reforms — outweighed their differences. When Bulwer wrote that the Radicals ought to form themselves into a distinct body, independent of the Whigs, Mill applauded the sentiment, insisting that, despite differences on certain issues, he and Bulwer agreed on essentials, and that "I am no 'impracticable,' and perhaps the number of such is smaller than you think."[51]

Despite Mill's efforts to find common ground with Bulwer, the latter's days as a promoter of a Radical party were rapidly coming to an end. There were a number of reasons for this, none more important than Durham's announcement in 1837 that he had no intention of leading a Radical party.[52] With his chief seeking reconciliation with the Whigs, Bulwer had every reason to follow suit.

He found this surprisingly easy to do, thanks to his friendly personal relationship with the Whig leader, Lord Melbourne. Whereas the previous Whig Prime Minister, the chilly Lord Grey, had personified Whig exclusivity, Melbourne was warm and avuncular. He had known Bulwer for many years.[53] Moreover, Melbourne proved willing to make up for past Whig ingratitude, and this went beyond the offer of a minor office in 1835. Two years later, we find Bulwer writing to the Prime Minister:

Will you allow me to remind you of our conversation at Brocket nearly a year ago [?] The present occasion, at the commencement of a new reign, is one not unfavorable to the kind wishes with which you have honored me. I desire not to boast pretensions nor to advance claims. I rather venture to believe that both will be viewed by your Lordship with enough prepossession to render such a task superfluous to you as it would be irksome to myself. All that I would say is, that I would not seek any distinction that I imagined would seem unmerited to my countrymen — or that I supposed would be unwelcome to my sovereign, or displeasing to her legitimate advisors.[54]

The following year, indeed, Bulwer received his long sought after symbol of recognition, in the form of a baronetcy.

While Melbourne's kindness was drawing Bulwer into the Whig camp, other factors were repelling him from the Radicals. Years later, in an effort to explain his break from the Radicals, Bulwer stressed ideological differences:

I was [he recalled] often opposed to the more extreme party commonly called the Radicals;. . . and the reason why the Radicals opposed me was because . . . [I stood for] the maintenance of an Established Church, opposition to the principle of household suffrage, and advocacy of . . . the just rights of the agricultural producer.[55]

These points of disagreement became increasingly acute over time. Earlier, Bulwer had, perhaps, stood apart from other Radicals more over tactics than objectives. He believed in making compromises in order to achieve the maximum degree of progress practically attainable; his settlement with Spring-Rice on the question of the stamp duties exemplified this. The more extreme Radicals condemned him for this willingness to compromise; they believed in holding out for all or nothing. Despite their quarrel, then, both Bulwer and his Radical critics were working toward the same end, only by differing means. Later in the 1830's, this ceased to be the case, as Bulwer's substantive disagreements with the Radicals became increasingly crucial. For example, his support for the Established Church led him to advocate the maintenance of Church schools, a view diametrically opposed to that of most Radicals. Similarly, he opposed household suffrage and the repeal of the tariffs on grain known as the Corn Laws. By 1838, clearly, Bulwer had parted company from the Radicals for good.[56]

This schism became obvious during the House of Commons debate on the Whig Ministry's conduct of the government of Canada, where a rebellion had erupted the previous year. While the Ministry's decision to send out Lord Durham as governor-general to investigate the situation won applause from Whigs and Radicals alike, other matters sparked dissension between the two groups. Certain Radicals, notably Grote and Joseph Hume, put the onus of blame for the bloodshed in Canada on the Melbourne Ministry's policies, which they termed repressive.   In particular, they attacked the suspension of the Canadian Constitution.[57]

Bulwer intervened in the debate to champion the Whigs. After enthusiastically vindicating the Whigs' Canadian policy, he turned his heaviest guns against the Radicals themselves:

> I wish the House and the country to observe that it is the same small and isolated knot of Gentlemen, who . . . declared so much contempt of the Reform Bill, and so much hostility to the Government, who now differ also from the whole people of England in their sympathy for a guilty and absurd revolt. Whether those Gentlemen call themselves Radicals or not, the greater body of Liberal politicians neither agree with them in their policy for Canada nor their principles for England. . . . They and the people of these realms cordially rejoice that the House supports her Majesty and her Ministers in this attempt to save Canada from the hell of her own factions . . . . [58]

The Radicals responded with vituperation of their own. Grote, for example, sneered at Bulwer as a "literary Whig."[59] But Bulwer was unmoved. Afterward, he commented, "The ultra Radicals abuse me like a pickpocket on the Canada question — See what a man gets for loving England better than party."[60]   After this debate, certainly, if Bulwer loved any party, it was not an independent Radical one. By the end of the year, Mill had written him off, and, in fact, lumped him among the "herd of professing Liberals" who opposed the independent Radical movement.[61]

To Bulwer, the Radicals in the late 1830's were extremists demanding changes the spirit of the age did not require. By so doing, they threatened to undermine the social stability upon which, Bulwer believed, the progress of liberty and morality ultimately depended. Their tactics could well end in revolution. Bulwer, accordingly, opposed both Chartism and the Anti-Corn Law movement.

As to Chartism, a movement advocating various democratic reforms, he wrote that off simply as a revival of the movement to abolish the New Poor Law, a measure Bulwer had advocated and now defended. As Bulwer put it:

> The People's Charter is but the Anti-Poor law agitation in disguise! The re-ascendancy of pauperism — the right of the sturdy beggar to pick the pocket of industry, these are the real objects. . . . The People's Charter . . . crusades against property itself . . . .
>
> And in the breath of these inciters to physical force — these declaimers against all rich men as robbers . . . breaks out the spirit of ferocious pauperism itself.[62]

In the new climate of political affairs, it was natural for Bulwer to alter his attitude toward the Whigs. Before, he had deprecated their impeding the progress of radical measures; now, he applauded them, for the same reason. As he wrote in an article vindicating the Whigs in 1839, it was a

> necessary condition of a free people and a representative government — that any possible administration — must always be more moderate in its views than many of those who favour it with their support . . . . That government is the best which unites the greatest degree of progress and improvement with the greatest degree of tranquillity and safety — which is best suited to the people, and therefore most popular — which is most conducive to order, and therefore most conservative.[63]

For the latter reason, Bulwer preferred the Whigs with all their faults, to the Radicals. Moreover, he deprecated Radical opposition to the Ministry as serving only to aid the Tories, whom, as ever, Bulwer abominated. In 1840, he thus outlined the essential differences between the two major parties:

64

> In a Parliamentary government there must be always two great and
> leading divisions. . . — the one, a party which, feeling confidence in the
> people, will . . . favour all propositions for the extension of public
> liberty, so far as is consistent with order and with security; the other, a
> party distrusting the judgment and virtue of the people, and which seeks
> to confine their contentment and obedience.

To Bulwer, at this stage, the Whigs were the party that "acts upon the
principle of confidence of progress," and the Tories the party of "mistrust
and restraint."[64]

Over the course of the 1830's, then, Bulwer's political orientation had
undergone substantial change. From a caustic critic of the Whigs, he had
become their champion. He viewed the Whigs as a selfish clique, but
came to believe that their party embodied the best political instrument for
satisfying the demands of liberty while securing social stability. With
this remarkable transition behind him, little could Bulwer have imagine
that the ongoing controversy over the Corn Laws would set into motion
an even more extraordinary transformation, one that would culminate in
his elevation to the rank of Cabinet Minister, — in a *Tory* Government.

NOTES

1. Quoted by Asia Briggs, *The Making of Modern England* 1783-1867 (New York: Harper
& Row, 1965), 268.

2. Bulwer took the view that children's hours of work must be limited in order to allow
them to preserve their health and obtain an education. In a speech prepared for the debate
on the Factory question which he never delivered, Bulwer observed: "These children are
to be citizens hereafter — it is impossible to forget that every year the manufacturing towns
are gaining greater political influence . . . . The State is bound . . . to see that the
members of this important class may be fairly fitted for the new duties entrusted to them.
I fear Sir that if you suffer them to grow up . . . with bodies broken by premature decay,
with minds soured by an early and familiar fellowship with misery and a belief that
labour is but another name for Exhaustion and Disease I do fear that you only rear men
who must be disaffected not only with your Laws and institutions but with Society itself."
Thus, Bulwer argued that the "strong directing state" must at times make exceptions to
the laws of political economy that condemned interference with the right freely to enter
into contracts, in order to elevate the moral character of the people and thus protect social
stability. See Lytton Papers D/EK W101.

3. Edward Bulwer, "Politician IV, in *New Monthly Magazine* (October 1, 1832).

4. Bulwer, *Pelham*, 209.

5. Sadleir, *Bulwer: A Panorama*, 207.

6. Bulwer, *Paul Clifford*, 78-79.

7. Bulwer, *Edward and the English*, II, 160-168.

8. On this point, see Sadleir, *Bulwer: A Panorama*, 193-195.

9. *Ibid.*, 322.

10. Bulwer, *England and the English*, I, 23.

11. *Ibid.*, I, 71-72.

12. [Edward Bulwer-Lytton], "Pitt and Fox," in *Quarterly Review*, 97 (September, 1855), 529.

13. [Edward Bulwer-Lytton], "England and Her Institutions," in *Quarterly Review*, 120 (October, 1866), 555-556.

14. Edward Bulwer, *Rienzi* (New York: Charles Scribner, 1902), 631.

15. Sadleir, *Bulwer: A Panorama*, 336.

16. Bulwer, *England and the English*, II, 191.

17. *Ibid.*, I, 72.

18. He also dabbled with some more imaginative ideas, but, as a pragmatist, tended to dismiss these as impracticable. In the early 1830's, for example, Bulwer wrote an article advocating the reduction of the House of Commons to one hundred members, on the grounds that it is "the unavoidable consequence of all democratic assemblies" that the "individual character" of the members "merges in the general emotion," and thus they "cease to be sages." This proposal revealed Bulwer's Carlylean contempt for "talking shops" that undermined the efficiency of government. He realized however that the House of Commons would not scuttle eighty percent of its membership, and therefore quietly let the idea drop. See, Edward Bulwer, "Character of the Last Unreformed House of Commons," Lytton Papers, D/EK W102.

19. *Hansard*, XXIII, 1080.

20. *Ibid.*, 118-119. This notorious case concerned six agricultural laborers who were transported out of the country for the crime of organizing a union.

21. *Ibid.*, XV, 238-244.

22. See, for instance, Earl of Lytton, II, 156-157.

23. Benjamin Disraeli, for example, became a Radical in 1832 because he considered the Tories "worn out." See Robert Blake, *Disraeli*, (New York: Anchor Books, 1968), 84. On Bulwer's war of words with the Tories, see Sadleir, *Bulwer: A Panorama*, 166-186 and 226-260.

24. Bulwer, *England and the English*, II, 178.

25. Bulwer, "The Politician XVIII," *New Monthly Magazine* (August, 1833).

26. Edward Bulwer to Benjamin Disraeli, June 17, 1832, Hughenden Papers, Box 104, B/XX/Ly/13. Robert Blake interprets this letter to mean that Bulwer intended to use his influence with the Whigs to see to it that Disraeli got in unopposed; but since Grey had appeared on the hustings of Wycombe at least a week earlier, that interpretation would seen untenable. See Blake, *Disraeli*, 84-85.

27. Bulwer to Lord Durham, January 13, 1835, Lytton Papers, D/EK C26.

28. Bulwer to Albany Fonblanque, January 18, 1835, *Ibid.*

29. Bulwer to Edward Bell Drury, November 26, 1834, in Parrish Collection, Firestone Library, Princeton University.

30. Quoted by Earl of Lytton, I, 481.

31. *Ibid.*, 484-485.

32. *Ibid.*, 484-485.

33. T. H. S. Escott, *Edward Bulwer* (London: George Routledge, 1910), 216.

34. Earl of Lytton, 494-495.

35. Edward Bulwer-Lytton, Speech at Hitchin, June 22, 1852, Lytton Papers, D/ED W98.

36. Sadleir, *Bulwer: A Panorama*, 133.

37. Bulwer's later novels, such as *The Caxtons*, rely for humor on a sort of good natured joviality which was quite different from wit. Bulwer attempted to compensate for his weakness in that area by clipping and saving humorous fillers and jokes that appeared in newspapers, in order that he might rework them and fit them into his own writings when he felt comic relief was called for.

38. For an excellent and complete account of Bulwer's marriage and the reasons for its failure, see Sadleir, *Bulwer: A Panorama, passim.*

39. Quoted by Devey, *Letters of Bulwer to His Wife*, 399.

40. Edward Bulwer to Rosina Bulwer, July 4, 1834, *Ibid.*, 394-398.

41. As part of this campaign, Rosina actually published a novel of her own, *Chevely, or The Man of Honour*, to poke fun at Bulwer. The subtitle of the work clearly showed her awareness of his extreme sensitivity — and vulnerability — when it came to the concept of honor. On the unhappy aftermath of their marriage, see Chapter Seven.

42. Bulwer to Lady Blessington, October 23, 1834, Lytton Papers, D/EK C26.

43. Lady Blessington to Bulwer, n.d., quoted by Michael Sadleir, *The Strange Life of Lady Blessington* (Boston: Little, Brown, 1933), 212.

44. Bulwer to Lord Durham, January 21, 1835, quoted in Earl of Lytton, I, 497.

45. Bulwer to Lady Blessington, October 23, 1834, Lytton Papers, D/EK C26.

46. Bulwer to Lord Durham, January 21, 1835. Quoted by Earl of Lytton, I, 496-498.

47. Lord Durham to Bulwer, January 26, 1835; Bulwer to Lord Durham, February 2, 1825. *Ibid.*, 498-500.

48. John Stuart Mill to Albany Fonblanque, March, 1835. See Frances E. Mineka, ed., *The Earlier Letters of John Stuart Mill* (Toronto: University of Toronto Press, 1963), 251.

49. John Stuart Mill to Bulwer, November 29, 1836. *Ibid.*, 313-314.

50. Bulwer to Lord Durham, January 212, 1835, quoted in Earl of Lytton, I, 497; Same to same, n. d. Stuart J. Reid, *Life and Letters of the First Earl of Durham 1792-1840* (London: Longmans, Green, 1906), II, 96-99.

51. Mill to Bulwer, quoted by Earl of Lytton, I, 511-512.

52. On Durham's renunciation of the Radical party, see Harriet Grote, *The Philosophical Radicals of 1832* (New York: Burt Franklin, 1970), [first published 1866], 33.

53. Bulwer, like Byron before him, had had an affair with Lady Caroline Lamb, wife of the future Lord Melbourne. Melbourne viewed these escapades indulgently. In Bulwer's case, the thrill no doubt came more from his imitation of Byron than from his admiration of Lady Caroline.

54. Bulwer to Lord Melbourne, August 15, 1837, Parrish Collection, Firestone Library, Princeton University.

55. Bulwer, Speech at Hitchin, June 22, 1852, Lytton Papers, D/EK W98.

56. When Bulwer received his baronetcy, the Radicals charged that he obtained it in exchange for his surrender, as they saw it, on the stamp duties issue. See Earl of Lytton, II, 245. On the stamp duties questions, see Chapter Two of this biography. On Bulwer's support for the Church of England, see also Chapter Two, and *England and the English*, I, 7, 207-209, 235-237.

57. *Hansard*, XL, *passim*.

58. *Ibid.*, 393-399.

59. *Ibid.*, 399.

60. Bulwer to Lady Blessington, January 31, 1838, Lytton Papers, D/EK C26.

61. Mill to John Robertson, November, 1838, in Mineka, *The Earlier Letters of John Stuart Mill*, 391-392.

62. [Edward Bulwer], "The People's Charter," in *Monthly Chronicle* (October, 1838), 297-302.

63. [Edward Bulwer], "Defense of the Whigs," in *Edinburgh Review*, 70 (October, 1839), 259.

64. [Edward Bulwer], "Present State and Conduct of Parties," in *Edinburgh Review*, 71 (April, 1840), 277-278.

CHAPTER FOUR

THE MAKING OF A CONSERVATIVE

In the early years of his political career, Edward Bulwer held views then fashionable among intellectuals and radicals. It was not therefore remarkable that he advocated free trade. Yet, during the course of the 1830's, he reevaluated his position and became a protectionist, a transformation that would profoundly affect the course of his career.

To account for it, we must return to 1832, when the Reform Act abolished the Parliamentary borough of St. Ives, for which Bulwer had sat since the previous year. With a view to the General Election in the fall, three boroughs invited Bulwer's candidacy. Of these, he chose to stand at Lincoln.

Some of his biographers[1] have written that Bulwer selected Lincoln because its voters, as residents of an agricultural district, opposed the abolition of the Corn Laws. But these writers incorrectly assumed that Bulwer held in 1832 the protectionist views that would later distinguish him. Such was not the case. Shortly before the Lincoln election, there appeared in the *New Monthly Magazine*, which Bulwer was then editing, an article that denounced the Corn Laws as "bread denying ordinances" and urged that Britain should obtain cheap bread from abroad in exchange for manufactured goods.[2] The following year, Bulwer showed that he shared these sentiments. In *England and the English*, he ridiculed the "typical" Tory protectionist squire under the pseudonym "Sir Harry Hargrave":

Sir Harry Hargrave is never dishonest nor inhumane, except for the best possible reasons . . . . Sir Harry Hargrave gives away one hundred and two loaves every winter to the poor; it is well to let the labourer have a loaf of bread now and then for nothing; would it not be as well, Sir Harry, to let him have the power always to have bread cheap? Bread cheap! What are you saying? Sir Harry thinks of his rents, and considers you a revolutionist for the question. But Sir Harry Hargrave, you answer, is a humane man, and charitable to the poor. Is this conscientious? My dear sir, to be sure; he considers it his first duty — *to take care of the landed interest.*[3]

Not only did Bulwer advocate cheap bread, but he also made it clear that he favored free trade as a general principle:

> Industry is . . . *the* distinguishing quality of our nation, the pervading genius of our riches, our grandeur, and our power! . . . We should break down all barriers that oppose it; foresee, and betimes destroy, all principles that are likely to check or prevent it . . . . We cannot too zealously guard it from all obstacle . . . and [from] bounties, prohibitions, and monopolies, that amputate the sinews of action.[4]

This endorsement of free trade did not prevent Bulwer from easily winning his election at Lincoln. Consequently, it seems reasonable to conclude that, as large scale agitation against the Corn Laws had not yet begun, the question influenced neither Bulwer's decision to contest Lincoln nor the outcome of that election.

It is likely, however, that the strength of the agricultural interest at Lincoln later led Bulwer to mute his opposition to the Corn Laws. When, in 1834, the issue came up for a vote in the House of Commons for the first time during his Parliamentary career, Bulwer actually paired off on the side of the protectionists. Deference to the wishes of his constituents, rather than a genuine change of heart, probably accounted for this reversal of form, for we find that a year later Bulwer was, in private at least, still opposed to the Corn Laws:

> The rural ignorance, as far as I have seen, passes all understanding — and it is quite enough with most that a man is popular with the town to be terrible in the counties — I am sure that till the Corn Laws are properly settled — the feud between town and country must ever go dangerously on. . . . [5]

With free trade views and a protectionist constituency, no wonder that Bulwer considered the Corn Laws an issue best left alone. Probably he was indicating his own attitude when he suggested, in 1834, that his political idol "Lord Durham should carefully avoid committing himself about the Corn Laws or against the Agricultural Interest."[6]

Bulwer did not genuinely adopt protectionist views until the later 1830's, when he was also transferring his political allegiance from the Radicals to the Whigs. At that same time the Anti-Corn Law League was making protection a major issue, and their agitation no doubt led Bulwer to give more thought to the issue than he ever had before. He eventually rejected the reasoning of the Anti-Corn Law League as emphatically as he did the hostile assessment of protection he had himself expressed only a few years earlier.

Instead, as the struggle over the Corn Laws approached its climax, he took the view that the entire question was "one in which political economy — mere mercantile loss and gain, has least to do. High social considerations are bound up in it." The effects of repeal, he warned, would be "felt in the next age." It was, in his view, a question of whether the industrial working class ought to make up an increasing proportion of the nation's population; whether

> by augmenting yet more, not the prosperity of commerce and manufacturing alone but the masses of men employed in them — you have not altered for the worse the staple character and Spirit of the people . . . . [7]

Clearly, Bulwer had come to consider agriculture an indispensable occupation, if not for economic reasons, then for the sake of the survival of those moral qualities in the population that he deemed essential if England were to continue to enjoy liberty and order.

To understand Bulwer's change of heart, we must recall certain events of his personal life. At the time he separated from his wife in 1836, Bulwer was burdened by anxiety and overwork. The one person who could offer him the solace and understanding he needed, was his mother. Once again they became close.[8] She offered him not only maternal affection, but security. He knew that, as her heir, he would someday own Knebworth House and its estates. The prospect of becoming a country squire suddenly appealed to him, whereas, a few years before, when he and Rosina were shining in the "gilded saloons" of Mayfair, this would have sounded a deadly bore, if not a complete impossibility. As he himself put it a few years later:

> There are two things in life which bring a man in connection with that grave happiness called Duty. One is a fortunate marriage, the other a landed property. As I missed the one, I am pleased to see

that the other compels one, *nolens volens,* to rouse oneself from one's egoism, and to one's amaze [sic] act for other people . . . .

I often think over the wisdom of a saying of Goethe's, "nothing keeps the mind more healthful than having something in common with the mass of mankind." Property and politics both help to do this, whereas literature takes one away from it.[9]

While the foregoing dates from the 1850's, Bulwer had, by the late 1830's, already recognized how much personal satisfaction he might derive from acting the part of a country squire. This is clear from his novel *Alice* (1838), in which he wrote of "Ernest Maltravers," who had returned to his rural estates after suffering disappointment in his worldly ambitions:

The effect which the presence of Maltravers produced among his peasantry was one that seldom failed to refresh and soothe his more bitter and disturbed thoughts . . . . They felt that his real object was to make them better and happier; and they had learned to see that the means he adopted generally advanced the end. Besides, if he was sometimes stern, he was never capricious or unreasonable; and then, too, he would listen patiently and advise kindly. They were a little in awe of him, but this awe only served to make them more industrious and orderly; to stimulate the idle man — to reclaim the drunkard. . . .

And Maltravers looked into his cottages and looked at the allotment ground; and it was pleasant to him to say to himself, "I am not altogether without use in life."[10]

Thus, long before Bulwer actually joined the Tory party, an element of "Tory Paternalism" had crept into his thinking. This certainly accelerated his separation from the more extreme Radicals who saw political democracy as a solution for all the nation's ills.[11] Bulwer regarded rapid political change as dangerous. He developed his ideas on this point as well in *Alice*; in this instance he spoke through the character "De Montaigne," a Frenchman who believed that the

tendency of all European states is towards Democracy, but he by no means looked upon democracy as a panacea for all legislative evils. He thought that, while a writer should be in advance of his time, a statesman should content himself with marching by its side; that a nation could not be ripened, like an exotic, by artificial means; that it must be developed only by natural influences. He believed that forms of government are never universal in their effects. Thus, De Montaigne conceived that we were wrong in attaching more importance to legislative than to social reforms.[12]

Then "De Montaigne" proposed that the paternalism of the English aristocracy should provide the model for this social reform policy; to "Maltravers" he stated:

> Do you not employ on behalf of individuals the same moral agencies that wise legislation or sound philosophy would adopt toward the multitude? For example, you find that the children of your village are happier, more orderly, more obedient, promise to be wiser and better men in their own station of life, from the new . . . excellent system of school discipline and teaching that you have established. . . . Again, you find that, by simply holding out hope and emulation to industry — by making stern distinctions between the energetic and the idle — the independent exertion and the pauper mendicancy — you have found a lever by which you have literally moved and shifted the little world around you. But what is the difference here between the rules of a village lord and the laws of a wise legislature? The moral feelings you have practiced are as open to legislators as to the individual proprietor.[13]

The foregoing, to be sure, has much in common with the views Bulwer had expressed as an avowed philosophic Radical. There is the same insistence on encouraging independence as a means of inculcating morality among the masses.[14] But there is also a difference. In *England and the English*, for instance, he had depicted the English aristocracy as an impediment to the aims of effective government.[15] But, by 1838, he had begun to regard himself as belonging to the landed class, and he therefore took a far more positive view of their role. Indeed, he was advancing rapidly toward the position he would express in 1852:

> I hold the Aristocratic Element in a State to be vitally essential to all elevation of Social Thought and all durability to free institutions. I would infinitely prefer an Aristocratic Republic to a Democratic Monarch. And connecting with this theory . . . the peril of disaffecting or greatly impoverishing the sole party in this state that counterbalances the inevitable democracy engendered in the manufacturing populations (I mean the agricultural) I have ever been opposed to total Repeal of the Corn Laws.[16]

Bulwer's increasing attachment to the aristocratic element no doubt helped bring about his abandonment of independent Radicalism in favor of Whiggism in the late 1830's. It also contributed, ironically, to his defeat for re-election at the agricultural borough of Lincoln in 1841. Bulwer lost his seat, as he himself stated, principally because he had supported the increasingly unpopular Whig Ministry.[17] Two issues in particular proved his undoing: the proposed reduction of the Sugar Duties and, of course, the question of the Corn Laws.

Bulwer found himself in an awkward position in 1841 as a result of the political strategy pursued by Lord John Russell, then the Secretary of State for the Colonies and the outstanding figure in Melbourne's Whig Administration. Lord John recognized that the Ministry could not long survive. But he believed that the manner in which it met its demise could help prepare the way for future political triumphs. He actually sought therefore to alienate various special interests — notably Agriculture, Sugar, and Lumber — which enjoyed the protection of prohibitory tariffs. Russell expected his chief rival, Conservative leader Sir Robert Peel, to defend these interests. This would cause the industrial middle-class, which was demanding free trade, to support Russell and the Whigs. Alternatively, should Peel make a bid for middle class backing by abandoning the principle of protection, he would lose forever the allegiance of the country squires who formed the bulk of the Tory Parliamentary party. Confident he could force upon Peel this choice of two equally fatal courses, Russell serenely awaited his own party's impending fall from power.[18]

On May 7, 1841, Russell put his plan into action by introducing a Bill to reduce the duty on foreign sugar. He argued that the institution of a revenue tariff in place of a prohibitory duty would help to balance the budget. He also took this occasion to denounce the Corn Laws — maintaining they should be replaced by a fixed duty of eight shillings per quarter on imported grain — thus leaving no doubt in the minds of the agriculturalists that the sugar bill represented the opening sally in an assault upon themselves. Thus Russell steered his sugar bill directly for the shoals.[19]

Meanwhile, Bulwer was resolved to demonstrate his loyalty to the Ministers by voting for their measure. It is unlikely he did so wholeheartedly. For one thing, the sugar bill would open the lucrative British market to foreign slave-grown sugar, at the expense of the British West Indian merchants who had recently turned to free labor. To Bulwer, who had delivered some of his most eloquent and effective addresses on behalf of the abolitionist cause,[20] this must have seemed as unwise as it was unjust.

Quite apart from this, the Whigs had placed Bulwer in a politically awkward position. As Russell had raised the question of the Corn Laws as well as the sugar duty, Bulwer knew that to support the Government meant offending his constituents. Paradoxically, now that he had become a genuine protectionist, he stood at greater peril than ever of losing his seat at Lincoln.

Despite such considerations, Bulwer both spoke and voted for the sugar bill. Perhaps he felt that he had cast his lot with the Whigs and did not want to change course again. In his speech, he denied that the sugar bill undermined the anti-slavery movement. Britain, after all, imported other slave-grown commodities. And, as far as foreign sugar was concerned, it had long since been coming into Britain — to be re-exported — in an arrangement that meant profits for British West Indian merchants. Why, Bulwer asked, could not this inexpensive sugar be sold in Britain to the advantage of British consumers, while at the same time, the proceeds of the revenue tariff helped balance the budget and thus lessened the need for imposing "new taxes on an already overtaxed and oppressed people?"[21]

In the same speech, Bulwer derided the idea that reduction of the sugar duties would lead to repeal of the Corn Laws. He knew that if the electorate linked these two issues, he would very likely meet defeat at Lincoln. That this consideration was much on his mind is clear from his speech:

> Being a Member representing an agricultural constituency, and entertaining, as I always have, even before I had the honour of appearing in this House as the representative of that constituency, a very strong feeling with regard to an adequate degree of protection [being] afforded to the landed interest . . . I confess I am not satisfied with the degree of protection which the noble Lord proposed to afford. . . . But. . . I do not see how these sentiments oblige me to band myself with the friends of all monopoly whatsoever. I believe, too, that the agricultural interests need no such alliance, but that the demands of their case will place them upon such a footing as that they will suffer no injustice at the hands of the House.[22]

In the division that followed, the sugar bill failed by 36 votes. Russell thereupon intended to push to a vote his proposal to replace the existing Corn Law with a moderate fixed duty, but Peel outmaneuvered him by passing a vote of no confidence against the tottering Government, thus forcing the Whigs to resign and face a General Election.

Bulwer stood once again at Lincoln, where he had already won three times. The City would elect two Members, and, in 1841, there were four candidates: Bulwer (Liberal), Charles Seeley (Liberal), William Collett (Conservative), and Colonel Charles Sibthorp (Conservative). Sibthorp, who had been Bulwer's colleague in the representation of Lincoln since 1835, ranked as one of the most extreme ultra Tories in the House of Commons, but he was very popular with the borough's agricultural interest. With Sibthorp thus virtually certain of heading the poll (as he had in the two preceding elections), the other three candidates were left to contend for second place.

Much of the campaign's oratory, of course, focused on the Corn Laws. Bulwer gave his views on this topic as follows:

> These are my sentiments on the Corn Laws. I will not vote for the abolition of them; I will not vote for the Government proposition of an eight or nine shilling duty, because I believe it to be but a step to that abolition. But I am ready to allow that you must take the matter of the Corn Laws into serious consideration; and I do believe that by a judicious mixture of the fixed duty and the graduated scale, you may give great relief to the manufacturers, and, at the same time not diminish the proper protection of the land.[23]

Land, he argued, deserved a special protection because a large proportion of the population depended on farming for their livelihood. He explained that, while he considered the existing sliding scale "defective and unjust," and likely to diminish the nation's commerce, he felt himself

> bound to look to the millions employed in agriculture whose hard fingers, as Mr. Collett well said, can never learn the art of handling threads and bobbins. I cannot be insensible to the one great danger of throwing large tracts of inferior land out of cultivation. It is this which would make me cautious in any alteration of the Corn Laws—and to prefer a fixed duty to any more searching and revolutionary change.[24]

Bulwer, then, was steering a middle course, attempting to conciliate the agricultural interest, without offending the Whigs and Liberals who had supported him in the past. In the end, however, this proved fruitless. He alienated the more radical free traders, but failed to attract any significant support from Tory protectionists.

But the results of the Lincoln election did not turn exclusively on the question of the Corn Laws. As is so often the case, purely local political considerations played a part in determining the outcome. The fact that Bulwer — on account of ill health and sagging spirits — had not even visited Lincoln for two years preceding this election, certainly did him no good in this respect.[25]

By the time of the election, a serious rift had taken place in the ranks of the Liberal party of Lincoln. Charles Seeley, a tradesman and formerly chairman of Bulwer's own election committee, had, upon the death of the man expected to stand, emerged as the second Liberal candidate, whereupon he began a vigorous campaign, enunciating the principles of middle class radicalism, and denouncing aristocratic and ecclesiastical influence in the City. Bulwer took a detached view of all this. As he put it during the campaign:

> It is not for me to dictate to any of those with whom my only connection is that of Representative . . . . Let my constituents and general supporters select the person they prefer as second candidate, let them decide, uninfluenced by me, whether we should cooperate and coalesce or stand separate and independent of each other.[26]

As Seeley's campaign went ahead, antagonism grew between his supporters and Bulwer's. Probably this owed more to mutual feelings of rivalry and resentment than to any substantive disagreement over the issues. Bulwer later wrote that all those who had voted for him in the past remained "satisfied with my political opinions." But because Seeley had been "inspired with the ambition of presenting himself as a candidate . . . , great jealousies were created . . . and the great liberal party was broken up in consequence of that step . . . ."[27] At the same time, Bulwer's supporters probably considered Seeley too radical, while the adherents of the latter may have felt that Bulwer, with his marked attachment in recent times to the Whig Ministry, had become too conservative.

Bulwer recognized that the antagonism between his supporters and Seeley's posed grave peril to the Liberal cause. He knew that most of the Seeleyites had voted for himself in elections past, and feared they might now withhold from him the second of their two votes, out of spite as well as to aid Seeley. Yet it was apparent that if the supporters of

78

each of the Liberal contenders systematically "cut" the other candidate, it would surely result in the election of both the Tories. To prevent that, Bulwer addressed a Liberal meeting and called for party unity:

> To gain . . . victory, one thing is necessary—union amongst ourselves . . . . For my own part I have not the shadow of a jealousy or a suspicion as to the upright, fair and honorable course that Mr. Seeley and his Friends wish to adopt with regard to myself. . . . I know that . . . strength depends upon mutual compromise. Some of Mr. Seeley's more immediate Friends have not approved of all my opinions but I count on their general support with the fullest confidence—some of my friends may dissent from Mr. Seeley—but I respectfully suggest to them that Mr. Seeley is in this instance the representative of a great Principle, the entire emancipation from [sic] this city from all corrupt—all Ecclesiastical and all Aristocratic domination in the choice of a British Representative.[28]

Bulwer had good reason to commend Seeley's stand against corruption. For, while the Liberals battled among themselves, the Tories were striving to entice the voters to their side with offers of free ale and other bribes. Such affronts infuriated Bulwer, whose nerves were probably near the breaking point anyway. At any event, with all his latent military instincts aroused, Bulwer exhorted his supporters at the hustings after the manner of Henry V before Agincourt:

> This contest, the severest ever known in this City— will be remembered long by those who . . . are identified with the progress of the People and the emancipation of the City. They shall tell their sons with pride of the threats that they disregarded, of the temptations that they resisted. Every man who will register his vote for this great cause shall say in his old age—"I would not have lost that vote for ten times the money for which a vote was ever sold."[29]

But the "happy few" who voted for Bulwer proved, in the end, too few. The results were: Sibthorp 541; Collett 481; Bulwer 443; Seeley 340. The difference between Bulwer's total and Seeley's suggests that the split in the Liberal party had indeed caused widespread withholding of votes.[30]

The election of 1841 affected the course of Bulwer's political career in two ways. First, he lost his seat in the House of Commons, to which he would not return for eleven years. Thus, in the prime of his life, he had no opportunity for advancement in Parliament or in party politics.

Secondly, and more fundamentally, the election of 1841 clearly marked the beginning of the end of Bulwer's rapprochement with the Whigs. Although, in the late 1830's, he had broken his ties with the Radicals and loyally supported the Whig Ministry, he had little to show for his trouble. True, the Government had granted him a baronetcy in 1838, but that honor scarcely satisfied Bulwer's ambition. Then, when he lost the election, his support for the Government seemingly contributed to his defeat. Accordingly, he wrote to the Prime Minister, Lord Melbourne, to ask

> for the merely nominal dignity which perhaps I might have reasonably attained had I held any subordinate office in your Lordship's administration. In support of that administration I have gone through 5 contested elections entirely at my own expense and am now defeated solely on account of my votes on the sugar duties and Sir Robert Peel's motion in want of confidence. During that period, not only as a Member of Parliament, but far more efficiently perhaps as an author, I have defended the measures and policy of the government — without the usual rewards of place or emolument connected with Political and Parliamentary exertion.[31]

Apparently not yet realizing that the Whigs were being soundly beaten in the General Election and that Melbourne would soon have to resign, Bulwer asked to be made a privy councillor.[32] This, however, was not forthcoming. Although Bulwer was to remain a Liberal for the duration of the decade, the disenchantment that ultimately caused him to leave that party dated from this occasion.

Following the election of 1841, Bulwer put a happy face on his defeat, acting as if he really preferred private life to the anxiety involved in holding the office he had so recently sought. "I can well bear being out of Parliament at present," he wrote to John Forster nine days after his defeat, implying he no longer cared about having a political career.[33] But, during his years outside of Parliament, he remained an interested and discerning observer of public affairs. He had by no means shaken the political bug. When he learned of Sir Robert Peel's decision to repeal the Corn Laws, Bulwer-Lytton[34] did not even try to disguise his determination to return to the political fray:

> This stupendous treachery of Peel's excites my gall and recalls my
> political fervor. I long again to be in Public Life—though the old
> illusions are dispelled and the career neither elevating nor happy.[35]

Unfortunately for his attempts at a political comeback,
Bulwer-Lytton had not lost all of his political illusions. He failed to
perceive how drastically the political situation had altered since his last
campaign, and remained a Liberal protectionist, though this stance had no
longer a semblance of plausibility. The Liberal party had made free trade
part of its platform. Whereas in 1841 Lord John Russell had seemed
radical when he advocated a moderate fixed duty on imported grain, such
a proposal now suited virtually no one except certain Tory Protectionists.
Russell himself had endorsed free trade in 1845 and had replaced Peel as
Prime Minister the following year. If Bulwer-Lytton had hesitated to
follow Russell's lead in 1841, it made no sense for him to do so in 1847.

The logic of events, then, dictated he join his fellow protectionists
in the Tory party. But he had always opposed Toryism and, unable to
break the political habit of a lifetime, he remained a Liberal. It would
take a sharp jolt to awaken him to political reality; and events at Lincoln
were shortly to provide just that jolt.

Strangely enough, it seemed for a time that Bulwer-Lytton's
Liberal/protectionist views would work to his advantage at the next
Lincoln election. Sibthorp, the reactionary incumbent, and Seeley, the
radical outsider, were both definitely in the running again, except the
latter now seemed a far more formidable candidate than he had in 1841.
As Bulwer-Lytton later described the situation:

> There had been a reaction in the prevalent opinions of the town, the
> agriculturalists were dispirited, the repealers could return a member.
> If I had then acquiesced in Repeal the person [Seeley] who opposed
> me on the liberal interest would have had no pretense to stand. . . .
> I did not acquiesce in the repeal . . . . [36]

The Tories of Lincoln wanted desperately to defeat Seeley, but their
chances of doing so seemed slim, especially since Collett, the other
incumbent, had apparently decided not to seek re-election. This
circumstance disposed them to support any candidate who would support
the principle of protection and who seemed capable of defeating Seeley.

Such was the state of affairs that led William Rudyard, an influential
Lincoln politician who had long had friendly relations with
Bulwer-Lytton, to write the latter urging him to stand once again at

Lincoln. Rudyard informed Bulwer-Lytton that Sibthorp would do everything to prevent Seeley's return, and offered the following advice:

> I should have no hesitation in advising you to come forward for you would have a great weight of Sibthorp voters divide with you and I have assurance of the principal agriculturalists . . . (who opposed you at the last election) that they would do all they could to promote your return.[37]

According to Rudyard, Seeley had no chance against the combination of Sibthorp and Bulwer-Lytton. The latter would pick up a substantial share of Tory votes (assuming Collett kept out of the contest) and would also retain the support of many of the Liberals who had supported him in the past. The fact that he was both a protectionist *and* a Liberal placed him in a particularly strong position, given the peculiar circumstances then prevailing in Lincoln politics. Rudyard underscored this fact when he praised Bulwer-Lytton for "remaining constant in your opinions of general Liberal government," while also noting "I agree with you that Peel's new Corn Law is 'an hazardous experiment'. . . ."[38]

Although Bulwer-Lytton agreed to become a candidate, he felt less than pleased about the electoral tactics he was bound to employ. It struck him as unethical to campaign as a Liberal, and appeal to the old loyalties of Liberal voters, while acting simultaneously in friendly cooperation with the Tories, thereby serving Tory interests by assisting their efforts to exclude an avowed reformer from the House of Commons. As Bulwer-Lytton wrote to John Forster:

> I don't like my position at Lincoln at all. I may come in, but it will not be by a straight forward contest but a war of . . . tact and management, in other words, tricks and craft.[39]

Meanwhile, Seeley, who was not above employing "tricks and craft" himself, was proving a formidable antagonist for his erstwhile leader. He insinuated that Bulwer-Lytton had become a Tory by noting that he employed a lawyer, William Loaden (who represented him at certain political meetings at Lincoln) whom the Seeleyites termed "a London TORY lawyer."[40] In addition, the Seeleyites circulated a pamphlet which struck at the heart of Bulwer-Lytton's strategy. It charged that Bulwer-Lytton has been brought into the field, solely to defeat our Citizen Candidate [Seeley] . . . .On former occasions Sir Lytton Bulwer was the zealous opponent of Col. Sibthorp and the Tories; now he says nothing of his old antagonists, but his whole hostility is directed against Mr. Seeley and Liberals . . . . There is no man I should more have wished to support than Sir Bulwer Lytton [sic], if he had come forward as an avowed Liberal, but I cannot help to return a man who is brought forward solely for the purpose of defeating another Liberal candidate.[41]

Seeley's campaign proved effective, assisted no doubt by the fact (which he also played up) that Bulwer-Lytton had been away from Lincoln for six years. Loaden reported to Bulwer-Lytton a few weeks before the balloting that many Liberals in the borough had decided, to their regret, that they could not vote for Bulwer-Lytton unless Seeley's election were certain.[42] Thus, Bulwer-Lytton found himself increasingly dependent on Tory support.

But misfortune plagued him in that regard as well, for William Collett, the Tory incumbent, unexpectedly declared his candidacy for re-election. This was bound to cost Bulwer-Lytton the support of many protectionists. Rumors spread that Bulwer-Lytton had decided to withdraw, and Rudyard summoned Loaden to Lincoln to meet with the election committee to determine whether or not Bulwer-Lytton should remain a candidate. Perhaps because he believed Collett would not be able to regain much of his former strength, Bulwer-Lytton remained in the contest.[43]

He concentrated his efforts on winning back support among the Liberals. Nine days before the election, he wrote his friend John Forster to request "a few lines in the *Examiner* and *Daily News* on behalf on my election." Significantly, as Bulwer-Lytton was walking a political tight rope, he added that these lines should not be directed "against either Tories or Radicals," but should simply present Bulwer-Lytton as "a man of merit . . . and integrity." Bulwer-Lytton explained to Forster that "a large portion of the voters for Seeley the Radical . . . withhold their second vote from me . . . [and] I want to get their 2nd votes by strong appeals to my claims independent of personal considerations." At the same time, he added, he was counting on some help from Tory voters and "any violent anti-Tory paragraph would therefore do more harm than good."[44]

In his election address, Bulwer-Lytton made a final appeal for Liberal support, while remaining careful to signal to the Tories his continuing support of protectionism:

> It is probable that, in the general severance of old party ties throughout the country, and the absence of questions creating strong party excitement, I may obtain the aid of many who have formerly opposed me; I shall feel honored by such confidence, and in those points we do agree, they will not find they have misplaced that confidence . . . . But . . . I am peculiarly anxious to obtain no votes given under erroneous impressions . . . . I am, as I ever have been, one of that class who call themselves "Reformers:" I shall offer to the existing Government such support as becomes an independent Member . . . . [45]

He remained hopeful of victory until the eve of the election, writing to Forster that "the general feeling of the Town is strongly with me and the Election depends on votes unpromised, which that general feeling may influence at the poll."[46] But, in the end, Bulwer-Lytton's attempt to appeal at once to both parties backfired. The support he got from Colonel Sibthorp, for instance, which should have helped by keeping Tory voters from deserting him in favor of Collett, had instead the effect of confirming Seeley's charge that Bulwer-Lytton was acting in collusion with his long time political foes. As Bulwer-Lytton noted afterwards, "I lost more from desertion than I gained from Conservative aid."[47]

As if that were not enough, Sibthorp's endorsement cost him more votes in another and totally unexpected way. Some Tory voters so resented Bulwer-Lytton's displacement of Collett that they determined to defeat him, even if it meant supporting Seeley instead.[48] Bulwer-Lytton explained this startling turn of events in a post-election letter to Lady Blessington:

> My election was lost, by votes being transferred from Collett the Tory candidate to Seeley the Radical. The night before the day, I seemed perfectly safe, having a clear majority of promises, and should have come in but for the most unexpected turn.[49]

The final count was: Sibthorp 659; Seeley 520; Bulwer-Lytton 437; Collett 277.[50]

Bulwer-Lytton took his defeat badly. Perhaps it was not so much the fact that he lost, but rather the degrading experience of the campaign itself. After all, he enjoyed international celebrity as an author. He aimed at literary immorality, and expected to become one of the great men of his age. As sensitive as he was proud, he thought it unseemly that he should have had to compete on equal terms with "nonentities" like Collett and Seeley. He thought that the Whigs, once again in power, owed it to him as one of their supporters to provide him with a safe seat. But he knew they would not do anything for him. As he told Forster, "I have little chance of another seat. Macaulay, Hobhouse, Howes, and others will get the Whig places . . . . "[51]

Bulwer-Lytton's second defeat at Lincoln, then, completed the process begun by his first, of revivifying his former anti-Whiggism. He made his feelings plain a few months later when Forster, who still regarded Bulwer-Lytton as a fellow liberal, requested he write for the *Examiner* in support of the Ministry. Bulwer-Lytton, in his reply, gave vent to his bitterness:

> I loathe politics. They are associated in my mind with the most bitter feelings . . . . I have met with what I call gross ingratitude from the leaders and the people . . . . After my last defeat, seeing myself probably thrust out of all fitting career in public life, I have shut myself up in my shell. . . .
>
> In much that unites the Liberal party, too, whether from prejudice or not, I have the misfortune to differ. Free Trade I regard as a delusion. . . , and as for the Government, my only feeling towards it and the Whigs is that if anything could excite me to interest, it would be an opportunity that would allow me conscientiously to destroy or help to destroy them.
>
> How in this condition of mind can I possibly serve *The Examiner?*
> . . . But these Whigs! they united to thrust me from my own country, to intrigue against me in every place that was open, to exclude me from Parliament, and they have succeeded.[52]

Despite his disgust with politics, Bulwer-Lytton, characteristically, did not hesitate to stand once again for Parliament at the first opportunity. The chance came when Seeley was unseated for bribery, necessitating a by-election at Lincoln in 1848. Bulwer-Lytton had anticipated this development and had obtained pledges of support from Tory protectionists and moderate Liberals alike, indeed from all factions except the radicals who had supported Seeley, and expected consequently to walk in. But Seeley — now a bitter antagonist — upset the applecart. He blandly reported to Henry Tufnell, the Government whip, that

Bulwer-Lytton did not intend to stand. Tufnell took this advice at face value and sent Thomas Hobhouse (brother to John Cam Hobhouse, then President of the Board of Control in the Whig cabinet) to Lincoln as the Ministerial candidate. Naturally, the Tories who pledged to let Bulwer-Lytton stand unopposed, felt themselves deceived when they saw a genuine Whig about to snatch the seat, and they riposted by nominating a candidate of their own, Lebbens C. Humfrey. With Humfrey taking the Tory votes and Hobhouse the Liberals, few remained for Bulwer-Lytton.[53]

When reports of these rapid and unexpected developments reached Bulwer-Lytton, who had been vacationing at Brighton, he hurried to London to lodge his protest. To John Cam Hobhouse, he wrote a note that resounded with his pent-up sense of resentment:

> That the brother of a Whig cabinet minister should be sent down to oppose me at Lincoln appears to me an act of political discourtesy and ingratitude without parallel. Mr. Tufnell, if he discharged his duty, would have informed your brother . . . that Mr. Seeley was my antagonist at the last election and that no reliance was to be placed upon anything he or his friends might say as to my intentions. And the laxest etiquette observed amongst the chiefs of a party to those to whom they have been indebted for support would at least have prescribed a personal application to myself previous to the departure of your brother.
>
> I have only to add that my friends will unquestionably bring me forward at the ensuing election, and that, if I am rightly informed, I shall be supported by an union of all parties and classes except Mr. Seeley's special faction.[54]

If Bulwer-Lytton believed the Whigs had not treated him fairly, the Whigs, for their part, believed they had done for him all he deserved. After receiving the above letter, Hobhouse made the following comment about Bulwer-Lytton in his journal:

> This novel writer is a strange, irresolute, conceited man; totally incapable of managing his own affairs, but not at all without selfishness.
>
> [James] Coppock [Parliamentary agent for the Liberals] told him to his face that his complaint of the ingratitude of the party was ridiculous. He had been a Baronet . . . ; he had been helped by the party purse at elections, and now he had turned half Tory, half

Protectionist . . . . If he had not made some noise in the world by his novels, I should not trouble myself to write so much about him.[55]

Despite their contemptuous attitude toward Bulwer-Lytton, the Whigs had for the moment to treat him with kid gloves, for if he persisted with his plan to stand at Lincoln, he would thereby divide the Liberal vote sufficiently to assure Hobhouse's defeat. To prevent this, Tuffnell, after paying an homage of apologies, struck a bargain. In exchange for Bulwer-Lytton's withdrawal from the contest at Lincoln, Tuffnell wrote a memorandum pledging that the Liberal party would support him for "the first seat that may become with [sic] a fair chance of success in preference to any Liberal candidate except a cabinet minister." It was also understood that this arrangement held good, as Bulwer-Lytton put it, "notwithstanding my opinions on the Corn Laws . . . ." Joseph Parkes and Tennyson D'Eyncourt witnessed the agreement.[56]

Bulwer-Lytton thereupon withdrew from the Lincoln election, throwing his support to Hobhouse, who then narrowly defeated his Tory opponent.[57] Tufnell, for his part, lived up at least to the letter of agreement, arranging for Bulwer-Lytton to stand as the Liberal candidate in a by-election at Leominster. But, upon arriving at the scene, Bulwer-Lytton discovered to his dismay that the electors of Leominster expected to receive bribes that "would have cost me four times the amount any contested election at Lincoln had ever done." He withdrew his candidacy, and, tongue firmly in cheek, posted a notice to that effect in the borough, expressing his "profound sense of . . . inadequacy to solve the doubts of the more cautious deliberators whom this farewell may find still stretched on the rack of conscientious suspense. . . ."[58]

This marked the last time Bulwer-Lytton stood for Parliament as a member of the Liberal party.[59]

Bulwer-Lytton was now on the verge of the political conversion he had so long deferred. But before discussing the steps he took to consummate it, one should understand his state of mind at the time. For the decade of the 1840's, during which he had played so small a part in the political affairs of the nation, was nonetheless assuredly the turning point of his career.

It had not been a happy decade for him. A letter he wrote to Forster in 1850 aptly expressed his prevailing mood:

> I return to England with a reluctant spirit; hard stepmother has that *arida nutrix leonum* been to me. When I see how Whigs and liberals have united to thrust me from Parliament, and critics and authorlings from my due place in letters, I find little to reconcile me to the fogs and east winds of the White Isle — little but the pleasure of greeting such friends as you, who are not to be found abroad.[60]

Clearly, Bulwer-Lytton was suffering from a profound sense of being taken for granted. We have seen the reasons for his resentment against the Whigs and Liberals; but it should also be noted that the 1840's witnessed an ebb tide in his literary career. Earlier, in the years immediately following the death of Sir Walter Scott, Bulwer-Lytton had shone as the brightest light of English letters. Considering his youth and seemingly unlimited powers of invention, he had every reason to expect that in the years ahead he would maintain and consolidate this position, ultimately to take his place among the masters of world literature. Instead, with the emergence of Dickens in the late 1830's and Thackeray in the late 1840's, Bulwer-Lytton, while his books continued to sell well, entered a period of relative decline. He still stood high among his contemporaries, but no longer in the first rank.[61]

From the perspective of posterity, it seems obvious that Bulwer-Lytton lacked the talent of the men who became his competitors. This, however, was not apparent to him. For one thing, he seldom made the mistake of underrating his own abilities; as often as not, the reverse held true. Beyond that, Bulwer-Lytton had ready to hand a different explanation for his decline. He, alone among the major authors of the day, had been the victim of a systematic and persevering campaign of denigration at the hands of a clique of journalists and critics, most notably, William Makepeace Thackeray and Dr. William Maginn who, as Bulwer-Lytton himself not unreasonably put it,

> long continued to assail me, not in any form that can fairly be called criticism, but with a kind of ribald impertinence offered, so far as I can remember, to no other writer of my time.[62]

This campaign of abuse had begun, as we have seen, owing to political motivations.[63] Maginn and Thackeray wrote for *Fraser's Magazine*, a Tory journal, and, in the 1830's, the young Radical Bulwer seemed to them an inviting target. But Thackeray kept up the vendetta well into the 1840's. His ardor owed both to jealousy of Bulwer-Lytton's lofty stature in the literary world, and to a genuine antipathy to what he termed Bulwer-Lytton's "premeditated fine writing,"[64] as well as to his conception generally of what a novel should be.[65]

Bulwer-Lytton was always excessively sensitive to criticism of any sort, and all the more so to ridicule such as came from Thackeray. In fact, he seriously intended for a time to challenge Thackeray to a duel, in order to bring him to account for his insults, but was dissuaded by his friends.[66] In light of all this, how galling it must have been for Bulwer-Lytton when, with the appearance of Thackeray's *Vanity Fair* in 1847-1848, this despised critic who had so undermined his own literary reputation, suddenly emerged as a major novelist, even surpassing in the general estimation Bulwer-Lytton himself.

Thus, as the decade of the 1840's neared its end, Bulwer-Lytton felt threatened on several fronts. His literary reputation had been diminished and his political career lay in ruins. Perhaps matters seemed to him all the worse because he had no one to console him, no one to stand with him against the world and buttress his self-confidence. He had been estranged from his wife since the early 1830's. Following the break-up of his marriage, he had only his mother to look to for support. But she had died in 1843, a severe blow that left Bulwer-Lytton bemoaning the loss of the "the great shelter-roof of my life. . . ."[67] Then, in 1848, the only person who could have taken over this role, his daughter Emily, died tragically at the age of twenty.[68] For Bulwer-Lytton, there remained no one in the world who would care for him above all other men.

Equally unfortunate, he had very few friends. As his grandson put it:

> Neither in literature nor in politics did he belong to any intimate set. He went little into society. . . ; at the end of the summer he always went to some health resort, generally on the Continent, to recover from the fatigues of the London life which was most distasteful to him, and the winter months were spent either in the south of England or the south of France. He had great affection for his Knebworth home . . . , but the large empty house only increased his sense of loneliness . . . . His chief literary friend was John Forster, and his chief political friend Disraeli, but his intimacy with both these men was on an intellectual rather than a personal basis.[69]

In fact, Bulwer-Lytton was not an easy man to befriend. He was aloof, haughty, and shy. His sensitivity, moreover, made him peculiarly quick to take offense at the slightest affront, and thus to alienate acquaintances who might otherwise have become admirers. Even unintentional "insults" infuriated him, as when he came near to terminating his friendship with Forster out of pique because the latter had dozed off during a reading of one of Bulwer-Lytton's plays.[70]   Then there was the episode that occurred when, in 1852, Oxford University invited him to receive the honorary degree of Doctor of Civil Laws. The ceremony was to extend over two days, with the political figures so honored to receive their degrees on the first day, and the literary men (including Bulwer-Lytton) to receive theirs on the second. Sir Archibald Alison, another of the literary men at Oxford to receive this degree, described Bulwer-Lytton's reaction to this "insult":

> In the evening, as Lady Alison and I were sitting at tea in our hotel, a message came in requesting me to see him, which I immediately did, and the first thing he said was, "Well, Sir Archibald, what are you going to do? I am off in the first train for London. I never wanted any of their d-d degrees; it was their own doing sending for me, and I am resolved not to submit to the slight now put on us. What! to think of postponing such men as you and me to a parcel of political drudges, who will never be heard of five years after their death. The thing is intolerable . . . ." During this vehement harangue he was impatiently quaffing the fumes of a huge Turkish pipe, the volumes of which came out between each fresh ebullition of wrath.[71]

This facet of Bulwer-Lytton's personality affected the course he followed in politics. The Whigs had slighted him. Despite all he had done for them with his speeches and pamphlets, they had not seen fit to secure him a seat in Parliament. Now he would turn his talents against them, and make them reckon with the man they had disdained.

There remains one factor more to consider with regard to Bulwer-Lytton's political conversion, his reaction to the series of revolutions that broke out on the Continent in 1848. As we have seen, his health began to fail in the early 1840's; indeed in 1843 he suffered a nervous breakdown following his mother's death,[72] and he lived the rest of his life a semi-invalid, due to various genuine ailments as well as hypochondria. Consequently, he spent a part of nearly every year at French or Italian resorts. The phenomenon that swept across so much of Europe in that period, of violent revolution sweeping away established governments, only to be succeeded by repressive counter-revolution, as in Italy, or military dictatorship, as in France, made a deeper impression upon him than it did upon many of his countrymen. Not remarkably, then, his perception of the events of 1848 served to strengthen his belief in the necessity of maintaining stable national institutions in order to preserve liberty and order; and this, of course, made him more conservative in English affairs.

We should also note, moreover, that Bulwer-Lytton's interest in European affairs did not begin in 1848. How thoroughly he had studied Continental political systems is apparent from *England and the English*.[73] Beyond that, he, like many other Englishmen of his generation, virtually founded his political philosophy upon the principle that nothing like the French Revolution and Reign of Terror should ever occur in Britain. To avert such catastrophes, he emphasized the importance of liberty, morality, and order.

Indeed, he wrote in 1842 that, more than anything else, a decline in moral values in France had paved the way for the Reign of Terror. The Church, he explained, had concerned itself more with maintaining her own special powers and privileges than with tending to the spiritual well-being of the faithful. And, since the State had suppressed religious dissent, those discontented with the Catholic Church had no alternative except to reject all religion, and "in the educated . . . classes, infidelity and liberalism found the earliest favour." Thus, there arose that "irreligious spirit which desecrated the land under the Reign of Terror."[74]

This dangerous spirit of "infidelity and liberalism," by rejecting the institutions of the old order and demanding rapid restructuring instead of cautious reform, had forced the pace of change, eventually culminating in chaos. To Bulwer-Lytton, this was the great alarm signal Englishmen had better heed. As he put it:

> Above all, perhaps, this revolution teaches communities that to *institutions* alone liberty must be confided, and that institutions to be permanent must not too materially differ from the ancient habits they seek to reform.[75]

He therefore distrusted the idealists who, in their zeal to remake society, ignored the importance of institutions to social stability. It was no wonder he opposed the philosophical radicals who figured so prominently in the Liberal party. He equated them with the French *philosophes* whose hammer blows against the established order cleared the way for the Robespierres and Marats. In his novel *Zanoni*, Bulwer-Lytton wrote as follows of the Reign of Terror:

It roars — the River of Hell, whose first outbreak was chanted as the gush of a channel to Elysium. How burst into blossoming hopes fair hearts that had nourished themselves on the diamond dews of the rosy dawn, when Liberty came from the dark ocean, and the arms of decrepit Thraldom, — Aurora from the bed of Tithorn! Hopes! ye have ripened into fruit, and the fruit is gore and ashes! Beautiful Roland, eloquent Vergniaud, visionary Condorcet, high hearted Malesherbes! — wits, philosophers, statesmen, patriots, — dreamers! behold the millennium for which ye dared and labored![76]

In England in the 1840's there were once again radicals and dreamers who dared and labored for the new millennium, and who apparently had no qualms about sweeping aside all established institutions to achieve their goal. Bulwer-Lytton believed it possible that these men and the ideas they unleashed might prove the undoing of the British Monarchy. In this regard, he singled out the "Manchester School" as especially dangerous, writing to Forster:

> Those miserable Cobdens! and visionary Peace Dreamers! What fools they are, and these are the men by whom England herself has been half driven to the brink of revolution. Wise Daniels indeed. The babyism of giving up indirect taxation, to be driven to direct in a country like this, . . . when the only substitutes are direct taxes or loans, unless indeed they will come to a proper reduction, not of Army and Navy, but of *Monarchy* itself. *A la bonne heure!* A Republic is cheap, but if ever that hour arrives it shall not be, if I and a few like me live, a Republic of millers and cotton spinners, but either a Republic of gentlemen or a Republic of workmen — either is better than those wretched money spiders, who would sell England for ls. 6d.[77]

Bulwer-Lytton wrote the foregoing letter just as the Revolution in France was getting underway. The fear of revolution, which his studies of the earlier French Revolution had engendered, had come to the fore. But he did not become a reactionary; instead, the events in Europe served to strengthen his belief that liberty and order, far from being opposed, rather depended one upon the other. At the end of the year, he stated in a political address:

> I am for the principle of progress, because I believe that the people of this country may be trusted with a greater degree of freedom than any other people in Europe, without endangering the safety of the

constitution. . . . The reason is, we have been taught in the school of freedom. . . . But the people on the continent, who have hitherto known little or nothing of freedom, have rushed to greater extremes than we ourselves ever contemplated. This is why the fabrics of liberty which they erect today are blown to the winds tomorrow; and we cannot at this moment say whether one single free constitution amongst the many that have so recently been gained on the continent, will survive the storm. . . . We have been a thousand years striving to become freer and freer, and . . . have managed to approach to a higher state of rational constitutional freedom than any other country . . . with the exception of the United States of America.[78]

Nonetheless, the events he witnessed on the Continent unquestionably left him convinced that henceforth the progress of liberty should proceed only at a deliberate pace, an opinion that completed his alienation from the Liberal party. Early in 1850, he summed up the matter in a letter to Tennyson D'Eyncourt:

One thing seems to me clear--*viz.*, that any change in England will be for the worse, and every change in France for the better. And, if our Liberals had their way, England would very soon become a France. As poor Julia finds no rest for her conscience but in Popery, so I see none for my doubts but in good, old Toryism.[79]

"Doubts" certainly had much to do with Bulwer-Lytton's decision to join the Conservative party. While he continued to believe in the ideal of liberty, he also felt, as he always had, that the degree of liberty compatible with stability and order depended upon the moral character of the people. And on that score, he was now less optimistic than he had been in his youth.[80] The Revolutions in Europe, the Chartist movement in England (which he had deprecated since its inception),[81] and the rising influence of the "visionary" Cobdenites, caused him to take an increasingly pessimistic view of the future. By 1850, he certainly no longer shared that confidence in "progress" implicit in nineteenth-century liberalism.

As far as his active political career was concerned, it was fortunate his thinking had taken this conservative bent. Had he remained a Liberal, he probably would not have been able to return to Parliament for years, if ever; and he could never have risen very high in the councils of that talent-laden party. The Conservative party more readily offered opportunities for advancement. And it was not long after he had committed himself to that party that he got the chance at last to find out whether he had the makings of a statesman.

NOTES

1. Mark Rochester, *The Derby Ministry* (London: G. Routledge, 1858), 163. This account was also given by, among others, the Earl of Lytton, I, 424.

2. "The Politician III," *New Monthly Magazine* (September 1, 1832).

3. Bulwer, *England and the English*, I, 70-71.

4. *Ibid.*, 57-58. Bulwer himself later gave the impression, for obvious political reasons, that he had always been a protectionist, which probably accounts for the widely held misconception on that point among his biographers. For example, he denied, in a letter written when was an outspoken protectionist, that he had been a "convert" to that cause. When his correspondent challenged him by referring to the free trade views he had expressed in *England and the English*, Bulwer-Lytton answered that "ever since 1834, when I voted against Mr. Hume's motion, I remained invariably opposed to the repeal of the Corn Laws. Now, the book you quote was published in 1833. . . . The fact is, that I had never thoroughly considered the question . . . until Mr. Hume's memorable motion, and my convictions were decided by the arguments employed in the debate." Bulwer-Lytton to unknown correspondent, July 16, 1852, and n.d. Lytton Papers, D/EK C28. I would suggest that, possibly, while he opposed repeal in Parliament from 1834 on, he did not genuinely come around to protectionist convictions until a few years later. But the main point is clear: Bulwer was not a protectionist in 1832, but rather, at that time, he went along with the free trade views fashionable among his fellow Radicals, without really analyzing the question for himself.

5. Bulwer to Albany Fonblanque, January 18, 1835, Lytton Papers, D/EK C26.

6. Bulwer to Lady Blessington, quoted in Earl of Lytton, I, 464.

7. Bulwer to John Forster, January 26, 1846, Lytton Papers, D/EK C27; Bulwer to Lady Blessington, April 17, 1846, Lytton Papers, D/EK C26.

8. Earl of Lytton, I, 243-244.

9. Edward Bulwer-Lytton to Lord Walpole, August 11, 1850. Quoted in Earl of Lytton, II, 130-131.

10. Edward Bulwer-Lytton, *Alice* (New York: J. F. Taylor, 1897), 194-195.

11. See above, Chapter Three.

12. Bulwer-Lytton, *Alice*, 352-353.

13. *Ibid.*, 355-356.

14. See above, Chapter Two.

15. Bulwer, *England and the English*, II, 160-168, and *passim.*

16. Edward Bulwer-Lytton to Lord Lansdowne, January 6, 1852, Lytton Papers, D/EK C23.

17. *Ibid.* See also Bulwer to [Lord Melbourne], n.d., Lytton Papers, D/EK C28.

18. John Prest, *Lord John Russell*, (London: Macmillan Press, 1972), 173-177.

19. *Ibid.*

20. See Earl of Lytton, I, 520-526.

21. *Hansard*, LVIII, 373-374.

22. *Ibid.*, 374-375.

23. Quoted by Escott, *Edward Bulwer*, 219.

24. Bulwer, [Address at Lincoln], Lytton Papers, D/EK W99.

25. *Ibid.*

26. *Ibid.*

27. Bulwer-Lytton, quoted in *Hereford Times*, December 16, 1848.

28. Bulwer, Address at Lincoln, Lytton Papers, D/EK W99.

29. Bulwer, Speech at Lincoln, *Ibid.*, D/EK W48.

30. Charles R. Dod, *Electoral Facts from 1832-1853* (Brighton: Harvester Press, 1972), 186-187.

31. Bulwer to [Melbourne], n.d., Lytton Papers, D/EK C28.

32. *Ibid.*

33. Bulwer to John Forster, July 9, 1841, Lytton Papers, D/EK C27.

34. He changed his name to Bulwer-Lytton upon his mother's death in 1843.

35. Bulwer-Lytton to Lady Blessington, February 13, 1846, Lytton Papers, D/EK C26.

36. Bulwer-Lytton to Lord Lansdowne, January 6, 1852, Lytton Papers, D/EK 023.

37. William Rudyard to Bulwer-Lytton, May 18, 1846, Lytton Papers, D/EK 023.

38. *Ibid.*

39. Bulwer-Lytton to John Forster, July 10, 1847, Lytton Papers, D/EK C28.

40. Quoted in *List of the Poll . . . For the City of Lincoln* (Lincoln: John Stanton, 1847), iv-v.

41. *Ibid.*, xix.

42. *Ibid.*, xx; William Loaden to Bulwer-Lytton, June 16, 1847, Lytton Papers, D/EK 023.

43. "Memorandum of Committee to Elect Edward Bulwer-Lytton at Lincoln." June 11, 1847; *List of the Poll*, iv-v; Bulwer-Lytton to John Forster, August 3, 1847, Lytton Papers, D/EK C27.

44. Bulwer-Lytton to John Forster, July 20, 1847, Lytton Papers, D/EK C27.

45. Quoted in *List of the Poll*, i-ii.

46. Bulwer-Lytton to John Forster, July 23, 1847, Lytton Papers, D/EK C27.

47. Bulwer-Lytton to Tennyson D'Eyncourt, n.d., Lytton Papers, D/EK C26.

48. Bulwer-Lytton to John Forster, August 3, 1847, Lytton Papers, D/EK C27; *List of the Poll*, iv-xx.

49. Bulwer-Lytton to Lady Blessington, n.d., Lytton Papers, D/EK C26.

50. Dod, *Electoral Facts*, 186-187.

51. Bulwer-Lytton to John Forster, August 3, 1847, Lytton Papers, D/EK C27.

52. Bulwer-Lytton to John Forster, October 29, 1847, Lytton Papers, D/EK C27.

53. Bulwer-Lytton to Lord Lansdown, January 6, 1852, Lytton Papers, D/EK 023.

54. Bulwer-Lytton to John Cam Hobhouse, March 12, [1848], Lytton Papers, D/EK C26.

55. Lord Broughton, *Recollections of a Long Life*, VI, ed. by Charlotte Hobhouse Carleton (London: John Murray, 1911), 208.

56. Bulwer-Lytton to Lord Lansdowne, January 6, 1852, Lytton Papers, D/EK 023.

57. The results were: T. Hobhouse 552; L. Humfrey 550. See Dod, *Electoral Facts*, 187. On Bulwer-Lytton's role in this election, see also Earl of Lytton, II, 156-157.

58. Bulwer-Lytton, "A Notice to the Electors of Leominster, January 22, 1849," in Lytton Papers, D/EK 023. Bulwer-Lytton to Lord Lansdowne, January 6, 1852, Lytton Papers, D/EK 023.

59. Bulwer-Lytton to Lord Lansdowne, January 6, 1852, Lytton Papers, D/EK 023. There were other occasions when Bulwer-Lytton received offers from various constituencies to stand as the Liberal Candidate, but as all of these were predicated upon his renunciation of protectionism — which he refused to make — they came to nothing. Bulwer-Lytton refers to this in his "Speech at Hitchin," January 22, 1852, Lytton Papers, D/EK W98.

60. Bulwer-Lytton to John Forster, May 20, 1850, in Earl of Lytton, II, 129.

61. Justin McCarthy, *A History of our Own Times*, (New York: Harper & Brothers, 1881), I, 555-556.

62. Quoted in Earl of Lytton, I, 81.

63. See above, Chapter Three; also, Sadleir, *Bulwer: A Panorama*, 166-186, and 226-260.

64. *Ibid.*, 229-233.

65. Hollingsworth, *The Newgate Novel*, 224-228.

66. *Ibid.*, 199-200.

67. Bulwer to Mrs. Hall, quoted Earl of Lytton, II, 21-22.

68. *Ibid.*, 99-103. Bulwer-Lytton's extreme grief at his daughter's death, along with his lifelong interest in the occult, led him to believe he could — and did — communicate with her through a medium. See Sir Archibald Alison, *My Life and Writings* (Edinburgh: William Blackwood, 1883), II, 52-53.

69. Earl of Lytton, II, 376-377.

70. *Ibid.*, I, 544-545.

71. Alison, *My Life and Writings*, II, 51. Alison managed to assuage Bulwer-Lytton's anger by suggesting the delay had been intended as a compliment, rather than as a slight. Bulwer-Lytton remained and accepted the degree.

72. Earl of Lytton, II, 22-24.

73. Bulwer, *England and the English*, I, 190-194, 234-238.

74. Edward Bulwer, "The Reign of Terror: Its Causes and Results," in *Foreign Quarterly Review*, July, 1842, LVIII, 275-309.

75. *Ibid.*, 309.

76. Edward Bulwer-Lytton, *Zanoni* (Boston: Little, Brown, 1893), 407.

77. Bulwer to John Forster, quoted by Earl of Lytton, II, 161.

78. Bulwer, quoted in *Hereford Times*, December 16, 1848.

79. Bulwer-Lytton to Tennyson D'Enycourt, March 31, 1850, Lytton Papers, D/EK C26.

80. See above, Chapter Two.

81. See above, Chapter Three.

CHAPTER FIVE

THE POLITICS OF PROTECTION

In the summer of 1850, Bulwer-Lytton explored the possibility of returning to Parliament as a protectionist. He knew it would not be easy. All his political life he had been a Liberal. Nearly all the people he knew in politics, both on the national level and in his home county of Hertfordshire (which he now intended to make his political base), were Liberals. Accordingly he had to wonder whether he might more readily effect his return to the House of Commons by persuading Hertfordshire Liberals to back his candidacy in spite of his protectionist views.

For a time, this seemed the more practical approach, even though the Liberal party had made free trade an article of faith. As a matter of fact, Bulwer-Lytton had good reason to expect the support of William Cowper, the Hertfordshire Liberal county chairman, who had urged him to stand for the county twice in the past: in the 1845 by-election and the general election two years later. On the latter occasion, Bulwer-Lytton told Cowper he would only stand as a "Whig protectionist,"[1] and Cowper had agreed to that stipulation. Although local considerations finally dissuaded Bulwer-Lytton from taking up Cowper's offer,[2] he naturally supposed it would hold good in the future. As Bulwer-Lytton later put it, with reference to the period 1847-1850,

> I was invited by several gentlemen of the Liberal party in Herts to become their candidate for that county whenever a vacancy should occur. They were fully aware of my unchanged opinions on the Corn Laws and did not then consider them objectionable . . . . [3]

At the same time, however, Bulwer-Lytton had reservations about standing as a Liberal protectionist. He had done that in 1847 at Lincoln,[4] and the strategy backfired when he failed to get the expected Tory votes. He thus discussed this matter with Cowper:

> With regard to myself and the county . . . I don't think I could stand without depending rather on the Tories than the liberals which would be against my feelings of right if the dissolution takes place upon the question of the Corn Laws, and therefore in that case I must not be thought of. If [the dissolution takes place] after that question [has been settled], I think I should be as likely as any liberal to succeed. But this doubt may certainly serve to shackle the liberal party and cramp their present operations. They may wish to be provided with some one ready in either event to stand. At all events, don't let me be in the way. I have a strong wish to return to Parliament if the question is settled — none till it is. I . . . leave myself in your hands.[5]

While this letter made clear Bulwer-Lytton had no wish to repeat the error he had committed at Lincoln, it was in other respects disingenuous. He had no intention of shelving his plans for returning to Parliament just to suit the convenience of the Liberal party in Hertfordshire. Perhaps he feared that if he definitely attached himself to that party, they might "shackle and cramp" *his* operations, instead of the reverse. Bulwer-Lytton was keeping all his options open. He had no reason to expect the Corn Law question to fade away, and he knew that, in contrast to Cowper, many other influential Hertfordshire Liberals opposed him, presumably on account of his protectionism. Meanwhile, he also knew that there was in the county "a numerous body of . . . farmers . . . most favourable" to his candidacy.[6] In view of these considerations, Bulwer-Lytton, while careful not to close off the possibility of a Liberal candidacy, moved quietly to open up lines of communication with the Tories.

While he knew few Tories, he did know one of the most important, Benjamin Disraeli, that party's second in command overall (under Lord Stanley) and its leader in the House of Commons. Back in the 1830's, in the days of their *jeunesse dorée*, Bulwer and Disraeli had been best friends. Then Disraeli had described Bulwer as

> one of the few [men] with whom my intellect comes into collision with benefit. He is full of thought, and [has] views at once original and just.[7]

Then, too, they had seemed two of a kind, both of them novelists of promise and politicians of limitless ambition; and all the while each tried to outdo the other in displays of dandyism. No one else could understand them as they did each other. Once, reflecting on the ordeal of ambition, Disraeli wrote in his diary (September 1, 1833):

> I remember expressing this feeling to Bulwer as we were returning from Bath together, a man who was at that moment an M.P., and an active one, editing a political journal and writing at the same time a novel and a profound and admirable philosophical work. He turned round and pressed my arm and said in a tone, the sincerity of which could not be doubted: "It is true, my dear fellow, it is true. We are sacrificing our youth, the time of pleasure. . .—but we are *bound* to go on, we are *bound*. How our enemies would triumph were we to retire from the stage! And yet," he continued in a solemn voice, "I have more than once been tempted to throw it all up, and quit my country, for ever."[8]

But this intimacy did not last. The cooling off between the two men can, in large measure, be attributed to the influence of Mary Anne Wyndham Lewis, whom Disraeli married in 1839. Once a close friend of Rosina Bulwer's, Mary Anne had spread a report, as the Bulwers' marriage neared collapse in 1836, that Rosina had discovered her husband with another woman. This was almost certainly untrue, and Bulwer sharply rebuked Mary Anne for meddling. The latter, afterward, probably realized she had been in the wrong, but took offense anyway. To quote from Michael Sadleir's account of the incident, Mary Anne,

> after her marriage with Disraeli, when she came to possess great political and social influence. . . saw her chance of revenge and quietly took it. Wherefore, among the various causes which were to cheat Bulwer in middle life of the material and social rewards to which his intellect and political assiduity would normally have entitled him, must be numbered this hostility of a woman who having long before been detected in spiteful gossip, and called to account for it, was thereafter full of resentment against the man she had herself sought to injure.[9]

As a result, during the decade of the 1840's, Bulwer-Lytton and Disraeli seldom saw one another. And when, in August 1850, Bulwer-Lytton invited the Disraelis to Knebworth, it was not an incident in an ongoing relationship, but an attempt to revive a friendship long dormant.[10]

We have already discussed some of the political considerations that underlay Bulwer-Lytton's decision to seek out his old friend; it is equally important to consider how Disraeli, in a political context, may have regarded Bulwer-Lytton in 1850. On a strictly personal level, perhaps, Disraeli no longer relished Bulwer-Lytton's company, as he once had done. He probably found him an uncomfortable reminder of his own extravagant youth, a period of his life of which he had become ashamed and generally preferred to forget.[11] Politically, however, Disraeli must have recognized that Bulwer-Lytton, if he chose to join the Tories, could become a valuable ally.

For one thing, Disraeli had every reason to expect, based on their old friendship, that he could count on Bulwer-Lytton's personal loyalty and support. This meant much, for at the time Disraeli had only the shakiest hold on the Conservative leadership in the Commons. Lord Stanley had made it clear he preferred a more conventional figure for that post. And the country squires, who made up the majority of the party's backbenchers, for the most part persisted in regarding Disraeli as nothing more than a political mercenary who had sold his sword to the Tories, but who otherwise had nothing in common with them. To be sure, both Stanley and the backbenchers respected Disraeli's abilities as a debater, and they realized his departure from the leadership would leave a void no other Protectionist could satisfactorily fill. There was a sorry dearth of talent among the Tories, since the party's most brilliant and experienced figures — men like William E. Gladstone and James Graham — had left it to support Sir Robert Peel and the repeal of the Corn Laws. Disraeli could not ignore the fact that should the Peelites decide to return to the Tory fold, many in the party would demand Disraeli make way and resign the leadership. Thus, to secure his hold on the leadership, Disraeli needed all the friends he could get.[12]

And there was a second reason Disraeli would have especially welcomed the accession of Bulwer-Lytton to the Tory party. The defection of the Peelites, which had in the first place given Disraeli his great opportunity, at the same time made the day-to-day business of leading the party in the House of Commons an inordinately arduous task. As Robert Blake put it, in this period Disraeli

> stood alone, trying to answer most of the great orators of the day ranged against him on the opposite benches. His tongue-tied colleagues in the early days of his leadership could give him little support, save their goodwill.[13]

Here, Bulwer-Lytton could really help out. During his days as a Liberal M.P., he had demonstrated his ability as a debater. Granted, few would regard him as a great, or even a good orator. But, then, neither could anyone call him tongue-tied. However mediocre the manner in which he delivered his speeches, their content stood comparison with those of Parliament's most celebrated speakers. On numerous occasions, Bulwer-Lytton's powers of analysis profoundly impressed the House.

If Disraeli regarded Bulwer-Lytton as a man to be won over, he made a good start toward that goal when he and his wife visited Knebworth in August 1850. Old grudges forgotten,[14] the reunion went off perfectly, and the Disraelis, who had planned to stay only a few days, remained two weeks. Disraeli adopted his most charming manner — calm, indolent, and witty — and seemed to Bulwer-Lytton once again the boon companion he had known twenty years before. As Bulwer-Lytton put it in a letter to Lord Walpole,

> Disraeli is . . . very agreeable, indeed taken from his politics and restored to his sofa and chit chat. If he would but smoke he would be the same man as ever.[15]

In light of later events, it is reasonable to speculate that some of this "chit chat" may have related to the policy of the Tory party in the wake of the repeal of the Corn Laws. Disraeli had come to regard protectionism as "dead and damned," and he believed the Tories would remain a minority until they accepted free trade. He could not as yet express such sentiments openly, for only a few years before he had castigated Peel for reversing himself on this very issue. In private, however, Disraeli liked to get the matter off his chest. As G. E. Buckle put it, "With friends and political acquaintances not belonging to his own party Disraeli seems to have made no concealment . . . of the direction which his thoughts were taking."[16]

It may have surprised Bulwer-Lytton to find how similarly he and Disraeli thought about this question. Only a few months before, Bulwer-Lytton had privately criticized Disraeli's policies as undermining public credit.[17] In particular, he condemned certain schemes Disraeli had advocated in order to reduce both taxes and interest rates for farmers.[18] But if Bulwer-Lytton disapproved of these expedients, at least he agreed with Disraeli's aims. Like the Tory leader, Bulwer-Lytton considered old fashioned protectionism utterly unrealistic. As he observed earlier in 1850, "there is a disposition in the House to do something for the Land — but not to renew protection."[19] The failure of so many Tories to recognize that fact made Bulwer-Lytton all the more hesitant to join that party.[20] Ever conscious of the need to preserve social stability, he must have recognized that a renewal of the Corn Laws would certainly stir up dangerous anti-aristocratic sentiments among the middle class. But his concern for order made him, at the same time, determined to find an alternative to protectionism that would effectively relieve agricultural distress. The country would be in danger, he believed, if it failed to check "the disaffection of its only conservative class."[21]

The best means to do this, Bulwer-Lytton maintained, as, indeed, he had since 1841, lay in a moderate fixed duty, "the just compromise between rival interests."[22] That was his public position, and no doubt he believed what he said. But what linked him to Disraeli was his fundamentally pragmatic approach to the problem. He wanted to see agricultural prosperity, and did not wed himself to any single means to achieve that end. As he later advised a political supporter:

> It will be well not to press the fixed duty — but to argue . . . that . . . whatever can be done for the agricultural interest will be done . . . .
> Everything that can be got by the farmers is worth contending for . . . . Protection may come through other quarters than a tax on foreign grain. . . . Protection is not thrown over, if one mode of seeking it be substituted for another.[23]

Thus, Disraeli and Bulwer-Lytton had compatible attitudes towards this issue. But Disraeli did not control the Conservative party. Bulwer-Lytton, therefore, would not join the Tories until such time as Lord Stanley modified his own views and led the party away from their inflexible protectionism. As matters were to turn out, that time was not far off.

In the meantime, Disraeli tried to help Bulwer-Lytton return to Parliament. They must have discussed this matter — perhaps not in detail — when they met August. About six weeks later, Disraeli reported back that he had learned from Lord John Manners, a prominent Tory and longtime Disraeli lieutenant, that Bulwer-Lytton looked "safe for Lincoln," if he cared to give that city one more try, presumably with Protectionist support. Disraeli added, however, that Bulwer-Lytton might do better to stand for Hertfordshire: "I am all for the county . . . if we can manage it." His use of the word "we" certainly suggests that he considered Bulwer-Lytton practically a Tory already.[24]

Bulwer-Lytton agreed with Disraeli about standing for the county. "Lord John Manners . . . confirms what I have heard about Lincoln," he wrote, "but, certainly I do not feel that venerable city offers the same temptations to public life that the Natale Solum does. . . ."[25] This euphemistic phrasing, typical of what Michael Sadleir called "Bulwerese,"[26] meant in effect that Bulwer-Lytton had had his fill of Lincoln politics.

But Hertfordshire politics could also be rough and tumble. In the letter already quoted, Bulwer-Lytton asked Disraeli to find out "what are the views of Lord Verulam, or any other of the Conservative and Protectionist magistrates" in Hertfordshire, concerning, presumably, Bulwer-Lytton's availability to become a candidate. But Bulwer-Lytton may have had an additional reason for taking this interest in the views of Lord Verulam, and for wanting Disraeli to speak to Verulam on his behalf. Verulam was a prominent Hertfordshire Tory and Lord Lieutenant of the county. As such, he had the responsibility for nominating each November three men for the office of High Sheriff. Perhaps Bulwer-Lytton had reason to expect his own name to appear on the list. Certainly, he wanted no part of this honor, as a High Sheriff could not stand for Parliament in his own county. This legal technicality was to weigh heavily on his mind for the next year and a half.[27]

Just as he had feared, Bulwer-Lytton was nominated for High Sheriff in November 1850. Politics may well have influenced Verulam's choice, since two of the men he nominated, Bulwer-Lytton and Wynn Ellis, were former Liberal M.P.'s, and possibly he wanted to keep at least one of them from standing for the county in the event of an election. But Verulam did not have the final say in the matter. According to tradition, the High Sheriff was chosen by the Crown at random from among the nominees. For his part, Bulwer-Lytton left nothing to chance. He contacted Lord Lansdowne, then Lord President of the Council and one of the few Whigs with whom he had remained on friendly terms, and requested he use his influence to keep Bulwer-Lytton from being "stuck" with the shrievalty.[28] Under the circumstances, it was fortunate Bulwer-Lytton had not yet formally abandoned the Liberal party.

Lansdowne, no doubt under the impression he was helping a member of his own party, responded favorably. Bulwer-Lytton did not become High Sheriff in 1851, and instead resumed his quest for a seat in the House of Commons. He knew he could not afford to defer much longer committing himself to one party or the other. Disraeli had advised him the previous autumn that a dissolution of Parliament appeared imminent,[29] and, moreover, it seemed that a by-election in Hertfordshire might come sooner yet, since one of the sitting M.P.'s, Thomas Trevor, was in line to succeed to the peerage of Lord Dacre, a man then in failing health.[30] As we have seen, Bulwer-Lytton had received offers of support from certain Hertfordshire Liberals, and it is possible he might have stood as their candidate had the anticipated by-election occurred in 1850. Near the end of that year, however, any hopes he had entertained in that regard dimmed abruptly. As Bulwer-Lytton later described what happened:

> I heard to my surprise that some of the gentlemen of the Whig party had been proposing to a Mr. [Christopher] Puller, a highly respectable person but of small property, new family, and wholly unknown in public life, to become their candidate.

He thereupon protested to a "noted Whig," who tried to placate him. Despite this, Bulwer-Lytton learned soon afterwards that Puller had become the Liberal candidate.[31]

The time had come to play the Tory card. But he worried that, while the Tories might nominate him on account of his general reputation as a Protectionist, they would desert him at the election, once they found out he supported only a moderate fixed duty, not the full restoration of the Corn Laws. To avoid such a misunderstanding, he resolved to set forth his views precisely and in such a way as would assure them a wide circulation.

The opportunity came in February 1851, when the Prime Minister, Lord John Russell, resigned after his anti-Catholic Ecclesiastical Titles Act had alienated the Peelites and the Irish. After some hesitation, Lord Stanley began an attempt to form a Government. In view of the scarcity of talent among the Protectionists, he hoped to persuade either Lord Palmerston or the Peelites, or both, to join him. Disraeli, of course, assisted in the complex negotiations that followed. While these proceedings were underway, Bulwer-Lytton wrote to Disraeli:

> If you make up your Government, or even if you don't, I think of writing a short pamphlet which will contain my own honest views of the state of affairs and parties; and in which there may probably be something that, consistently with those views, might do you some service, if the pamphlet proved a hit.[32]

Perhaps Bulwer-Lytton had in mind repeating the triumph he had scored in 1834, when his pamphlet *On The Present Crisis* helped turn the results of an election.[33] But he was denied this chance when Stanley, having failed to put together a coalition, declined to take office. Stanley, nonetheless, aided Bulwer-Lytton's personal ambitions immeasurably when, on the following day, he addressed the House of Lords to explain why he had not formed a Government; for, as part of this speech, Stanley, in response to a request from Prince Albert, outlined what policies he would have followed had he become Prime Minister, and stated, among other things, his support for a moderate fixed duty on imported grain.[34] The official position of the Conservative party was now identical with Bulwer-Lytton's. The latter had the opening he had wanted. His pamphlet, which appeared the following spring, eloquently upheld the agricultural interest and the idea of a moderate fixed duty, and thus placed him at last emphatically among the followers of Lord Stanley.

In the pamphlet, entitled *Letters to John Bull*, Bulwer-Lytton derided the popular idea that free trade would prove a panacea for all the world's problems. He granted it had certain benefits, but went on to argue that:

> *A State can adopt no dogma for universal application, whether of Protection or Free Trade.* In those branches in which it produces more or better supplies at less cost, it must naturally court Free Trade; in those branches where its produce is less or its cost greater than that of its neighbors, it must either consent to the . . . possible ruin . . . of that department of industry, or it must place it under Protection. Free Trade, could it be universally reciprocal, would therefore benefit Manchester *versus* Germany, and injure Lincolnshire versus Poland. The English cotton manufacturer thoroughly understands this when he says, with Mr. Cobden, "Let us have Free Trade, and we will beat the world!" But the world does not want to be beaten! Prussia, France, and even America, prefer "stupid selfishness" and protected manufactures to enlightened principles and English competition.[35]

Bulwer-Lytton thereby recognized that English agriculture would collapse if left unprotected from foreign competition. Most opponents of free trade have argued that no nation can afford to dispense with farming, since in wartime it might find itself cut off from its overseas supplies of food. But Bulwer-Lytton emphasized the need to preserve the moral influence of farmers for the sake for the stability of the state and the liberties of the people:

108

> You must be conscious that the evil which modern civilization has most to apprehend, lies . . . in the struggle and ferment . . . in the heart of your great manufacturing towns; the heated desires for a change, never circumscribed in the mild limits of reform; the tendencies to whatever can revolutionize institutions . . . . It is good for democracy itself that the state should contain a fair proportion of the elements of conservation. Political liberty could not last a year, if there were not in the community some retentive and tenacious principle which preserves liberty itself from the eternal experiments of fanatics . . . .
>
> Is there then, no danger in converting the sole conserving and retentive classes . . . into those most indifferent to your institutions and least interested in that order of things, which has condemned *them* alone to sacrifice and calamity . . . ?[36]

After thus setting forth the dangers involved in alienating the "tillers of the soil," Bulwer-Lytton proposed as a solution the imposition of a moderate fixed duty on imported grain, a measure he regarded as a reasonable compromise between the demands of the industrialists and the requirements of the agriculturalists:

> I own that the benefit of the agriculturalist, in a moderate fixed duty would be small in comparison to the loss he has sustained and the risks he must encounter; but in consenting to that compromise, through the mediation of the chief [i.e. Lord Stanley] to whom he has entrusted his cause, he shows that he will accept what can least interfere with the experimental policy you have begun, and that he has due consideration to the exports of the manufacturer — the price of bread to all classes. Small it may be, in actual pecuniary relief to the agriculturalist, but large indeed . . . in . . . reconciling class, — smoothing obstacles to progressive legislation, — lessening dangers in those crises in which progress is exchanged for convulsion.[37]

Although this pamphlet appeared at a relatively quiet time in national politics, it enjoyed a brisk sale, going through ten editions.[38] And, despite Bulwer-Lytton's contention that he was offering a compromise between rival interests, it was widely perceived as a partisan tract, thus ending all doubts as to his future political affiliations. Disraeli and other Protectionists praised it warmly.[39] The Liberal *Hertford Mercury* denounced it, adding significantly:

We regret that he [Bulwer-Lytton] is likely to become a candidate for
the representation of this county, upon the "adverse side." A
candidacy based upon opposite principles would, as we believe, have
been more fortunate to his own fame, and would have more assured
him of success.[40]

But Bulwer-Lytton cared more about the opinions of Hertfordshire's
Tories. Even before the publication of *Letters to John Bull*, they had
expressed interest in having him as their candidate. On March 6th, the
county's branch of the Agricultural Protection Society, a great force in
Tory/Protectionist politics, met to select a candidate for the anticipated
by-election. After several prominent contenders announced they would
not stand, it was noted that "Rumors had been afloat of the intention of
Sir Edward Bulwer-Lytton to become a candidate." The Society decided
to inquire of Bulwer-Lytton whether, in fact, he intended to stand.
Possibly, too, some members of the Society had reservations about
supporting a former Radical. Accordingly, they delegated the Reverend
Charles Pearson to communicate with Bulwer-Lytton, and to determine,
first, whether he would stand, and, second, how he stood on such issues
as the Ballot, extension of the suffrage, and the political role of the
Church of England. Evidently Bulwer-Lytton's replies were satisfactory,
for, when the Society met again in April, it endorsed his candidacy.[41]

Bulwer-Lytton took all this in stride. He wrote to his son Robert
(then twenty years of age) that,

I am asked by the Protectionists of Herts to stand for the county at the
next vacancy which is daily to be expected — and shall probably do
so — though it is with a heavy heart I foresee all the abuse I shall meet
. . . .[42]

He worried, too, about how the Tories would react to his advocacy
in *Letters to John Bull* of a moderate duty, which, after all, would have
seemed radical only a few years earlier. But attitudes had altered more
drastically than he realized. In the end, the pamphlet served to cement
the Tories' support of Bulwer-Lytton.

This support became evident very quickly, thanks to Lord
Salisbury,[43] an important figure in the Tory party nationally, a man of
unsurpassed influence in Hertfordshire, and, significantly, a good friend
of Disraeli's. Possibly at the latter's suggestion, Bulwer-Lytton visited
Salisbury in April and found him "most kind about the county."[44] The
matter remained unsettled, however, as *Letters to John Bull* was not to

appear until later that month. When it did, Bulwer-Lytton sent Salisbury a copy, and, almost apologetically, advised him that,

> until you shall have found leisure to read it — and see how far my views agree with your own, I feel another reason for suspending decision upon the subject on which you did me the honor to speak with so much generous frankness and friendly feeling.
>
> You will perceive . . . that I advocate the theory and abstract principle of protection as the policy of a commercial as well as agricultural state, — but . . . that in the temper of the public mind . . . I am for the moderate measures and policy suggested by Lord Stanley. And it may be a matter of question how far that meets the views of the more sanguine Protectionists.[45]

Salisbury gave the pamphlet his seal of approval. Shortly afterward, Bulwer-Lytton apparently let it be known that he would after all accept the Agricultural Protection Society's offer that he stand for the county; at all events, Salisbury wrote him in May from the Carlton Club, to say that he was "very glad to find that we have anticipated your wishes." He added that the Agricultural Protection Society would shortly hold another meeting for the sake of "proposing the suggestion to you and to our present Members to defend our cause in Parliament whenever a dissolution will take place."[46]

But when would the dissolution take place? Now that Bulwer-Lytton was ready to run and had a party at his back, there was just one thing wanting: an election. Months passed, and it became clear that there would be no election in Hertfordshire in 1851. Nonetheless, Bulwer-Lytton officially declared his candidacy that September.[47] Possibly he did this for fear of being saddled with the shrievalty for 1852, and hoped his declaration of candidacy would foreclose that eventuality.

Sure enough, in November, he saw his name placed at the head of the list of candidates for High Sheriff. He immediately protested, writing to one county official that there was

> a general suspicion that there is some most unusual and unhandsome attempt to thwart my candidature and interfere with the free representation of the county. And I confess that I myself can look on it in no other light until I find myself set free from liabilities which the ordinary etiquette of public life does not impose on one who has actually entered the field as a candidate for the county.[48]

Soon Bulwer-Lytton began to suspect the Whigs had perpetrated this political "dirty trick." They had dealt unfairly with him in the past, and now that he had joined the Tories they at least had a good reason to strike against him.

Even though he had become a Tory, Bulwer-Lytton had no qualms about writing to the Whig Lord Lansdowne for help, just as he had done the year before. Bulwer-Lytton informed Lansdowne that Wynn Ellis had seemed intent on becoming High Sheriff. Consequently, "I felt assured of safety in accepting the requisition to stand for the county. My committee was formed, my opponent in the field." Then, he saw his name placed ahead of Ellis's. "The under sheriff informed me," he reported to Lansdowne, "that the transposition was made at the suggestion of Chief Justice [Thomas, Lord] Denman and [Chancellor of the Exchequer] Sir Charles Wood," both leading Whigs. He argued that, despite the report that Ellis had withdrawn on account of illness, it seemed "this unusual transposition of names was influenced by some desire to frustrate my candidature for the shire." He concluded by stating he would be happy to serve as High Sheriff in his proper turn in 1853, assuming he was not then in Parliament.[49]

Lansdowne was a gentleman of the old school, scarcely an ardent partisan. But even he balked at a request for help from a man who had just joined the opposing party. Consequently, Bulwer-Lytton wrote him a long letter, describing the slights he had received from the Whigs in the past, and justifying his joining the Protectionists. He expressed his gratitude to Lansdowne, "the only Member of the present cabinet for [sic] whom I have received personal kindness," but he had no similar feeling toward the Whig party as a whole. He had, after all,

> deserted no principle previously entertained, but remained faithful to those cherished during the whole of my humble political career . . . .
> I have never been inconsistent in my opinions nor ungrateful to a party — I have adhered to the one, and it may be allowed, that I owe nothing to the other.[50]

This may have done the trick; at any rate, Wynn Ellis, despite his purportedly poor health, agreed to take on the burdens of the shrievalty, and Bulwer-Lytton was off the hook.[51]

Now he had again to await an election, but it soon became clear that this time the wait would not be long. In February 1852, the Ministry of Lord John Russell at last collapsed, largely due to the opposition of Lord

Palmerston, whom Russell had the year before dismissed from the Foreign Office. The Queen called for Lord Derby,[52] who unhesitatingly took office at the head of a purely Protectionist cabinet. Disraeli became Chancellor of the Exchequer and Leader of the House of Commons. But, despite the formidable talents of Derby and Disraeli, the Ministry was among the weakest of the century. The majority of the Ministers (including Disraeli) had never before held office, and few of them were fast learners. It was, moreover, a minority Government, in office at the sufferance of its more numerous opponents. Consequently, the Ministry would have to hold a general election within a few months, in hopes of winning a genuine majority in the House of Commons.[53]

Bulwer-Lytton viewed the new Government with surprising detachment. Writing to his friend Lord Walpole, he remarked that

> the present men have a very good chance of staying in, unless they do something very silly or break down for want of absolute debating ability in the House against such a phalanx of speaking talent. Mrs. Disraeli in the 7th heaven; and he himself sublimely joyous.

Regarding his own career, he acknowledged that the next election would "decide my future mode of life." But, he characteristically hastened to add that, if he should lose, "I could bear that misfortune with equanimity."[54]

Certainly he liked to appear disinterested and unambitious; but long before the dissolution actually occurred, he was working hard to make sure he would *not* lose. He made several speeches in the county that spring, and he sent a number of electioneering directives to William Pollard of the pro-Tory Hertford *Guardian*. For one thing, Bulwer-Lytton did not want to be singled out from among the three Tory candidates: "support us *all three*," he instructed Pollard, "support the cause in fact." Then, he continued, Pollard was not to reply to attacks from opponents because strident controversy frightens off votes. "Allow me . . . to recommend great moderation in tone: Violence hurts us all. . . . " As for protection, "I offer my policy itself as a conciliator between two extremes: this is the line to take." Taking no chances, Bulwer-Lytton also demanded to see every reference to himself before it actually appeared in the paper.[55]

If Bulwer-Lytton sounded somewhat overbearing in these communications, it was understandable in view of the confusion among the Tories generally as to how they should handle the question of protection. Supposedly, their advocacy of tariffs on imported grain defined them as a party; the label "Protectionist" was applied to them at least as often as that of "Tory." Yet, there was no denying that the tide had turned in favor of free trade, both politically and economically. A party whose program was to raise the price of bread could scarcely expect electoral success. Nor could die-hard Protectionists look to their party leaders for encouragement. Disraeli hardly bothered any longer to hide the fact that he regarded protection as an electoral albatross, the sooner shed the better. And Derby, while he still insisted on paying lip service to the cause, openly acknowledged that even if the Tories won the upcoming elections they could not restore agricultural protection. All this left the party's Parliamentary candidates to fend for themselves as best they could, and they tended to follow the line of least resistance. They were in many cases protectionists in the counties, and free traders in the boroughs. Or, they simply shouted "No Popery," and left the tariff question alone.[56]

In fact, "Papal aggression" proved such a congenial theme for Tory orators that this issue actually overshadowed protectionism during the campaign. Many Conservatives genuinely felt that the Pope's re-establishment of a Roman Catholic hierarchy for England in 1851 somehow threatened English liberties; but others took up the cry out of expediency, for they feared the electoral consequences of leaving uncontested to Russell and the Whigs the still popular cause of anti-Catholicism. Even Bulwer-Lytton, who had long championed religious liberty, showed that he was not above pandering to the prejudices of the masses in his determination to win an election. In a speech at Bishop Stortford School in April, he declared:

> Last year you witnessed one determined aggression upon our civil liberties from the Court of Rome. Depend upon it that this aggression is but the commencement of a premeditated system.

Having thus shown himself on the side of the angels, he turned to the more congenial work of turning the Whigs' own issue against them. He denounced Russell's anti-Papal "Durham Letter" as "inflammatory," and ridiculed the Ecclesiastical Titles Act as a "thimbleful of paltry legislation." For his part, he preferred "calm and vigilant resolve" to "defend our own rights as Protestants," rather than Russell's "idle language." Generalities of this kind best suited his purpose. But he did not hesitate to preserve his "Protestant" credentials by coming out against the Maynooth grant (a subsidy for a Roman Catholic College in Ireland), when a questioner raised that topic.[57]

In this speech, Bulwer-Lytton used his discussion of the threat posed to English liberties by "Papal aggression" as a lead-in to a discussion of a very different sort of threat, one which he actually considered far more significant: the rise of Cobdenism. This would be his principal theme, not only in this campaign, but for the remainder of his political career; as he put it on this occasion:

> I see danger to our liberties, and our constitution, in that species of democracy which threatens to place all the general interests of trade and agriculture, all the institutions which preserve Monarchy and order, in the hands of reckless and excitable manufacturing populations. Mr. [Richard] Cobden has told us the great towns should rule the country, and at the head of these great towns will be the men of Manchester.

The fundamental conflict in the nation, he continued, matched the Conservatives against the Cobdenites. While the Whigs also opposed Cobden, they would help his cause if they turned out Lord Derby, the true bulwark against the men of Manchester. In the present state of affairs, the Whigs had become an irrelevancy, and Bulwer-Lytton predicted they would soon realize this and join with the Tories against the forces of disorder and democracy. As for the present election, he told his listeners they had best make their "choice manfully between the Government of Lord Derby or the principles of Mr. Bright."[58]

For the time being, however, Bulwer-Lytton's warnings against the onset of democracy must have sounded somewhat theoretical and vague to the voters of Hertfordshire. Most of them were worried about a more pressing problem—low prices for farm producers. Bulwer-Lytton, of course, addressed himself to that issue as well. He strongly supported Derby's proposal for a moderate fixed duty on imported grain, but, as we have seen,[59] he recognized the necessity of finding alternative means of helping farmers. In a speech at Hitchin, he called for the abolition, or reduction, of the malt tax. Temperance-minded Liberals supported that tax because it reduced farmers' incentive to raise that grain to sell to brewers. Elimination of the tax would compensate British agriculturalists for the losses they incurred after the Corn Laws were repealed, and, for once, apply the principle of free trade to benefit them. As Bulwer-Lytton put it:

I say that Free Trade to the farmer, and the raising of six millions by
the duty on malt are wholly incompatible one with the other.[60]

Bulwer-Lytton was certainly telling the voters what they wanted to
hear. The campaign, indeed, was going extremely well, and, in his
Hitchin speech, he confidently predicted victory for himself and for his
two colleagues, the Conservative incumbents Thomas Halsey and Sir
Henry Meux. Of course, practically all political candidates predict
victory at every opportunity, but in those days of open voting it was
possible for Bulwer-Lytton to speak with a degree of confidence — and
candor — that would be startling today:

> I must say that unless promises are actually broken, unless we are
> deserted at the poll by those who have assured us of support, I don't
> see a chance of defeat for any one of us three, Halsey, Meux, or
> myself.[61]

Nonetheless, the election was hard fought. On July 15, 1852 (two
weeks after the dissolution of Parliament that officially commenced the
campaign), the candidates appeared at the hustings in Hertford to deliver
their election addresses. They faced a crowd of rowdy Liberal
partisans — the "metropolitan mob," as one account described them — who
had stationed themselves directly in front of the stand. When Halsey and
Meux tried to speak, the crowd drowned them out. Then came
Bulwer-Lytton's turn. After meeting a similar reception, he suddenly
jumped off the hustings and onto the press table directly beneath it,
knocking over ink bottles and sending startled reporters scurrying for
cover. This unexpected distraction got the audience's attention, and he
did his best to take advantage of it, saying:

> I do not know whether it is your intention to hear me or not; but I
> have left the place appropriated by custom to a candidate, and you see
> me here; because it is a maxim of my life to get as close as I can to
> my enemies, and to stick as firmly as I can to my friends.

This banter won a cheer from the friendlier part of the crowd, and
Bulwer-Lytton then worked his way into his prepared speech, a partisan
denunciation of the Russell Ministry.[62]

He spoke directly to the hecklers: "You are friends to reform and
progress, but where is the reform and where is the progress?" But the
mob did not give up either, and began to drown him out. Bulwer-Lytton

tried a different tack. He approached the man who seemed to be their leader. "Come, my good friend," he said, "why should you so obstinately interrupt me?" He then shook the man's hand, while the crowd cheered.[63] It would make for a better story if one could report that thereafter Bulwer-Lytton held the crowd spellbound. In fact, the heckling continued unabated, and the man whose hand Bulwer-Lytton shook caused such commotion he had to be led away by police. Bulwer-Lytton remained undaunted, however, and he thus ridiculed the uproar:

> Why can't you be quiet for a moment? Ah, I see one honest fellow there. I have my eye on you, sir. Keep your neighbor quiet. Come, I count on you (cheers and laughter). Are you in earnest about Reform? . . . Then, pray, what is that last cabinet to you?

Eventually, he made it to the end of his address, concluding by declaring himself "not disheartened by that zealous clamour which mistakes noise for votes. . . ." And, it was reported, even the Radical mob joined in the cheers for him at the end.[64]

The voting took place one week later. It soon became clear that Bulwer-Lytton would in fact return to Parliament, after an absence of eleven years. It was, however, somewhat anticlimactic, following his spirited performance at the hustings, that he trailed the other Tory candidates. The final results were: Thomas Halsey (C), 2225; Sir Henry Meux (C), 2219; Sir E. Bulwer-Lytton (C), 2190; Hon. Thomas Trevor (L) 2043; Christopher Puller (L), 1890; George Jacob Bosanquet (L), 1868.[65]

The election of 1852 marked Bulwer-Lytton's emergence as an advocate of certain ideals for which he would stand during the remainder of his political career. To be sure, the tariff question, which had loomed so large during the preceding years, soon receded into the background. But Bulwer-Lytton would continue to oppose Cobdenism in other areas. In the years ahead, he emerged as a spokesman for an aggressive, sometimes bellicose foreign policy; for development of the Empire; and for the maintenance of the national institutions and the aristocratic order. He was, in short, a conservative nationalist, — and the uncompromising foe of Cobdenite internationalism.

Certainly he now regarded the Cobdenites (and not Whiggism) as the real enemy. The Cobdenites' emphasis on breaking down barriers between nations — and their perceived lack of patriotism — he denounced as "the sentiments of slaves" which undermined "the love and pride of country, without which no community can endure long."[66] Their antagonism to the landed class, he believed, threatened one of the principal bulwarks of English liberty. And their proposals for granting the franchise to the urban working classes would mean, Bulwer-Lytton believed, the extension of political power to those least able to exercise it intelligently, a step that would lead to sudden and ill-considered changes, and the collapse of the social order.[67]

Perhaps most fundamentally, Bulwer-Lytton opposed the Cobdenites because, he believed, they concentrated on the financial aspects of every question, and ignored the underlying moral considerations. They applied the abstract principles of political economy, "as if they were describing lifeless things, and not dealing with human beings . . ." who acted on the basis of their "passions, and habits, and prejudices. . . ."[68] For example, Cobden and "the recruits to his financial standard" would, "under the cry of economy," undertake to

> reduce the empire of Great Britain to a fourth-rate state, leaving none
> of the defenses which other fourth-rate states concur in maintaining
> . . . . From a modern school, politicians have arisen who seem to
> make it their boast that they know how to make great states small.[69]

Even worse, they applied the same criteria when analyzing the ancient institutions of England. These "wretched money spiders," Bulwer-Lytton charged, would even do away with the Monarchy because "a Republic is cheap."[70]

Bulwer-Lytton believed no one could place a price tag on a nation's heritage. The traditions of "old England," however anomalous they had become, added immeasurably to the stability of the state, and thus helped maintain the continuity that he regarded as essential for the survival of liberty. In an essay entitled "The Spirit of Conservatism," that appeared a few years after the period we have been discussing, Bulwer-Lytton wrote with regard to the necessity for continuity:

> Conservatism accepts cheerfully the maxim of Bentham, "the greatest
> happiness of the greatest number," provided it may add this
> indispensable condition, "for the longest period of time." . . .
>
> Duration is an essential element of the plans for happiness, private
> or public; and conservatism looks to the durable in all its ideas of
> improvement.

118

> But duration means the duration of a something definite in politics;
> that something is the body politic—the Nation. A conservative party
> must be national, or it is nothing.
>
> Patriotism is a safer principle, both for a state and the human race,
> than Philanthropy.[71]

Continuity, then, did not mean blind adherence to the ways of the past.
Indeed, he argued, without progress the body politic would "languish and
die." But, he added,

> progress does not mean transformation; it means the advance toward
> the fullest development of forces of which any given human
> organization . . . is capable. What is progress in one state may be
> paralysis to another. Each state is an integral unity; it has, when free,
> not otherwise—. . . the powers within itself to improve all the
> faculties which it takes from birth. It can not, any more than a man
> can do, alter its whole idiosyncrasies into those of another organized
> unity which you present to it as a model. . . .
>
> Conservatism, rightly considered, is the policy which conserves the
> body politic in the highest condition of health of which it is capable,
> compatible with longevity.[72]

It is clear from this that Bulwer-Lytton, like Edmund Burke before
him, viewed the state as a living organism. He regarded the nation's
"integral unity" as an indispensable precondition to progress. No wonder,
then, he so ardently opposed those radicals who, he asserted, portrayed
patriotism as an obstacle to advancement, or undermined national unity
by stirring up class conflict. Progress, he wrote, should always be
encouraged

> with a due regard to the idiosyncratic character of a state, such as it
> has been made by time and circumstance—[and] to the institutions
> which have not only become endeared to it by custom, but have
> contributed to consolidate the national unity by forming and
> systematizing the national spirit and mind.[73]

No account of Bulwer-Lytton's campaign against Cobdenism would
be complete unless it took into consideration the series of novels—which
comprised *The Caxtons* (1849), *My Novel* (1853), and *What Will He Do
With It?* (1858)—that he wrote to popularize his conservative/nationalist
philosophy. These books, generally known as the Caxton series,
constituted, as his grandson the Earl of Lytton put it, "a complete

departure from the romantic style of all his previous works." And, if the Earl's prediction that these books would prove the most lastingly popular of all Bulwer-Lytton's works has not been borne out,[74] at least the author achieved the aim he expressed at the time, "to create the kind of interest which secures popularity . . . [even] independent of its merely literary merit."[75] This popularity enabled him to inculcate his ideas among the largest possible number of people.

Bulwer-Lytton's purpose in writing these novels was to glorify the "idiosyncratic character" of the English people, the customs, peculiarities, and traditions whose preservation he considered essential for the healthful development of the nation.[76] Consequently, these works were avowedly nationalistic. The fundamental "sentiment of the work" was to foster feelings that would "cement" society. "My endeavor," he wrote, was

> to strengthen the Old English cordial feeling — & bind together those classes which the Manchester School are always trying to separate & the French School would dip into the fusing pit altogether.[77]

The Caxton series proved a great popular success and, in a real sense, revitalized his literary career.[78] This series was also remarkable because it showed that, to a greater extent than ever before, Bulwer-Lytton was popularizing as a novelist the philosophy he propounded as a politician. It remained to be seen, following the election of 1852, whether he would be as effective in Parliament as he had been with his pen.

NOTES

1. Edward Bulwer-Lytton, Speech for Nomination at Hertford, Lytton Papers, D/EK W99.

2. When Thomas Brand, the nephew of Lord Dacre (an influential Hertfordshire Liberal), unexpectedly announced his candidacy in 1847, Bulwer-Lytton decided not to enter the contest. It seems reasonable to infer that, since Brand stood to succeed to the Dacre peerage, Bulwer-Lytton may have done this to secure Brand's backing in an election following the latter's elevation to the House of Lords. *Ibid.* See also, below, note 30.

3. Bulwer-Lytton to Lord Lansdowne, January 6, 1852, Lytton Papers, D/EK 023.

4. See above, Chapter IV.

5. Edward Bulwer-Lytton to William Cowper, n.d., in Parrish Collection, Firestone Library, Princeton University.

6. J. S. Foster to Edward Bulwer-Lytton, August 1, 1847, Lytton Papers, D/EK 023.

7. Quoted by Blake, *Disraeli*, 80.

8. *Ibid.*

9. Sadleir, *Bulwer: A Panorama*, 368-369.

10. Monypenny and Buckle, *Life of Benjamin Disraeli*, III, 337.

11. See Blake, *Disraeli*, 129.

12. *Ibid.*, 253-257, 720.

13. *Ibid.*, 544.

14. One can infer this from the tone of a friendly, rather chatty letter Bulwer-Lytton wrote to Mrs. Disraeli shortly after this meeting. Edward Bulwer-Lytton to Mrs. B. Disraeli, October 26, 1850, Hughenden Papers, Box 104, B/xx/ly.

15. Edward Bulwer-Lytton to Lord Walpole, August 27, 1850, Lytton Papers, D/EK C26.

16. Monypenny and Buckle, *Life of Benjamin Disraeli*, III, 241.

17. Edward Bulwer-Lytton to Lord Walpole, May 10, 1850, Lytton Papers, D/EK C26.

18. See Blake, *Disraeli*, 278-280.

19. Edward Bulwer-Lytton to Lord Walpole, March 3, 1850, Lytton Papers, D/EK C26.

20. Bulwer-Lytton told Lansdowne that, up until February, 1851, he had refrained from joining "the party styled the Protectionists because their demands had hitherto appeared to me vague and exaggerated. . . ." Bulwer-Lytton to Lord Lansdowne, January 6, 1852, Lytton Papers, D/EK 023.

21. Bulwer-Lytton to Lord Walpole, March 3, 1850, Lytton Papers, D/EK C26.

22. Bulwer-Lytton to Lord Lansdowne, January 6, 1852, Lytton Papers, D/EK 023.

23. Edward Bulwer-Lytton to [William Pollard], April 7, 1852, Huntington Library, Letters of Edward Bulwer-Lytton, Box II. Bulwer-Lytton was a Tory candidate for Parliament at the time he wrote this letter to Pollard, a pro-Tory newspaperman, to advise him as to the line he should take in the campaign.

24. Benjamin Disraeli to Edward Bulwer-Lytton, October 16, 1850, Lytton Papers, D/EK C5.

25. Edward Bulwer-Lytton to Benjamin Disraeli, October 19, 1850, Hughenden Papers, Box 104, B/xx/ly.

26. Sadleir, *Bulwer: A Panorama*, 192.

27. Disraeli to Bulwer-Lytton, October 19, 1850, Hughenden Papers, Box 104, B/xx/ly.

28. Bulwer-Lytton to Lord Lansdowne, January 6, 1852. Lytton Papers, D/EK 023.

29. Disraeli to Bulwer-Lytton, October 16, 1850, Lytton Papers, D/EK 05.

30. Thomas Trevor had changed his name from Brand (see above, note 2). His uncle, the 20th Lord Dacre, died on March 21, 1851, and was succeeded by his brother (the father of Thomas Trevor, M.P.). This gentlemen, the 21st Lord Dacre, died on June 2, 1853, whereupon Thomas Trevor succeeded as the 22nd Lord Dacre. He had, however, already lost his seat in the House of Commons (in the general election of 1852); consequently, no by-election resulted from his succession to the peerage.

31. Bulwer-Lytton to Lord Lansdowne, January 6, 1852. Lytton Papers, D/EK 023.

32. Edward Bulwer-Lytton to Benjamin Disraeli, February 27, 1851, in Earl of Lytton, II, 163-164.

33. See above, Chapter III.

34. Wilbur Jones, *Lord Derby and Victorian Conservatism* (Athens: University of Georgia Press, 1956), 149-150.

35. Quoted by Earl of Lytton, II, 168. For an analysis of this aspect of the pamphlet, see *Ibid.*, 164-165.

36. Edward Bulwer-Lytton, *Letters to John Bull* (London: Chapman & Hall, 1851), 100-101.

37. *Ibid.*, 103-104.

38. Earl of Lytton, II, 172.

39. Benjamin Disraeli to Edward Bulwer-Lytton, May 2, 1851, quoted in *Ibid.*, 173.

40. Hertford *Mercury*, May 3, 1851.

41. "Report Passed by (Hertfordshire) Agricultural Protection Society, April 24, 1852." Charles A. Pearson to Edward Bulwer-Lytton, March 28, 1851, Lytton papers, D/EK 023. It should be noted that, in the course of these negotiations, Bulwer-Lytton's great concern was that the Agricultural Protection Society should agree to help him with the election expenses. George Passingham to Edward Bulwer-Lytton, April 16, 1851, *Ibid.*

42. Edward Bulwer-Lytton to Robert Lytton, April 14, 1851, Lytton Papers, D/EK C26.

43. Father of the future Prime Minister.

44. Edward Bulwer-Lytton to Lord Salisbury, n.d., Lytton Papers, D/EK 023.

45. Edward Bulwer-Lytton to Lord Salisbury, n.d., Lytton Papers, D/EK 023.

46. Lord Salisbury to Edward Bulwer-Lytton, May 22, 1851, *Ibid.*

47. Edward Bulwer-Lytton to Benjamin Disraeli, n.d. [September, 1851] Hughenden Papers, Box 104, B/xx/ly.

48. Edward Bulwer-Lytton to Phillip Longmore, November 17, 1851, Lytton Papers, D/EK 023.

49. Edward Bulwer-Lytton to Lord Lansdowne, January 19, 1852, *Ibid.*

50. Same to same, January 6, 1852, *Ibid.*

51. Sir John Bernard Burke, *History of the Landed Gentry of Great Britain and Ireland* (London: Harrison, 1871), I, 393.

52. Stanley had succeeded to this title in June 1851.

53. On this Government, see Blake, *Disraeli*, 300-309.

54. Edward Bulwer-Lytton to Lord Walpole, February 28, 1852, Lytton Papers, D/EK C26.

55. Edward Bulwer-Lytton to William Pollard, April 21, 1852, Huntington Library, Letters of Edward Bulwer-Lytton Box II.

56. Blake, *Disraeli*, 309.

57. Edward Bulwer-Lytton, Speech at Bishop Stortford School, April 29, 1852, Lytton Papers, D/EK W99.

58. *Ibid.* John Bright was the principal ally of Richard Cobden in the free trade movement.

59. See above, page 104.

60. Bulwer-Lytton, Speech at Hitchin, June 22, 1852, Lytton Papers, D/EK W98.

61. *Ibid.*

62. *The Times*, October 7, 1874; Bulwer-Lytton, Speech for Nomination at Hertford, July 15, 1852, Lytton Papers, D/EK W99.

63. *Ibid.*

64. *Ibid.*

65. Dod, *Electoral Facts From 1832 to 1853*, 145.

66. Quoted by Earl of Lytton, II, 167; Bulwer-Lytton, *Letters to John Bull*, 99.

67. Bulwer-Lytton, Speech at Bishop Stortford School, April 29, 1852, Lytton Papers, D/EK W99.

68. Quoted by Earl of Lytton, II, 170.

69. Bulwer-Lytton, *Letters to John Bull*, 99.

70. Bulwer-Lytton to John Forster, March 1, 1848, Lytton Papers, D/EK C27.

71. Edward Bulwer-Lytton, "The Spirit of Conservatism," in *Caxtoniana* (New York: Harper & Bros., 1864), 436-437.

72. *Ibid.*, 435-436.

73. *Ibid.*, 439-440.

74. Earl of Lytton, II, 30, 104.

75. Quoted by Allen C. Christensen, *Edward Bulwer-Lytton* (Athens: University of Georgia Press, 1976), 139.

76. Bulwer-Lytton, *Caxtoniana*, 435-440.

77. Quoted by Christensen, *Edward Bulwer-Lytton*, 141-142.

78. During the decade preceding the appearance of *The Caxtons* in 1849, Bulwer-Lytton published a great many popular works; and yet, during this time, his standing as a novelist unquestionably declined. It seemed he was merely reworking familiar themes, and

seldom breaking new ground. The two most original of his writings during these years, moreover, illustrate another aspect of the problem. These were *Zanoni* (1843), which was probably Bulwer-Lytton's favorite among his novels, and *King Arthur*, an "epic" poem, undoubtedly the author's favorite among all his works. Both were steeped in the occult mysteries of which Bulwer-Lytton was so fond, and both, consequently, struck the public as at best esoteric, at worst obscure. *Zanoni* did not sell as well as many of Bulwer-Lytton's other novels; *King Arthur* was a straightforward failure. It was clear the author was writing more to please himself than to interest the public. As indicated, this approach changed with the Caxton series. His purpose in those works was to popularize certain ideals; and, significantly, Bulwer-Lytton's writing improved when he was striving for popularity. Thus the Caxton novels had a freshness and vigor their immediate predecessors had lacked. They constituted, along with *Pelham* and *The Last Days of Pompeii*, one of the three landmark successes of his literary career, and secured his reputation as a great novelist, at least during his own lifetime.

CHAPTER SIX

SPEAKING FOR ENGLAND

The General Election of 1852 sealed the fate of the Derby Ministry. The Tories had failed to win a majority in the House of Commons, and, accordingly, their Government would fall whenever the several opposition factions united against it. Despite their gloomy prospects, the Ministers had one great consolation: the opportunity to demonstrate their capacity to govern, a capacity few thought they had. If, however briefly, the Tories competently managed the nation's business and held their own in debate, they would improve the future prospects of their party.

As a newly elected backbencher, Bulwer-Lytton had no role in the formulation of Ministerial policy; but the Tory leaders did expect he would add much to the party's debating strength. In this regard, his performance was to meet these expectations only intermittently, as became apparent after two major debates that took place soon after the new Parliament convened in November 1852.

The first of these debates concerned a motion by the veteran free trader Charles Villiers, which declared, among other things, that the repeal of the Corn Laws had been "a wise, just, and beneficial measure." Clearly, passage of this resolution would humiliate the Tory Ministers, who had of course opposed repeal of the Corn Laws, and force them to resign in disgrace. There seemed real danger this would occur, especially after Lord John Russell, anxious as ever to return to office, threw his weight behind the Villiers motion.[1]

Fortunately for the Tories, Lord Palmerston, with Peelite backing, offered a compromise in the form of a substitute pledge that the "policy of unrestricted competition [would be] firmly maintained and prudently extended." This phrasing the Ministers could accept, as it suggested no censure against those who had opposed free trade in the past. Certainly Disraeli did not regret seeing another nail driven into the coffin of protection, and he promptly endorsed Palmerston's motion.[2]

The debate over the two motions lasted for four days in late November. Shortly before it began, Disraeli had asked Bulwer-Lytton to participate, assuring him with a typical hint of flattery that "the occasion would not be unworthy of the speaker."³ As it turned out, Bulwer-Lytton was not to contribute significantly to the Tory cause; apparently his nerves failed him. He managed to speak briefly on the 25th, principally to point out that repeal of the malt tax would make for a "fair and impartial application of free trade." But this was scarcely the oration Disraeli was expecting. The next day, Bulwer-Lytton wrote his Leader to excuse himself from making another speech on the grounds of ill health: he was suffering from a "constitutional" heart problem. He assured Disraeli, however, that he remained "most anxious to serve your Government" in the future.⁴

Such incidents would recur all too frequently in the years ahead. To be sure, genuine ailments, as well as hypochondria, played a part in constraining Bulwer-Lytton's Parliamentary activities, and it would be pointless to speculate as to which factor was the more significant. What is certain is that Bulwer-Lytton did not become the ready, reliable debater Disraeli needed to back him up in the House of Commons.

This was regrettable because Bulwer-Lytton could make an excellent speech when he felt up to it. He demonstrated his ability less that three weeks after his disappointing showing in the free trade debate, when he spoke in support of Disraeli's Budget. On that occasion, indeed, Bulwer-Lytton gained the distinction of taking a prominent part in one of the most famous debates in all of British Parliamentary history.

It became evident, after the Ministers succeeded in defeating the Villiers motion,⁵ that the Government would stand or fall on the Budget. As Chancellor of the Exchequer, Disraeli undertook to find some method of compensating the agricultural interest, on whose support his party depended, for the loss of income they had suffered as a result of the repeal of the Corn Laws. He proposed therefore to reduce both the malt tax and the tax on farm income. To make up for the loss in revenue, he hoped to increase the inhabited houses duty. This "bundle of expedients" did not impress the House of Commons. T. B. Macaulay neatly summed up the general reaction to the plan when he described it as "nothing but taking money out of the pockets of the people in towns and putting it into the pockets of growers of malt." More ominously, Gladstone termed it "the least conservative budget I have ever known."⁶

When the actual debate on the Budget began on December 10th, the strength of the opposition became manifest. Three former Chancellors of the Exchequer denounced Disraeli's plan,[7] as did such formidable figures as Richard Cobden, Robert Lowe, and James Graham. The Ministers who rose to defend the Budget, notably Lord John Manners, Sir John Pakington, and Spencer Walpole, were no match for such an outstanding array of talent, although Walpole at least made an excellent speech. Among Tory backbenchers, Bulwer-Lytton alone contributed significantly to the cause, and the very weakness of the Ministerial side made his spirited oration all the more welcome to that party.[8]

The speech consisted of two distinct parts. First, he defended the specific proposals Disraeli had made. He argued that reduction of the malt tax was essential in order to relieve distress among British farmers; and, citing J. S. Mill as an authority, maintained that the inhabited houses tax was one of the fairest of all possible taxes. As if to answer the criticism by Macaulay quoted above, he continued:

> because this question is accompanied indirectly with benefit to the farmer, and is accompanied by a double house tax, [sic] we are told that this is a question of town against country. No, Sir, it is a question of Free Trade against restriction; it is a question whether you will . . . remove a check which operates directly against an important branch of the industry of the country—and it is accompanied with a direct tax which would be fair and just, and as such is recommended by all political economists . . . . You say you object to the house tax being doubled for the benefit of the farmers, but that is simply to say that you object to the further extension of Free Trade when it operates against the other classes whom you represent.[9]

Then, in recognition of the fact that this was really his first speech as a Tory M.P., he moved on to a justification of his own political conversion, which concluded with an encomium upon the Derby Ministry itself:

> The support which I now tender to the Government is not any question connected with agriculture; it is not any party consideration; it is simply this—the disposition they have shown to promote general measures for the improvement of the laws, and for advancing the welfare of the people . . . . I see a . . . Government which, while it will be conservative of the great principles of the constitution, will make that constitution suffice for all purposes of practical reform. It is by measures and sentiments like these that the Government have shown already that they do not come into office

as the exclusive advocates of a single class, or the inert supporters
of a retrograde policy.[10]

This speech proved such a success as to surprise even
Bulwer-Lytton himself. He had felt dissatisfied with his delivery, and
regretted that, owing apparently to a lapse of memory, he had omitted
what he considered his best argument. But the warm praise of his
colleagues gave his self-confidence — which was never very secure despite
his proverbial vanity — a badly needed boost.[11]

Bulwer-Lytton's laudable effort notwithstanding, the fact remained
that the Tories were outgunned in the House of Commons. Disraeli went
down fighting. On the last night of the debate, he spoke for two and a
half hours, hammering at the coalition of critics who had lambasted his
Budget. It was a remarkable speech: spirited, combative, and replete
with the withering sarcasm that made Disraeli so feared an opponent in
debate. One observer thus described the memorable scene:

> During the invective of Disraeli's speech, the Opposition presented
> a most remarkable appearance; not speaking to each other, pale in
> the gaslight. It reminded one of the scenes in the National
> Convention of the French Revolution. To complete the effect,
> although in midwinter, a loud thunderstorm raged; the peals were
> heard and the flashes of lightning could be seen in the Chamber
> itself.[12]

When Disraeli finished, at one o'clock in the morning, Gladstone
unexpectedly rose to reply. His brilliant dissection of the Budget not
only established him as Disraeli's great rival among the coming men in
the House of Commons, but also demonstrated his mastery of orthodox
economics and effectively extinguished whatever glimmering hopes the
Tories had of remaining in office. The Budget was defeated 305 votes
to 286, and Derby resigned the next day. A coalition Government then
took office under the leadership of the Peelite Lord Aberdeen, with
Gladstone as Chancellor of the Exchequer. The Tories became once
again the opposition party, as they would remain, with only two brief
interruptions, for the next twenty-one years.[13]

During these long years out of office, Disraeli seldom failed to act
upon the principle that it is the duty of an opposition to oppose. In this
task, he demonstrated remarkable energy and resilience; as Gladstone
once put it, Disraeli was "a man who is never *beaten*. Every reverse,
every defeat is to him only an admonition to wait and catch his

opportunity of retrieving and more than retrieving his position."[14] Of course, he could not carry on the fight unaided, and Bulwer-Lytton, after his fine speech in support of the 1852 Budget, seemed likely to become one of Disraeli's most valuable Parliamentary allies.

And, indeed, during the next five years, Bulwer-Lytton ranked as one of the principal spokesmen for the opposition in the House of Commons. In this role, he had at last an opportunity to play a conspicuous part in national politics. But whether he would succeed or fail in this endeavor depended, above all else, on his ability as a Parliamentary debater.

Any assessment of Bulwer-Lytton in this regard should note at the outset the comment contemporaries most frequently made about his speeches: they read better than they sounded.[15] In reality, he presented to the House carefully prepared "oratorical essays,"[16] well worthy of so preeminent an author. But their impact was often dissipated by faulty delivery. William White wrote that Bulwer-Lytton was

> not an effective speaker; not, however, because his matter is not good, but because his action spoils all. It is well known that he studies his speeches carefully beforehand—would that he would, under proper guidance, study how to deliver them! His manner is this: He begins a sentence, standing upright, in his usual tone; as he gets to the middle he throws himself backwards, until you would fancy that he must tumble over, and gradually raises his voice to its highest pitch. He then begins to lower his tone and bring his body forwards, so that at the finish of the sentence his head nearly touches his knees, and the climax of the sentence is lost in a whisper . . . . [17]

This description, if hyperbolic, was close to the truth. A source friendlier to Bulwer-Lytton noted that his articulation was "not as clear as articulation should be in an orator, and his delivery was . . . too monotonous."[18]

He recognized his shortcomings, once remarking that "We English are accustomed to clip our consonants and drop our voices at the end of our sentences (that as a Public Speaker is my own besetting fault)."[19] His inability to cure this bad habit resulted mainly from nervousness. White once observed how, "When Sir Edward has made up his mind to speak, he is restless, uneasy, and wanders about the House and the lobby with his hands in his pockets and his eyes upon the ground."[20] It is hardly remarkable, then, that he often forgot his resolve to enunciate each syllable, with the result that his words frequently became "inarticulate — mere sounds, conveying no meaning."[21]

This problem was aggravated because Bulwer-Lytton was losing his hearing.[22] Not only did this affliction make it difficult for him properly to modulate his voice, it also restricted his effectiveness in debate. As Sir Archibald Alison reported:

> I have often heard it said by the best judges in the House of Commons that Bulwer-Lytton was for an opening the best speaker in that assembly. His unfortunate deafness shut him out from the chance of a reply, unless he had time to see his opponent's speech in the newspapers.[23]

Severe as this handicap was, it is also true that Bulwer-Lytton could hear something of what was said on the opposite side of the House.[24] But, owing to his high-strung temperament, as well as to his hardness of hearing, it suited him to recite from memory the speeches he had carefully written in advance. He himself readily admitted that he lacked as a speaker the fluency that so distinguished him as a writer; as he put it:

> I have little repartee, my memory is slow, and my presence of mind not great. My powers of speaking are very uncertain, and very imperfectly developed. I have eloquence in me but . . . I cannot speak without either preparation or the pressure of powerful excitement. It would cost me immense labor to acquire the ready, cool trick of words with little knowledge and no heart in them, which is necessary for a Parliamentary debater.[25]

As a result, too often the impact of his premeditated eloquence was lessened for lack of spontaneity. The comment Arthur Balfour once made about Winston Churchill, who similarly memorized his speeches, might apply as well to Bulwer-Lytton:

> The Right Honorable Member's artillery is very powerful. But it is not very mobile. It has continued firing away at a position we have never occupied.[26]

For all his faults, Bulwer-Lytton also possessed powerful artillery. We have already noted Alison's remark on how highly esteemed were his speeches. Bulwer-Lytton's strengths as an orator were, however, less obvious than his weaknesses. As Disraeli observed in a description of one of Bulwer-Lytton's most successful speeches:

> Deaf, fantastic, modulating his voice with difficulty, sometimes painful — at first almost an object of ridicule to the superficial — Lytton occasionally reached almost the sublime, and perfectly enchained his audience.[27]

Thus did Bulwer-Lytton's intellectual strength overcome his physical frailty. We can sense this again in Alison's description of a speech Bulwer-Lytton delivered in Edinburgh, in 1854:

> The speech . . . was listened to with breathless attention. Its language was so terse and elegant, that . . . it revealed the labor of previous composition; but it was so thoroughly committed to memory, and delivered with so much fervor and animation, that it had all the charm of extempore speaking. Never was an effort more successful. . . . Genius broke out almost in every sentence. . . . They obviously came from the heart, and were inspired by the hidden fire of sympathetic genius.[28]

While this speech took place "out of doors," where Bulwer-Lytton probably felt more at ease and performed better than in Parliament, there were occasions in the House as well when the brilliance of his intellect shone through the fog of faulty elocution and exaggerated gesticulation. He would at once seize upon the heart of an issue, and develop the successive points of his argument with apparent frankness and faultless logic, until it seemed his conclusion was the only one any reasonable person could possibly reach.

I would cite as perhaps the best illustration of his powers of persuasion the debate over the repeal of the stamp duty in 1855. At that time, Sir George Cornewall Lewis, the Chancellor of the Exchequer in Lord Palmerston's Ministry, proposed to repeal the stamp duty on newspapers, a step which, as we have seen, Bulwer-Lytton had forcefully advocated some twenty years earlier.[29] In this debate, Bulwer-Lytton repeated what he had said on the question before, with the difference that now he was a Tory, and the bulk of that party opposed repeal, while the Liberals supported it. Consequently, he emphasized that aspect of his argument most likely to appeal to Conservatives: that making newspapers cheaper was the most effective means of counteracting the immoral and incendiary publications then circulating among the working classes, as it would facilitate the dissemination of moral precepts and conservative ideas. And, it would seem, his argument caused some Conservatives to take a different view of the issue than they had before. George Jacob Holyoake described Bulwer-Lytton's performance:

> While Mr. Deedes [Tory M.P. for East Kent] moved an amendment . . . to defer the second reading of the Bill, a fashionably-dressed, slenderly-built Member appeared on the right of the gangway, taking notes. From the Speaker's Gallery he seemed a young man. Before the dull Deedes had regained his seat, the elegantly-looking lounger from the Club threw down his hat and caught the Speaker's eye. Rebuking his "honourable friend" (Deedes) for assuming that the House had not had time to understand the Bill before it, he announced that 20 years ago he (the lounger) had introduced a similar Bill into Parliament. Strangers then knew that Sir Edward Bulwer-Lytton was the Member addressing the House.

After quoting a portion of Bulwer-Lytton's speech, Holyoake went on to comment:

> This fine passage was worthy of the occasion. Nothing comparable to it was said during the debate . . . . Those who say old convictions are never shaken, nor votes won by debate, should have stood in the lobby at midnight after his division. A burly country squire of the Church-and-King species — fat and circular as a prize pig — a Tory "farmer's friend," born with the belief that a free press would lead to an American Presidency in St. Stephen's. . . — this obese legislator, nudging a Liberal who had voted in the majority, said, "I gave a vote on your side to-night! Lytton convinced me." A triumph of oratory that for Sir Edward! 215 voted for a free press on this night — 161 against; majority 54.[30]

Bulwer-Lytton's strengths as a Parliamentary debater were as remarkable as his weaknesses. He became, with all his failings, a major force in the House of Commons. While different observers would have given different assessments of his standing in that body, it would not be going too far to regard him as, next to Disraeli, the most important figure among the Tories in the House of Commons in this period. This is not to say, however, that he was Disraeli's chief lieutenant or right-hand man. Bulwer-Lytton was never a professional politician; and habitual ill health, hypochondria, or just plain nerves rendered him an unreliable colleague. He simply could not be counted on to perform steadily in the day-to-day conduct of business. It is significant how few speeches he actually made. In all of 1853, for instance, he addressed the House only once.[31] Granted that his health was particularly poor during that period,[32] and that the position of the Aberdeen Ministry was then so strong the opposition really had little to say for itself. But during the session from December 1854 to March 1855, when Bulwer-Lytton was again reasonably healthy and the political scene had become unstable, he spoke only twice; while, in the same period, Disraeli delivered fifteen speeches, and Sir John Pakington, Joseph Henley, and Spencer Walpole each made at least eight.[33]

But when Bulwer-Lytton did speak, he usually had something of importance to say. If his delivery was poor, that did not matter to those who read his words in the newspapers the next day. Unquestionably, his orations had an impact that resounded beyond the walls of Westminster. As evidence of his standing with the public, one can cite a work entitled *An Anecdotal History of the British Parliament* (1881), which includes chapters on the outstanding Parliamentarians from the sixteenth century to the 1880's. Only three men who served as Ministers in Tory Governments in the 1850's received mention: Lord Derby, Benjamin Disraeli, and Bulwer-Lytton.[34]

Bulwer-Lytton's importance derived from his intellectual prowess. He stood out particularly in this regard among the Tories. While the sobriquet J. S. Mill gave them, "the stupid party,"[35] may not have been deserved, the fact remained that, in the early 1850's, the Conservatives seemed out of step with the times, and appealed only to the agricultural classes whose economic interests they championed. This base, though substantial, was too narrow to afford them a majority in Parliament. Thus it became incumbent upon Bulwer-Lytton, as a man of ideas, to seek out ways the Tories might gain broader support. It was in this task that he was to prove his value to his party.

In 1853, for instance, Bulwer-Lytton set forth the novel idea of an alliance between the Whigs and Tories against the Radicals. In a series of essays entitled "Letters to the Whigs" that appeared under the pen name "Manilius" in the Tory weekly the *Press*,[36] he wrote:

> I see the sole hope for England in the union of those men who will defend England as she is. History has buried in the past all of the old feuds of the Tories and the Whigs . . . . Both have now to protect from a common fate the constitution which has been corrected and ennobled by their ancient collision of opinion. A

manly alliance upon the broad understanding that reforms are to
cement the foundations of monarchy . . . would at once give the
Whigs all that they require for the resumption of their historical
influence — electoral numbers — and strengthen the liberal disposition
of Lord Derby's partisans by the accession of all that they need to
make the public fully comprehend their views — viz., colleagues
experienced in office and eloquent in debate.[37]

Thus did Bulwer-Lytton foresee the Whig accession to the Tory
camp. Unfortunately for Bulwer-Lytton, however, it takes time for
prescience to be appreciated, and his proposal brought no results in his
own day. In the 1850's the Whigs still maintained great influence upon
the conduct of affairs, and no cataclysmic controversy had as yet arisen
to drive asunder the Liberal coalition. If the Whigs recognized the
underlying logic of Bulwer-Lytton's argument, they chose, for the time
being, not to do anything about it.

Important as was the idea of a coalition with the Whigs, it was not
Bulwer-Lytton's most significant contribution toward the forging of a
Tory majority. For he was among the first to understand the means by
which the Conservatives might become the party of the middle-class.
Certainly radicalism was losing much of its former appeal for that class,
now that the goal of free trade had been achieved. In the 1850's,
however, the beneficiary of this conservative trend was not the
Conservative party, but Lord Palmerston. As Asa Briggs has written:

In almost every respect Palmerston was the perfect epitome of the
politically articulate England of his day. . . . Averse to strong
government and uninterested in organic reforms, he believed in
gradual "improvement" and the continued prosecution of an active
foreign policy. . . . The extent of Palmerston's victory [in 1857]
entailed the almost complete destruction of the Manchester School
. . . and demonstrated how much the cries of the 1840's had faded
into the background.[38]

Palmerston came so completely to symbolize the aggressive,
nationalistic foreign policy that so many middle class electors supported,
that there was little the Conservatives could do to assail his supremacy.
After he died in 1865, however, Disraeli aspired to inherit his mantle and
succeeded in identifying the Tory party with jingoism and imperialism.[39]
And ever since, much of the strength of the party has derived from its
claim to represent British nationalism, or even British patriotism, as

opposed to the more cosmopolitan approach of its opponents. This strength was perhaps Disraeli's most important legacy to the party he led so long.[40] But it was Bulwer-Lytton who pointed the way toward that policy in the 1850's — once again, it would seem, well ahead of his time.

Bulwer-Lytton distinguished himself as a spokesman for bellicose nationalism in the debates over the Crimean War. In fact, he played a more conspicuous role in Parliament during this period than ever before in his career. An outspoken advocate of *guerre à outrance*, he expressed the sentiments of the majority of Englishmen, who had no patience with the Aberdeen Ministry's hesitant and vacillating policies. It would not be going too far to say that, for better or worse, during the Crimean War, Bulwer-Lytton spoke for England.

The first of his assaults upon the half measures of the Ministry took place on May 15, 1854 (only two months after the outbreak of hostilities) in the debate on Gladstone's War Budget. It was characteristic of the curious inability of Aberdeen's "Ministry Of All The Talents" to measure up to the exigencies of the crisis, that Gladstone, the unrivaled master of finance, made such an inadequate wartime Chancellor of the Exchequer. The trouble was, as one of his admirers acknowledged, he "shrank from war in general, and was not yet quite certain whether England had any right to undertake this war. . . ."[41] Consequently, he saw no reason why so dubious a venture need necessarily require him to dispense with the time-honored strictures of orthodox finance. Instead he went ahead with an ill-conceived and ill-fated scheme to conduct the War on a pay-as-you-go basis, proposing to meet the costs of the conflict through taxes, rather than long term loans. He even proclaimed that the difficulty involved in "meeting from year to year the expenditure which . . . [war] entails" was a "moral check which it has pleased the Almighty to impose upon the ambition and lust of conquest . . . ."[42]

Bulwer-Lytton regarded all this as nonsense. He believed wholeheartedly in the war effort, and rejected the suggestion that Britain was fighting out of "ambition" or "lust of conquest." Nor did he accept Gladstone's grotesquely materialistic concept that war would be irresistibly attractive were it not for the "moral check" of high taxes. For the time being, in any event, he was less concerned with preventing future wars than he was with vigorously carrying on the one in which Britain was already engaged. Towards this end, he denounced Gladstone's tax proposals as inequitable,[43] and advocated instead the raising of long term loans; and in this speech, he set out in no uncertain terms the attitude he would thenceforth take concerning the Crimean War:

So much has been said about our not saddling posterity, that it seems as if it were intended to insinuate that this is not a war to be waged on behalf of posterity, but for some fleeting and selfish purpose of our own. If that be so, I call on our Ministers to recall our fleets and to disband our armies — a war which is not for posterity is no fitting war for us. But surely if ever there was a war waged on behalf of posterity, it is the war which would check the ambition of Russia, and preserve Europe from the outlet of barbarian tribes, that require but the haven of the Bosphorus to menace the liberty and the civilization of races as yet unborn. . . . It is that the liberties of our children may be secured from . . . the irruptions of Scythian hordes . . . [that] we might fairly demand the next generation to aid us in the conflict we endure for their sake.[44]

At this early stage of the War, however, the Ministry still held complete control of the House of Commons, and as a result Gladstone's Budget passed by a wide margin. But within a matter of months the political situation was to change dramatically, owing to the Government's palpable mismanagement of the Crimean campaign. Following the invasion of the Crimea in September 1854, the allied British and French armies fought a series of bloody battles against the Russians, and in each instance won the field, but little else. They failed in their plan to capture Sebastopol, and at the same time neglected to secure suitable winter quarters elsewhere. The end of autumn saw the War reduced to a frustrating stalemate, in which the encamped allied armies were left, as Bulwer-Lytton put it, "to moulder piecemeal, ragged, and roofless before Sebastopol. . . , subject to epidemics . . . yet . . . without ambulances, without hospital provisions, without even tents."[45]

Consequently, on December 12th, the Government called Parliament into an unusual special session in order to deal with the crisis. But, to general consternation, the Ministers' principal proposal turned out to be nothing more than a scheme to enlist 10,000 foreigners into the British army. Bulwer-Lytton joined Disraeli, Derby, and others in denouncing this Foreign Enlistment Bill. He termed it an "affront" to the "spirit of nationality," and ridiculed the Ministry which had undertaken a great war "on the niggard hypothesis that its cost could be defrayed out of our annual income," for finding itself now reduced to "this begging petition to petty potentates for ten thousand soldiers." Bulwer-Lytton was adept at playing upon British national pride, and there was no doubt of the success of his speech. Even Richard Monckton Milnes, who answered him on behalf of the Government, acknowledged that Bulwer-Lytton's address had "excited so much admiration," and that his arguments were "as sincerely offered as they were ably delivered."[46]

On this issue, the Ministry won a Pyrrhic victory. The Foreign Enlistment Bill passed, but by a majority of only 39 votes (the plan however was never put into effect). Meanwhile, the position of the army in the Crimea remained precarious, and the prestige of the Ministry continued to sink.

The political crisis came to a head immediately after the House of Commons reconvened following its Christmas recess. On January 23, 1855, the Radical John Arthur Roebuck moved for a select committee to inquire into the Government's management of the war effort. Scarcely had Roebuck given notice of his intention when Lord John Russell, then Leader of the House of Commons, resigned his position because he could not in good conscience oppose the motion. This untimely defection by one of its most famous figures doomed the coalition. "Appearances are," Disraeli wrote gleefully to Lady Londonderry, "that the Government will not survive the next ten days or so."[47] And he proceeded to lead the Tories in strong support of Roebuck's motion.

The ensuing debate can be taken as the high water mark in Bulwer-Lytton's political career. The Ministry had eloquent and able advocates in Gladstone and Palmerston; but, Bulwer-Lytton expressed what most Members were thinking.[48] No other speaker delineated more clearly than he did the case against the Government:

> And first, we accuse you of this: that you entered — not, indeed hastily, but with long deliberation, with ample time for forethought, if not for preparation — into the most arduous enterprise this generation has witnessed, in the most utter ignorance of the power and resources of the enemy you were to encounter, the nature of the climate you were to brave, of the country you were to enter, of the supplies which your army would need. This ignorance is the more inexcusable because you disdain the available sources of information. . . .

He then proceeded to catalogue the blunders the Ministers had committed, or, at least, those for which they bore responsibility: the failure to secure Odessa as a base for the siege of Sebastopol; the failure adequately to supply the troops, which had resulted in the British having to get their bread from the French; the wretched living conditions the troops had to endure; and the scandalous lack of suitable medical facilities. The real issue that the House had to consider in view of all of this, he argued, was whether it "should quietly acquiesce, not only in the continuance of their [*i.e.* the Ministers'] power, but in the mode by which their responsibilities have been discharged." Such acquiescence, he continued, would "make us the servile accomplices in the sacrifices of what remains of that noble army of whose deeds the country are so proud. . . ." He concluded by drawing an analogy between the Duke of Newcastle, who was serving as Secretary for War under Aberdeen, and the eighteenth-century Duke of Newcastle — the scatterbrained Whig magnate who had been forced to hand over the practical management of the Seven Years War to William Pitt — and by calling for the nation similarly to demand new leadership in the present crisis:

> Once in the last century there was a Duke of Newcastle, who presided over the conduct of a war, and was supported by a league of aristocratic combinations. That war was, indeed, a series of blunders and disasters. In vain attempts were made to patch up that luckless Ministry — in vain some drops of healthful blood were infused into its feeble and decrepit constitution — the people, at last, became aroused, indignant, irresistible. They applied one remedy; that remedy is now before ourselves. They dismissed their Government and saved their army.[49]

When the House divided over Roebuck's motion on January 29th, the result must have exceeded even Bulwer-Lytton's most sanguine hopes. Aberdeen's "Ministry Of All The Talents," which had taken office with such brilliant prospects scarcely two years before, met defeat by a vote of 305 to 148, a result the House received first in stunned silence, and then with derisive shouts of laughter.[50] The "aristocratic combination" had gone; but the question remained, who would play the part of Pitt?

The Queen quite properly called upon Lord Derby, as Leader of the Opposition, to form a Government. But, to the nation at large, Palmerston was clearly the man of the hour. Derby recognized this fact, and at all events he could not imagine forming a war ministry solely from among the parcel of mediocrities who had largely made up his 1852 cabinet. Consequently he solicited Palmerston's support, and, upon receiving a refusal, informed the Queen he could not take office. Possibly Derby acted as he did out of the belief that the public grossly overrated Palmerston's capacities, and that if the latter failed to form an effective administration, he himself could then take office in a much stronger position than he could otherwise have done.[51]

Disraeli viewed his Chief's action with disgust. He considered that
the Liberals' failure to meet the emergency of War had given the Tories
a golden opportunity, and that, had Derby taken office, he could — if
necessary — have dissolved Parliament and won a sweeping majority, thus
ushering in a new era of Tory hegemony.[52]   Instead, Derby had, as
Disraeli later put it, "shrunk . . . from the responsibility of conducting the
war."[53]   Disraeli was left as a result to console himself with the vain
hope that Palmerston, "the inevitable man," would soon be shown up as
an "imposter" after he had "tried and failed."[54]

As bitterly as Disraeli privately condemned Derby's timidity, he
nonetheless kept up a common front in public.   In his newspaper, the
Press, for instance, he advanced the hopeful view that the Tories could
control the course of events, and that they would achieve their objects by
remaining at once patient and vigilant.   "Your time will not be long
delayed," he told his party, "justice will be done you by the people."[55]

Bulwer-Lytton fully concurred with this view. He did not consider
that the party had "shrunk" from conducting the War.   Instead, he
believed that by overthrowing the indecisive Aberdeen, the Tories had
secured for themselves the enviable reputation of being the "warlike"
party, and that consequently the prospect of their eventually taking office
in "natural succession to Palmerston" was "increasing rapidly . . . [in]
popularity."[56]

Meanwhile, Bulwer-Lytton's prestige within the Tory party had
grown considerably, thanks to his prominent role in the debate on
Roebuck's motion.   He was now certainly a front bencher. Lord Derby
himself gave notice of this fact; when he explained to the House of Lords
his reasons for not forming an administration, he noted that, if he had
taken office, he

> should have received — and in a high office of the Administration I
> should have been proud to have received — the support and
> assistance of the unrivaled eloquence and commanding talents of Sir
> Edward Bulwer-Lytton.[57]

In the months ahead, Bulwer-Lytton served on several occasions as
the major spokesman for his party in important debates. On June 4th, for
instance, he delivered an address in support of Disraeli's attempt to
censure the Government, in the wake of the breakdown of the recent
peace talks at Vienna.[58]   Bulwer-Lytton left the House in no doubt of
how he believed Britain should proceed:

In order to force Russia into our object we must assail and cripple her wherever she can be crippled and assailed. I say . . . do not offer to her an idle insult, do not slap her in the face, but paralyze her hands . . . . No, we cannot crush Russia as Russia, but we can crush her attempts to be more than Russia. We can, and we must, crush any means that enable her to storm or to steal across that tangible barrier that divides Europe from a Power that supports the maxims of Machiavelli with the armaments of Brennus. . . ; we will crush the power of Russia to invade her neighbors and convulse the world.[59]

But Palmerston easily warded off this Tory assault. The failure to achieve a diplomatic solution had freed the Prime Minister to take a particularly bellicose line himself, which rendered futile Bulwer-Lytton's persistent efforts to outflank him politically; the "War party" in Parliament continued to prefer Palmerston to any Tory alternative.[60]

In light of this situation, it is paradoxical to find that when next Bulwer-Lytton acted as spokesman for his party, he actually helped keep Palmerston in office. This unexpected turn of events came about as a result of a motion by the Radical Henry Layard to censure the Government for maintaining aristocratic privilege in the Army, and the system of the sale and purchase of officers' commissions. This motion reflected the growing disposition in the country to blame bumbling aristocrats for Britain's lackluster showing in the War. Layard himself had been playing upon this feeling, addressing rallies all over the country in support of ending aristocratic monopoly of high offices in civilian government, as well as in the military. A formidable administrative reform movement was beginning to emerge, advocating the establishment of an independent civil service, in which recruitment and promotion would depend on competitive examinations as proposed in the Trevelyan-Northcote Report.[61]

Bulwer-Lytton viewed these developments with mixed feelings. As a lifelong advocate of efficient government, he certainly supported the principle of administrative reform. And there could be no doubt he agreed with Layard on the need for a more vigorous conduct of the War than Palmerston had provided. But Bulwer-Lytton, although he himself had achieved his success on the basis of his abilities and not his connections, could not support any motion intended to diminish the influence of the aristocracy. After all, who could have been more an aristocrat at heart than he?

As a result, he proposed an amendment to Layard's motion, which deleted its criticism of the Government, but called for the establishment of a committee of inquiry into the problem of aristocratic influence. This inquiry, Bulwer-Lytton hoped, would,

> by instituting tests of merit, as well as by removing obstructions to its fair promotion and legitimate rewards, [serve] to secure to the service of the State the largest available proportion of the energy and intelligence for which the people of the country are distinguished.

Possibly Bulwer-Lytton felt somewhat uncomfortable about pulling Palmerston's chestnuts out of the fire. Perhaps for that reason he indulged, in the same speech, in some partisan attacks on the Ministry, claiming for example that Layard's motion had gained so much popular support because Palmerston had failed to carry on the War effectively. He also got in some characteristic digs against the Whigs, blaming that sector of the aristocracy for the disrepute into which the entire class had apparently fallen:

> Can you deny that it has ever been the peculiar characteristic of the Whigs when in office to concentrate power as much as possible within their own narrow and exclusive coteries, and to make a marked distinction between the great body of their supporters and the high bred materials from which they construct their cabinets . . . ? Now it is because ever since the Whigs came into office . . . , the public have seen this applied to the more conspicuous departments of the State, that therefore now, when national disasters tend to magnify every abuse . . . , there has risen this cry against the governing classes . . . . [62]

The excesses of the Whigs notwithstanding, Bulwer-Lytton maintained it would be dangerous to insulate the civil service too completely from the political process. Opposed as always to anything that might undermine the stability of the State, he went on to argue that the preservation of national liberty depended upon the maintenance of the existing political order:

> The danger is to the fundamental principles of representative institutions. I do not think that those who are now so fiercely agitating against the influences of party and of Parliament are aware

of the logical consequences to which their agitation may lead. . . .
The influences of party are the sinews of freedom. Party and
freedom are twins — united at the birth by a ligament . . . , and if
you divide the ligament you kill the twins. Oh, yes, without the
influences of party you might, indeed, have able and efficient men
in your bureaux — England will never want such men [sic] under any
system; but you will have exchanged the nerve and muscle of
popular government for the clockwork machinery which belongs to
despotism.[63]

Bulwer-Lytton's cautious approach to the problem won broad
support in the House of Commons. Palmerston, of course, welcomed his
proposal because it enabled him both to parry Layard's hostile motion
and at the same time to satisfy the demand that existed in the House and
in the Country that he do something about administrative reform. Thus,
with support coming from Palmerstonians as well as from Tories, Bulwer-
Lytton's amendment passed easily, 359 to 46.[64]

If Bulwer-Lytton had done Palmerston a signal service in this
instance, he was to return just a month later to the more congenial
activity of attacking the Ministry. In July 1855, it appeared Palmerston
might well be overthrown, as a result of some extraordinary bungling by
his Colonial Secretary, Lord John Russell. This crisis grew out of
Russell's service as British plenipotentiary to the Vienna peace talks the
previous spring. During the course of those negotiations, Count Buol, the
Austrian Foreign Minister, proposed a compromise whereby, instead of
forcing the neutralization of the Black Sea upon Russia, the British and
French would increase their own strength in the Black Sea to balance off
Russia's forces. In addition, Austria would join Britain and France in a
treaty to protect Turkey. Russell agreed to this solution, but Palmerston,
who insisted that the Black Sea be neutralized, vetoed the plan. Russell
accepted this decision, and even went so far as to denounce the idea of
counterpoise in the House. This about-face irritated Buol, who thereupon
made public the substance of the negotiations and revealed Russell's
duplicity to the world.[65]

Russell's humiliation was the Tories' opportunity. Disraeli, ever the
optimist, believed nothing could save the Government, and passed on this
opinion to Derby, who morosely replied that he "lived in dread of a
telegraphic message" that would call upon him once again to take office.
Meanwhile, Bulwer-Lytton undertook to bring matters to a head by giving
notice that he would move for a vote of censure against Russell, a step
Palmerston tried to delay. "Palmerston may be able to save himself for

a time by throwing Johnny overboard," Derby commented, ". . . which would put an end to Bulwer's motion; but the shifts of putting off Supply from day to day, merely to evade it, shows the extremity to which they are driven. . . ."[66]

Considerable pressure was building up within the Ministerial party to force Russell to resign, as Bulwer-Lytton himself knew well. He still retained some contacts among the Whigs, and reported to Disraeli that his sources had told him that "JR[ussell] is *bona fide* out. . . ." But Bulwer-Lytton believed the Tories might still reap political advantage from the situation, provided they did not overplay their hand or make a martyr out of Russell by subjecting him to "hard or unfair" criticism. His inclination, indeed, was simply to withdraw the motion of censure should Russell resign. In the end, however, he deferred to the wishes of his party, and proceeded with this motion; but he decided to "soften" the attack on Russell, expressing "regret" at his behavior rather than strident condemnation. He advised Disraeli that the Whigs most feared a "weighty attack" and urged him to keep Russell's more violent critics quiet until he, Bulwer-Lytton, had had a chance to speak first. "I am sure from what I hear," he concluded, "these are our tactics."[67]

The first step was to get the motion onto the floor of the House. On July 12th, Disraeli tried to force the issue, reminding the House that the motion was still pending. When Palmerston implausibly accused Disraeli of making "much ado about nothing," Bulwer-Lytton alertly pounced upon the phrase:

> Sir, the noble Lord [Palmerston] has said that my right Hon. Friend has made "much ado about nothing." I am not surprised to hear such an observation . . . , for, if I am not much mistaken, in point of chronological order "Much Ado About Nothing" comes just after "The Comedy of Errors."

Finally, Palmerston agreed that Bulwer-Lytton could bring forward his motion on the following Monday, the 16th of July.[68]

When the day came, Russell spoke first and, as Bulwer-Lytton had anticipated, announced his resignation. Bulwer-Lytton then presented his motion, proceeded to review the course of Russell's conduct, and summed up the matter:

> The circumstances of the times require either peace in earnest or war in earnest. And I say you cannot have peace in earnest if your negotiator accepts terms upon one day which he shrinks from the

responsibility of adhering to them [sic] on the next . . . . Nor, I say, that when a Minister so recently as May had approved of the principle of the Austrian peace propositions, he is not a fit Minister to carry on the war in July. . . . For, if the noble Lord [Russell] tells us that the object of the war could have been attained in May, it is vain that he appeals to the military ardor of the people in July.[69]

Bulwer-Lytton was certainly hitting his target; but it was a matter of spearing fish in a barrel, so hopeless had Russell's position become. Bulwer-Lytton's speech would have fallen flat, were it not for the fact that he had anticipated Russell's resignation and had prepared a discussion of a larger issue, a moral issue that remained a matter for careful consideration:

There is something . . . which I think ought to be more lasting than any peace, and more glorious than any war—I mean that high standard of public integrity, without which nations may rot, though they have no enemies, and with which all enemies may be defied. On Friday week[70] that standard was debased. . . . You, the representatives of the people. . . have once more raised that standard to its old English level; and in now asking your leave to withdraw my Motion, I congratulate you on having successfully asserted that vital element of all free Governments which is lost the moment you divorce from the national Councils the recognition of that public virtue which demands that our actions shall not . . . give the lie to our convictions. . . . I am willing that the Government should not be removed, but I warn them that they will remain under the vigilant surveillance of public opinion. . . ; it remains to be seen whether that sacrifice [of Russell] has really removed the only obstacle to the earnestness of your purposes and the unity of your councils.[71]

By using this line of argument, Bulwer-Lytton established a criterion for future criticism of Palmerston: how successfully did the Prime Minister maintain that level of public morality essential for the survival of free government?

Bulwer-Lytton certainly intended as much as possible to redirect the focus of criticism against Palmerston, who still mattered politically, rather than Russell, who did not. Toward this end, he raised the question of whether the spectacle of a Cabinet evidently divided in its opinions on a major issue, did not both embarrass Britain and contravene the principle of Ministerial responsibility. He even went so far as to allege that the Foreign Secretary "Lord Clarendon is not the spokesman for the entire cabinet."[72] Despite the validity of this charge — certainly Clarendon and Russell had been very much at odds — [73]Bulwer-Lytton ought not to have made it. There was no way he could substantiate this accusation.

Palmerston, in his reply, was quick to seize on this point. With frequent reiterations of the exclamation "forsooth!" — apparently as a means of ridiculing Bulwer-Lytton's literary style — the Prime Minister took to the attack, charging that Bulwer-Lytton must have been guilty of either "deliberate insincerity . . . [or] the grossest possible ignorance of public affairs" when he stated that Clarendon did not speak for the cabinet. If Bulwer-Lytton believed that assertion, Palmerston went on, he must have been "more grossly ignorant — I will not say than any man in this House, but than any child who ever read a newspaper."[74]

It was evident that Bulwer-Lytton's speech and perhaps his earlier reference to "A Comedy of Errors" had profoundly angered Palmerston. Moreover, since he had such a weak case when it came to the major issue — there was really no way to defend Russell — Palmerston must have found this sort of personal attack an easy way out of a hopeless debacle. But he went too far, and no doubt did his own cause more harm than good, especially when, referring to Bulwer-Lytton, he stated that:

> The Hon. Baronet told us that these repeated changes in the Ministry expose us to the ridicule of Europe. Why, Sir, there might be a change of Government that would render us still more the ridicule of Europe; I mean if a man like the Hon. Baronet were to be placed in a high position in it.

This outburst brought down on Palmerston a memorable rebuke from Disraeli: that it was "not language which I expected from one who is not only the leader of the House of Commons — which is an accident of life — but is also a gentleman."[75]

In the end, this debate brought no results. Russell's resignation forced Bulwer-Lytton to withdraw his motion of censure. And Palmerston, if embarrassed, remained Prime Minister. The war of words continued at Westminster, as did the real War in the Crimea.

During the remainder of the War, curiously, Bulwer-Lytton was to find himself more in disagreement with Disraeli than with Palmerston.[76] Following the capture of Sebastopol in September, Disraeli concluded that Britain had achieved its only realistic military objective; therefore, he anonymously published a series of articles in the *Press* calling for an early peace. Bulwer-Lytton, still the war hawk, was appalled to find

Disraeli's newspaper taking this tack. Accordingly, he wrote his friend to protest:

> I cannot say, my dear Dis., how anxious I feel as to your views on the policy to be adopted with regard to the Peace and War question. Pray don't think me presumptuous if I most earnestly entreat you to pause long before you in any way commit yourself to the Gladstonian theory and sect. My convictions on that head are the strongest . . . . I am sure you know how cordial and brother-like my affection for you is, and how great my interest is in your fame and career. Pause — pause — pause, I entreat you again, my dearest fellow, before you lend your name to any of those argosies gone astray in the Pacific.[77]

Disraeli's reply was cordial, but disingenuous. He denied responsibility for the *Press* articles, and stated that he would "never have thought of taking up any new position with respect to so great a subject as the war, without previously consulting with those friends with whom I act, and certainly with yourself." Despite his lack of candor, Disraeli made clear enough the views he had adopted with respect to the War. He reminded Bulwer-Lytton of the "mortification" the Conservative party had suffered when Lord Derby refused to take office. A party which had "shrunk . . . from the responsibility of conducting the War," Disraeli maintained, was "bound to prepare the public mind for a statesmanlike peace." In short, Disraeli believed the Opposition party had a duty to oppose the policy of the Government. Otherwise, they would cease to be an Opposition, and would be reduced "to the level of the little boys who will cheer Palmerston on Lord Mayor's Day."[78]

This argument by no means set Bulwer-Lytton's mind to rest. He wrote back to say he was relieved to learn Disraeli did not feel "committed to the line of the *Press* articles," because a "concurrence with the views in those articles would either alienate from you or (if they were converted) oust from Parliament the most staunch and reliable of your friends, whose Constituencies are warlike to the core." Then he proceeded to answer Disraeli's argument about the proper role of an Opposition party, and clearly set forth his own view that the Tories would win power only if they identified themselves with the prevailing nationalistic spirit:

> Now, as to the theory that an Opposition must have a policy, and if it coincide in the policy of Ministers [sic] it ceases to be an

Opposition, with all deference to you, I think that theory might be fatal if pushed too far. This was the theory that wasted Fox's life out of office. The proper position for us to take seems to me not that of Fox in the French War, but that of Pitt versus Addington. Treat Palmerston as Pitt treated Addington — outwar him. Rely on it, that at this time, the country would allow no pacific advisers either to form a War Government, or to come in as a Peace one. *The Country will never take peace from a peace party.* It will take peace only from those whom it feels to have been thoroughly in earnest when the business was fighting.[79]

Bulwer-Lytton added that he too wanted an early peace. But he did not think Britain would gain a lasting peace if it should "creep out of the contest." To do that would only tempt other aggressors. In particular, he feared that if the French came to believe Britain had lost the will to fight, they might "subject us to a struggle . . . for our very existence."[80]

Returning to the political implications of the problem, Bulwer-Lytton assured Disraeli that

nothing could prevent the Conservatives coming into power, but a profession of peace policy and a junction with peace politicians. If that were to happen and we were to outvote Palmerston as too warlike, Palmerston would become the most popular Minister since Chatham. He would not resign, he would dissolve, and a Dissolution would scatter his opponents to the winds.[81]

In view of the state of public opinion, Bulwer-Lytton continued, the Tories had to "remove the suspicion and unpopularity those [*Press*] articles and rumors have engendered." He proposed to help the party do so by publishing an article of his own, taking what he considered the patriotic approach to the War: "I shall be general, English and hearty, because I feel English and hearty." This approach, of course, was exactly what Disraeli did *not* want, and he urged Bulwer-Lytton to give up the idea on the grounds that such an article would only divide the party. When the two men met, Bulwer-Lytton acceded to Disraeli's wishes, after the latter had persuaded him that he (Disraeli) had "had not hand nor voice in the Press articles — [and] that he had a substantial practical reason for not interfering against the paper . . . ."[82]

There the controversy rested. A few months later, Russia unexpectedly accepted the Allies' terms, and the War came to an end. Disraeli, then, had been right about the importance of preparing "the public mind for a statesmanlike peace." But surely Bulwer-Lytton had been right about the state of public opinion. The War, after all, had propelled Palmerston into power. The fact that the Tories had failed to "outwar" Palmerston would doom them to another twenty years as the minority party. Bulwer-Lytton had understood where his party's interests lay. But this is not to suggest that he had been trying to exploit the War for selfish partisan purposes. He sincerely believed that Britain was fighting for its national security, and that to settle for any peace agreement inconsistent with Britain's status as a great power would in the long run jeopardize that national security. Thus, he would have been willing to leave the Tory party had it officially adopted the pro-peace views expressed in the *Press*.[83] There is no question that Bulwer-Lytton placed patriotism above partisanship.

While it suited his philosophy to try to "outwar" Palmerston, he was not nearly so much of a "John Bull" as was the Prime Minister, who, after all, had built his career on gunboat diplomacy. The basic difference between the two men became evident when, in 1857, Britain became involved in the infamous "*Arrow* War" against China. This conflict began when Sir John Bowring ordered the bombardment of Canton as a reprisal against the Chinese seizure of a pirate ship, the *Arrow*, which had been flying the British flag. Actually, the Chinese had acted properly, for, as Bowring himself well knew, the *Arrow* had no legal right to claim British protection.[84] Nonetheless, Palmerston backed up Bowring, to the delight of British chauvinists.

It seemed a good issue on which to bring down the Ministry. Disraeli and Bulwer-Lytton joined forces with such strange political bedfellows as Cobden, Gladstone, Roebuck, Graham, and Russell, in denouncing Palmerston's high-handed behavior. As far as Bulwer-Lytton was concerned, there could be no question of protecting vital national interests in fighting the Chinese, as he considered there had been in the Crimean War. Nor did he believe that Palmerston was protecting national honor. "Sir, prevarication and falsehood have nothing to do with the honour of the English nation," he proclaimed in the House; "they appertain rather to the honour of an Old Bailey attorney." He went on to accuse the Government of

> lending the authority of the Crown to homicide under false pretenses, belying the generous character of our country, and offensive to every sentiment of right and justice . . . . In dealing with nations less civilized than ourselves, it is by lofty truth and

forbearing humanity that the genius of commerce contrasts with the ambition of conquerors. Talk not of the interests of trade! Your trade cannot prosper if you make yourselves an object of detestation to those you trade with.[85]

At the end of this debate, Palmerston was defeated in the House by sixteen votes. But he proceeded exactly as Bulwer-Lytton in 1855 had predicted he would: "if we were to outvote Palmerston as too warlike, Palmerston . . . would dissolve, and . . . scatter his opponents to the winds." Following the 1857 elections, Palmerston returned with a personal following of 370 Members in a House of between 650 and 660.[86] But even if Bulwer-Lytton had expected such an outcome, his scruples had not permitted him to attempt to "outwar" Palmerston in this instance.

It seemed then that Palmerston would remain Prime Minister as long as he lived. But in 1858, he momentarily lost his touch. In that year, an Italian named Orsini, who had resided in England, unsuccessfully attempted to assassinate Napoleon III. The French therefore demanded that Palmerston seek legislation to strengthen the laws against conspiracy to murder. Surprisingly enough, he agreed. This gave the Tories a rare chance to appeal to British national pride at Palmerston's expense. The Ministry was defeated, and Lord Derby undertook to form a Government. There could be no doubt but that Bulwer-Lytton, by virtue of the fact that for six years he had served as one of the Tory party's principal spokesmen in the House of Commons, would be among those the new Prime Minister would call upon to serve in the Cabinet. The recognition he had so long sought was now at hand.

NOTES

1. Blake, *Disraeli*, 321.

2. Monypenny and Buckle, *The Life of Benjamin Disraeli*, III, 411-421.

3. Disraeli to Bulwer-Lytton, November 20, 1852, Lytton Papers, D/EK C5.

4. *Hansard*, CXXIII, 494-495; Bulwer-Lytton to Disraeli, November 26, 1852, Hughenden Papers, Box 104, B/xx/ly.

150

5. Villiers' motion was defeated 366 to 256, while Palmerston's carried by 468 to 53. See Blake, *Disraeli*, 323.

6. *Ibid.*, 325-334.

7. They were Sir Charles Wood, Henry Goulburn, and Sir Frances Baring.

8. Monypenny and Buckle, *The Life of Benjamin Disraeli*, III, 437.

9. Quoted by Earl of Lytton, II, 187-188.

10. *Hansard*, CXXIII, 1231.

11. Bulwer-Lytton to William Kent, December 14, 1852, Boston Public Library.

12. Sir William Fraser, quoted by Monypenny and Buckle, *Life of Benjamin Disraeli*, III, 446.

13. Blake, *Disraeli*, 331-334.

14. Quoted in *Ibid.*, 573.

15. See, for example, *Bell's Weekly Messenger*, October, 1874.

16. Escott, *Edward Bulwer*, 327.

17. Quoted by Earl of Lytton, II, 282-283

18. *The Standard*, October 5, 1874.

19. Bulwer-Lytton to the Rev. Michael Greene, January 3, 1863, Lytton Papers, D/EK C26.

20. Quoted by Earl of Lytton, II, 303.

21. *Ibid.*

22. Bulwer-Lytton had suffered from recurrent earaches and impaired hearing since he was sixteen; the severity of the problem increased markedly after he reached his forties. Although he never became totally deaf, it was believed that an abscess in his ear ultimately caused his death. Owen Meredith, 140.

23. Alison, *My Life and Writings*, II, 99-100.

24. One incident that suggests Bulwer-Lytton was not as deaf as some accounts have indicated occurred in 1855. Gladstone was speaking in the House in defense of the Aberdeen Ministry's conduct of the Crimean War, arguing that rather than placing the blame on the Government for Britain's difficulties in the War, the House should first investigate to determine precisely where the fault lay. When Gladstone allowed that this would be a "slow process," Bulwer-Lytton interjected from the opposite side of the House: "The speech is a slow process." *Hansard*, CXXXVI, 1199.

25. Quoted in the *Times*, October 7, 1874.

26. Quoted by R. W. Thompson, *Winston Churchill, The Yankees Marlborough* (New York: Doubleday, 1963), 128.

27. Disraeli to Queen Victoria, March 22, 1859, in Monypenny and Buckle, *The Life of Benjamin Disraeli*, IV, 206.

28. Alison, *My Life and Writings*, II, 98-100.

29. See above, Chapter II.

30. Quoted by Earl of Lytton, II, 244-246. George Cornewall Lewis himself confirmed this account, commenting after the debate that "Bulwer's was an admirable speech. It even influenced some votes. I have no doubt it will be read all over the country, and will tend to fix opinion on the subject." G. C. Lewis to Abraham Hayward, March 28, 1855, in Henry E. Carlisle, ed., *Correspondence of Abraham Hayward Q.C.* (New York: Scribner & Welford, 1887), I, 251.

31. He spoke against Gladstone's Budget on April 25, 1853. See *Hansard*, CXXVI, 453-462.

32. His grandson described 1853 as "the least productive year in Bulwer-Lytton's life." Earl of Lytton, II, 192.

33. *Hansard*, CXXXVI, *passim*.

34. George Henry Jennings, *An Anecdotal History of the British Parliament* (New York: D. Appleton, 1881), *passim*. It is remarkable that Bulwer-Lytton, with his deficiencies as a speaker, played so prominent a part in Parliament. Many contemporaries noted and attempted to explain this paradox. Justin McCarthy, for example, after noting the "physical difficulties which stood in the way of his success as a Parliamentary speaker," wrote that Bulwer-Lytton nonetheless "seems to have determined that he would make a figure in Parliament. He set himself to public speaking as coolly as if he were a man, like Gladstone or Bright, whom nature had marked out for such a competition by her physical gifts. He became a decided, and even, in a certain sense, a great success. . . . He could pass for an orator; he actually did pass for an orator. . . . In fact, Lytton reached the same relative level in Parliamentary debate that he had reached in fiction and the

drama. He contrived to appear as if he ought to rank among the best of the craftsmen."
See McCarthy, *A History of Our Own Times*, II, 127-128.

35. Quoted by Blake, *Disraeli*, 376.

36. These articles were long thought to have been written by Disraeli—who was the
proprietor of the *Press*—but G. E. Buckle discovered some letters which clearly identified
Bulwer-Lytton as "Manilius." See Monypenny and Buckle, *The Life of Benjamin
Disraeli*, III, 496.

37. Cited by H. W. J. Edwards, ed., *The Radical Tory* (London: Jonathan Cape, 1937),
150-156.

38. Asa Briggs, *The Making of Modern England 1783-1867* (New York: Harper & Row,
1959), 420-421.

39. Blake, *Disraeli*, 514.

40. *Ibid.*, 721-722.

41. McCarthy, *History of Our Own Times*, I, 484.

42. Quoted by John Morley, *The Life of William Ewart Gladstone* (New York:
Macmillan, 1903), I, 513. Morley points out that Gladstone did not rule out recourse to
war loans if the income from the taxes proved inadequate. *Ibid.*, 515-516.

43. In particular, Bulwer-Lytton objected to Gladstone's proposal to increase the malt tax,
which he considered unfair to agriculture. Earl of Lytton, II, 214-215.

44. *Ibid.*

45. *Hansard*, CXXXVI, 1070-1071.

46. *Ibid.*, 519-534.

47. Disraeli to Lady Londonderry, January 23, 1855, quoted in Monypenny and Buckle,
The Life of Benjamin Disraeli, III, 556.

48. This was the opinion of G. E. Buckle, *Ibid.*

49. *Hansard*, CXXXVI, 1167-1178.

50. McCarthy, *A History of Our Own Times*, I, 504.

51. Jones, *Lord Derby and Victorian Conservatism*, 201-206.

52. See T. E. Kebbel, *Lord Beaconsfield and Other Tory Memories* (New York: Mitchell Kennerly, 1907), 13-14.

53. Disraeli to Bulwer-Lytton, November 6, 1855, in Earl of Lytton, II, 235-237.

54. Disraeli to Lady Londonderry, February 2, 1855, quoted by Monypenny and Buckle, *The Life of Benjamin Disraeli*, III, 566-567.

55. Quoted in *Ibid.*, 570.

56. Bulwer-Lytton to Disraeli, November 12, 1855, in Earl of Lytton, II, 237.

57. *Ibid.*, 224.

58. The conference broke down largely over Russia's refusal to accept restrictions on their naval strength in the Black Sea. McCarthy, *A History of Our Own Times*, I, 510.

59. Quoted by Earl of Lytton, II, 228-229.

60. See Jasper Ridley, *Lord Palmerston* (New York: E. P. Dutton, 1971), 446-447.

61. *Ibid.*, 440-442; Briggs, *The Making of Modern England*, 442-443.

62. *Hansard*, CXXXVIII, 2114-2222.

63. *Ibid.*, 2119.

64. *Ibid.*, 2222; Ridley, *Lord Palmerston*, 442-443.

65. Prest, *Lord John Russell*, 374-376.

66. Disraeli to Derby, July 11, 1855; Derby to Disraeli, n.d., in Monypenny and Buckle, *The Life of Benjamin Disraeli*, IV, 11.

67. Bulwer-Lytton to Disraeli, n.d., Hughenden Papers, Box 104, B/xx/ly; Bulwer-Lytton to Forster, n.d., Lytton Papers, D/EK C27.

68. *Hansard*, CXXXIX, 814.

69. *Ibid.*, 905-906.

70. A reference to Russell's speech in which he defended his remaining in office on the grounds that he had accepted the views of the Cabinet on the Black Sea question in preference to the opinion he had expressed when British plenipotentiary. See McCarthy, *A History of Our Own Times*, I, 511.

154

71. *Hansard*, CXXXIX, 913.

72. *Ibid.*, 910.

73. Prest, *Lord John Russell*, 374-376.

74. *Hansard*, CXXXIX, 915.

75. *Ibid.*, 916-925.

76. However, he was annoyed later that summer to hear of gossip that he had not replied to Palmerston's insults because he had been "cowed," a suggestion he heatedly denied. He consulted Forster about what he should do to dispel this idea. Bulwer-Lytton to Forster, August 5, 1855, Lytton Papers, D/EK C27.

77. Bulwer-Lytton to Disraeli, October 15, 1855, Earl of Lytton, II, 204-205.

78. Disraeli to Bulwer-Lytton, November 6, 1855, *Ibid.*, 235-237. Buckle confirmed that Disraeli was responsible for the *Press* articles in favor of a peace settlement. See Monypenny and Buckle, *The Life of Benjamin Disraeli*, IV, 18.

79. Bulwer-Lytton to Disraeli, November 12, 1855, in Earl of Lytton, II, 237-240, *emphasis in original.*

80. *Ibid.*

81. *Ibid.*

82. *Ibid.*; Bulwer-Lytton to Forster, November 21, 1855, Lytton Papers, D/EK C27.

83. *Ibid.*

84. McCarthy, *A History of Our Own Times*, II, 12.

85. *Hansard*, CXLIV, 1441-1446.

86. Monypenny and Buckle, *The Life of Benjamin Disraeli*, IV, 75.

CHAPTER SEVEN

COLONIAL SECRETARY

When Lord Derby became Prime Minister in February 1858, Bulwer-Lytton had every right to expect a place in the Cabinet. Characteristically, he liked to pretend that he did not relish this prospect. He wrote to Forster about his anxiety over "the difficulties in the way of office at present" and about how regretfully he had "no option" but to accept Derby's anticipated offer.[1] But in reality he had his heart set on receiving this recognition for the services he had rendered his party in the House of Commons. It was also typical of Bulwer-Lytton's high-strung personality that he managed to make something as simple as taking office the cause of considerable irritation, both to himself and to the leaders of his party.

At first matters went smoothly enough. Bulwer-Lytton had expected to be appointed either Chancellor of the Duchy of Lancaster or Secretary of State for the Colonies.[2] The former would have been little more than a compliment from the Prime Minister on his ability in debate, but the Colonial Office was the post for which he was clearly best suited.[3] Bulwer-Lytton's interest in the colonies dated from his days as a Philosophical Radical in the 1830's. Then he had been closely associated in Parliament with Charles Buller and other advocates of the policy — popularized by Edward Gibbon Wakefield — of developing the Empire by encouraging the emigration of "respectable" Englishmen and by granting the colonies self-government.[4] In 1838, the young Bulwer stated that,

> England is essentially a colonizing country — long may she be so! — to colonize is to civilize. Be not led away by vague declamations on the expense and inutility of colonies. When you are told to give up your dependent possessions — consider first whether you wish this island, meager in its population, sterile in its soil . . . to hold a first rate

empire, or to constitute a third rate nation. Ask any foreign statesman why England rates with Austria, with Russia, with France. He will point to India, to Australia . . . .[5]

In 1849, Bulwer-Lytton best expressed his enthusiasm for the Empire in his novel, *The Caxtons*, in which he depicted the colonies as the great hope and wellspring of renewal for the British people. The novel's hero, "Pisistratus Caxton," emigrates to Australia to raise sheep, and his success repairs the shattered fortunes of his family. One night, while in the bush, he muses on his surroundings, in words that clearly conveyed the author's own views:

> And this land has become the heritage of our People! Methinks I see . . . the scheme of the All beneficent Father. . . . How mysteriously, while Europe rears its populations, and fulfills its civilizing mission, these realms have been concealed from its eyes--divulged to us just as civilization needs the solution to its problems; a vent for fevered energies, baffled in the crowd; offering bread to the famished, hope to the desperate; in very truth enabling the "New World to redress the balance of the Old."[6]

Pisistratus makes a success of his endeavors in Australia, and returns to England a man of means. Bulwer-Lytton intended this to be a "parable," showing how the British nation could derive renewed strength from the colonies.[7] He also suggested that the various entities of the Empire comprised a single family, analogous to the "Caxtons" themselves in their affection for and dependence on one another. As Bulwer-Lytton himself once explained, the message of *The Caxtons* was that, "whether in an English country house or in an Australian sheep farm, the Englishman is equally at home, and the intervening oceans may separate, but need not disunite."[8] And that message was widely received. As T. H. S. Escott observed with pardonable hyperbole:

> The English people rose somewhat slowly to a right appreciation of the priceless treasure possessed by them in their settlements beyond the seas . . . . The true cult of the colonies at home was founded by Bulwer-Lytton in the *Caxtons* . . . .[9]

It therefore came as no surprise when, on February 24th, 1858, Lord Derby offered the office of Secretary of State for the Colonies to Bulwer-Lytton, who accepted at once. But the situation soon became confused. Later the same day Bulwer-Lytton received a report that the Liberals planned a formidable campaign to defeat him for re-election.[10] Whether this was a real danger, he would have no way of knowing until he consulted his supporters in the county; but there was no time for that, since the Cabinet would be announced within hours. Skittish as ever, he over-reacted and called on Sir William Joliffe the Conservative party whip, to tell him of his concern. The defeat of a Cabinet Minister, Bulwer-Lytton suggested, would seriously undermine the prestige of Derby's minority Ministry. It would also be a personal humiliation too galling to contemplate.[11]

Bulwer-Lytton probably suggested to Joliffe three alternative courses of action. He could, first of all, spare the party the risk of embarrassment by declining to take office. Actually, as we shall see, he had no intention of doing so, but he thought it proper to appear ready to sacrifice himself for the sake of the party. Bulwer-Lytton preferred that the party leadership, once duly informed of the risks of defeat, should coax him into standing anyway, thus taking upon themselves the responsibility in case the affair ended in fiasco. There remained a third alternative, which was from his standpoint the most attractive of the three. If only Derby would have him elevated to the House of Lords, Bulwer-Lytton could take his place in the Cabinet without risking the possible embarrassment of losing an election. He would thereafter be free to play the part of statesman, which he enjoyed, without having to descend again into the squalid world of electoral politics, which he despised.[12]

Bulwer-Lytton had indeed long desired to become a peer and, perhaps in his zeal to achieve that ambition, overplayed his hand. The party leaders had more pressing problems in their efforts to put together a presentable Government, and to Joliffe, Bulwer-Lytton was being nothing but a nuisance. Their meeting ended in mutual antagonism and misunderstanding. Joliffe reported the conversation to Derby, who thereupon wrote to Disraeli:

> Another hitch! Lytton informed Joliffe . . . that he could not face his county election! The fact is, he wants to be made a peer, which I will not do for him. *If* he is to be of *any* use, it must be in the H. of Commons. They parted on angry terms . . . . I wish you would come down here as soon as you can; unless you can *en route*, call on our refractory friend, and get him straight again . . . . I think it would not be amiss to hint to him that we are not without resources. I believe Sir J[ohn] Buller would accept, and would fill the office better than Lytton. . . .[13]

Derby's comments made sense. He could manage the House of Lords single-handed, but the party needed all the help it could get in the Commons. No doubt, had Disraeli followed Derby's suggestion and explained the situation to Bulwer-Lytton, the latter would have willingly faced his contested re-election. But Disraeli did not think this worth the trouble, as he informed Derby:

> Never mind — John Manners must have the Colonies . . . . I wished him to have it, and, indeed, never contemplated that Lytton should even have been in the Cabinet had it not been for our Chief's [i.e. Derby's] too gracious notice of him in 1855 . . . . I think Lytton too impudent.[14]

As a result, the misunderstanding was not cleared up. Whereas Bulwer-Lytton had meant to say he feared he might not be able to win his election, Derby got the impression he was certain to lose.[15] The Prime Minister therefore advised him that the Government could not afford to risk such a defeat.[16] Bulwer-Lytton, much to his chagrin, thus found himself out of office. He was furious with Derby, telling Lord Malmesbury that the Prime Minister had "acted with unjustifiable haste . . . . "[17] Matters grew even worse a few days later when unofficial lists of the new Ministers appearing in the press included Bulwer-Lytton as Colonial Secretary.[18] Characteristically filled with dread that he would appear ridiculous when, in the wake of these reports, it came out that he was not in the Cabinet after all, he complained to Disraeli that he "was not spoken to before my name was made use of without my knowledge or consent."[19] Disraeli managed to assuage his anger somewhat with a flattering letter, but Bulwer-Lytton nonetheless reminded him that,

> Still there rises the question what to say to the public. I see nothing but the plain truth that from complications of local circumstances in Herts I did not feel my re-election so sure as to warrant my exposing a new Government to the mere risk of one of its members not being returned, and therefore on the evening of the same day as I received Lord Derby's invitation, declined it.[20]

He added in another letter on the same subject that, "If well put, my position seems to me that of an honourable and unselfish scruple which all will understand."[21]

In the end, Lord Stanley, the Prime Minister's promising thirty-two-year-old son, became Colonial Secretary. Bulwer-Lytton professed to be delighted at this development, but he made no effort to disguise his own disappointment. He told Disraeli that "The chief ill luck of this affair has been in Joliffe's haste" which prevented the exploration of other possible courses of action, such as his giving up Hertfordshire to another Tory and standing instead for a safer seat elsewhere.[22] But he did not confine his resentment to Joliffe. Despite the seeming cordiality of his correspondence with Disraeli, the relationship between the two men had begun to sour. Two weeks later, Lord Carnarvon, the twenty-seven-year-old Under-Secretary of the Colonial Department, dined with Bulwer-Lytton and found him still "very much annoyed" at his exclusion from the Cabinet. Carnarvon further recorded that he "prophesied a speedy dissolution of the administration and denounced Disraeli's financial intentions."[23]

Thus matters remained until May, when a Cabinet shake-up gave Bulwer-Lytton an unexpected second opportunity. Lord Ellenborough, the President of the Board of Control, had had to resign,[24] and Stanley left the Colonial Office to replace him. Derby, who still did not realize that only a misunderstanding had prevented Bulwer-Lytton from taking office in the first place, again offered to appoint him Colonial Secretary, though fully expecting this gesture once more to be rejected.[25] Instead, of course, Bulwer-Lytton accepted, and was soon on his way to Hertfordshire to stand for re-election.

The situation there, at first, seemed far better than Bulwer-Lytton had been led to believe. He received a great many pledges of support,[26] and after consulting with local Tory leaders, concluded that he would have "nothing to fear from the result" of the contest.[27] At all events, a few days before the polling, his Liberal opponent withdrew, apparently unwilling to bear the election expenses.[28] Thus, there remained nothing more than for Bulwer-Lytton to make his election address at the hustings at Hertford on June 8, 1858. A routine matter, to be sure, but the day turned out to be one Bulwer-Lytton would never forget.

He had arrived at the town in most excellent spirits, having "achieved the object of my highest ambition" and feeling, as he characteristically put it, that the "destiny of millions was in my hands," and that "an opportunity would be afforded me of leaving my name as a household word to countless posterity."[29] But then the bubble burst. Bulwer-Lytton himself gave the best account of what occurred:

The brief ceremony of an unopposed election passed away with perfect tranquillity. . . . I had nearly finished my address, when I observed

. . . the vast crowd opening in the rear; and in its midst a passage
being formed, along which advanced a female of what appeared to me
gigantic proportions . . . . I am, as you know, slightly deaf I
leaned forward, placing my right hand to my ear; the first articulate
words that I caught were, "Monster! Villain! . . . " I stared in
astonishment: but in a voice of, I hope and believe, extreme courtesy,
I said, "Madam, allow me to ask your name." "My name? You know
me well enough. . . . I am your wife! . . ."[30]

At that, as Lady Lytton gleefully recorded later, Bulwer-Lytton's "head
fell *literally* as if he had been shot . . . ; he staggered against the post,
and seemed not to have the strength to move."[31] At this point she began
to harrangue her husband: "I am told that you had been sent to 'The
Colonies': if they knew as much about you as I do they would have sent
you there long ago."[32] To quote again Bulwer-Lytton's account:

> This was too much: I collapsed: I remember no more until I found
> myself at Knebworth, in bed, and surrounded by kind and sympathizing
> friends.[33]

With Bulwer-Lytton gone, Rosina treated the crowd to a lurid account of
his misdeeds, charging that he had forced her to live on charity and
blaming him for the death of their daughter.[34] Far worse, however, than
anything she had to say was the ridicule that would inevitably befall
Bulwer-Lytton as a result of this bizarre incident. And ridicule was the
one thing he could not bear.

In fact, this strange encounter at the Hertford hustings was only the
most dramatic event in the ongoing and seemingly endless hostilities
between Bulwer-Lytton and his wife. It would be appropriate at this
point briefly to review this topic, in order that the events of 1858 can be
understood in their proper perspective. For, as we shall see, Bulwer-
Lytton's troubles with Rosina undermined his mental and physical
well-being and impaired his ability to serve effectively as Colonial
Secretary.

Bulwer-Lytton and his wife had separated in 1836. It was agreed at
that time that he should provide her an annual allowance of £400. This
sum proved insufficient, and Rosina fell increasingly into debt. In 1847,
after long residence abroad, she returned to England determined to force
her husband to increase the allowance. Since he would not, Rosina,
knowing that his most vulnerable point was hypersensitivity, attempted
to change his mind by doing all she could to insult and embarrass him.

For instance, she scrawled obscenities on letters which she mailed to him at his clubs, hotels, the House of Commons, and—indeed—everywhere other people would be likely to see them. Even worse, she wrote equally abusive and insulting letters to his friends, including Disraeli, Dickens, and Forster. Perhaps the most astonishing of her "stunts" occurred in 1851, when the Queen was to attend a benefit performance of one of Bulwer-Lytton's plays at the home of the Duke of Devonshire. Rosina wrote the Duke threatening to "enter his house disguised as an orange woman and pelt the Queen with rotten eggs"; and she went on to accuse the Queen of being "the coldblooded murderess of Lady Flora Hastings."[35] It is no wonder that Bulwer-Lytton should have asked Forster in 1857 whether he thought Lady Lytton should be placed in an insane asylum.[36]

Rosina's conduct was certainly bizarre, but it was also calculating. Once she saw she would gain nothing by her campaign of vituperation but a counter-barrage of letters from Bulwer-Lytton's lawyers, she had sense enough to try another tack. In 1857, she asked her attorney, Charles Hyde, to begin proceedings for a divorce as the only means to secure what she considered adequate alimony.[37] But this, too, proved futile. English law did not allow divorce if both parties were at fault,[38] and in the case of the Bulwer-Lyttons there was plenty of blame for everyone. Even those who considered Rosina the innocent victim of a malicious husband recognized the impossibility of proving this in court. Hyde himself stated that "the enemy [i.e. Bulwer-Lytton] has been too cunning in all his proceedings to enable us to fix the wicked measures *personally* upon him."[39]

Such was the state of affairs when Bulwer-Lytton's elevation to the Cabinet and subsequent appearance at the hustings in Hertfordshire gave Rosina the opportunity to embarrass him as never before. That incident, however, seemed at first likely to backfire, for it drove Bulwer-Lytton to have his wife certified insane. He dispatched two doctors to examine her and form an opinion as to her sanity. This interview proved inconclusive, although one of the doctors did obtain from Lady Lytton a written statement which made clear her motives for acting as she had:

I have only to repeat to you in writing what I said *viva voce* and what has been represented to him, alas, in vain so often before, that let Sir Edward Lytton pay the debts of sixteen years' standing which his ceaseless persecutions have entailed upon me--to wit £2500, and allow me £500 a year for the remainder of my miserable existence (not his)

... and I solemnly pledge myself ... never even to mention his name verbally or otherwise.[40]

Following this examination, Lady Lytton proceeded to write one of the doctors a series of letters "of a violent and excited kind, full of the most monstrous allegations, and rambling reiteration of her imagined persecutions."[41] These led the doctor to advise Bulwer-Lytton to have Rosina committed. The necessary legal requirements were soon satisfied, and on June 23rd Lady Lytton was taken to Inverness Lodge, Brentford, a private nursing home for mentally disturbed patients.[42]

Whether or not this step was justified from a psychiatric point of view,[43] it proved a serious political blunder. Several newspapers, including the *Daily Telegraph* and the *Hertfordshire Gazette*, began demanding a public inquiry into the circumstances of Lady Lytton's detention.[44] This publicity was itself embarrassing to the Derby Ministry, but it was nothing compared to what would happen if such an inquiry were actually to take place. The prospect of giving Rosina a public forum at which to confront and denounce her husband utterly appalled both Bulwer-Lytton and his Cabinet colleagues. He therefore had no choice but to agree to her release, as the Liberal *Daily Telegraph* acidly reported on July 15th:

> Sir Edward Bulwer Lytton has succeeded in hushing up the scandal of his wife's arrest and conveyance to a madhouse at Brentford. . . . For the sake of the lady herself, the public will rejoice that such a compromise has been extorted from the Secretary of State . . . , but it must be remembered that Sir Bulwer Lytton alone has gained by the suppression of inquiry. . . . Justice may boast of a triumph, for though it would have been more satisfactory to have forced the entire transaction before an authentic tribunal, it may suffice to know that popular opinion has driven Lord Derby's choice and brilliant colleague into a virtual surrender . . . . Sir Bulwer Lytton, under Cabinet influence, has found it necessary to save the reputation of the Government as well as his own . . . ; and an explosion of national feeling having taken place, [Lady Lytton] . . . is to be released . . . .[45]

It is easy to conceive the corrosive effect of such commentaries upon Bulwer-Lytton's state of mind. The controversy, moreover, did not end with Lady Lytton's release, though there was at least a cooling off period, thanks to Robert Lytton, who took his mother to the continent for several weeks.[46] For Bulwer-Lytton, however, there remained the worry of negotiating a new financial arrangement with his wife. Rosina, upon returning to England, sensed that her husband's failure to constrain her had greatly strengthened her hand, and she increased her demand from £500 to £1000 per year.[47] Her lawyers, however, were more moderate. At last, in October, a new Deed of Separation was agreed to; it gave Lady Lytton essentially all she had originally demanded: Bulwer-Lytton would pay her £500 *per* annum for her lifetime, and would settle her debts amounting to £3000.[48]

This satisfied Lady Lytton, at least for the time being. Of course, Bulwer-Lytton could not have known this, and no doubt he continued to wonder when she might confront him with some new outrage in order to extract even more money. At all events, it is important at this point, as we return to an account of Bulwer-Lytton's service as Colonial Secretary, to bear in mind the unsettling effect this personal crisis must have had upon his capacity to perform the duties of office.

Perhaps because he so much wanted to forget his personal troubles, Bulwer-Lytton totally engrossed himself in his work at the Colonial Office when his tenure there began in June 1858. His frenetic energy startled the members of the permanent staff, who tended anyway to take a rather bemused view of their transient political chiefs. Sir Frederick Rogers, the permanent Under-Secretary, was amused to note that

> Both Lord Carnarvon [Parliamentary Under-Secretary] and Sir Edward
> Lytton work very hard; Sir Edward writes perfect volumes of minutes,
> and then tells me that he learned two great maxims in life, one to write
> as little as possible, and the other to say as little as possible![49]

Another bureaucrat, John Robert Godley, had a less sympathetic assessment, describing Bulwer-Lytton as

> literally half mad about his responsibilities, and fancies he is going to
> reform the whole colonial empire. He gets up in the middle of the
> night to write dispatches, and is furious if they don't actually go in
> twelve hours.[50]

Bulwer-Lytton often labored through the night. On at least one occasion he urgently summoned Carnarvon to his house before dawn, merely because he wished to discuss some idea which had just occurred to him.[51] Carnarvon, nonetheless, developed a real fondness for his chief;

164

he did not, however, consider him a great success as an administrator, observing that,

> His speeches on colonial matters have been remarkably good, but his powers of administration are by no means equal. He has no great capacity for business, or method in the small details and arrangement of the daily work, his ideas succeed each other when he takes up keenly any subject too rapidly and his plans undergo too many changes. But his views, when once fairly before him, are broad--and in his sympathies he is far more human than Stanley. . . .[52]

Despite his inefficiency in handling the day to day details of administration, Bulwer-Lytton proved adept in dealing with the larger questions that came to his attention. Perhaps his egotism was an asset here, giving him a certain crisp decisiveness in command. Certainly he demonstrated this quality early in his administration when he took the steps that led to the establishment of the new Colony of British Columbia.

In the spring of 1858, this vast territory on the fringe of British North America remained unincorporated. Even a few years earlier this status presented no problem, for then the area was still unsettled except for Indians, and the Hudson's Bay Company, which governed the nearby Vancouver Island Colony and which enjoyed a monopoly on trade with the Indians on the mainland, effectively kept outsiders from entering northwestern Canada. This static situation ended in 1856-7 with the discovery of gold along the Thompson and Fraser rivers, which soon brought tens of thousands of prospectors, representing a myriad of nationalities but overwhelmingly American, rushing into the territory.[53]

The Imperial Government proved sluggish in its response to this development, despite the urgent warnings of James Douglas, the Governor of Vancouver Island and Chief Factor of the Hudson's Bay Company, who feared the new American population would soon demand the area's annexation to the United States. In 1856, when Douglas asked Henry Labouchere, the Colonial Secretary under Lord Palmerston, for guidance as to how best to stem the then anticipated wave of immigration, he got no response. Douglas then suggested charging settlers a licensing fee, but Labouchere rejected the idea on the grounds that there was no governmental authority in the territory. Douglas, undeterred, acted on his own, declaring in December 1857, that all gold mines in the territory belonged to the Crown and that those who wished to work them would have to purchase licenses at a cost of a guinea. Since there was no authority to enforce the ruling, however, it became a dead letter.[54]

The solution, clearly, would have to come from London, and indeed the problem was discussed at the Colonial Office for months. But Labouchere, apart from suppressing the reports of the gold discoveries in order to postpone the influx of immigrants,[55] never formulated a policy. Lord Stanley, who became Colonial Secretary under Derby in February 1858, considered establishing a Crown Colony, but dropped the idea for fear the Hudson's Bay Company would demand compensation for surrendering its trading privileges. He then decided to name Douglas "Lieutenant-Governor" of the territory so as to give him the semblance if not the substance of authority. He abandoned this plan as well, when the law officers found it objectionable.[56]

In striking contrast to his predecessors, Bulwer-Lytton at once took strong and decisive action, canceling the Hudson's Bay Company monopoly west of the Rockies and proposing the establishment of a new Crown Colony which he called "New Caledonia." His plan for administering the new Colony, which he presented to Parliament on July 2, 1858, comprehended many of its author's fundamental political ideals. Citing the urgent need to "establish . . . law and order amidst a motley inundation of immigrant diggers," he planned to institute a government "which shall possess unhampered what powers we can give it, to secure . . . respect for recognized authority." He thought it best, therefore,

> to make laws for the district by Orders in Council, and to establish a Legislature; such Legislature to be, in the first instance, the Governor alone; but with power to the Crown, by itself or through the Governor, to establish a nominative Council and a representative assembly.[57]

Bulwer-Lytton believed it would take this regime no more than five years to lay solid foundations for orderly and more representative government. After that time, he continued, it would give way to liberal self-goverment. This transfer of authority, from the Crown to the colonists themselves, would assure stability, for, as he explained,

> if you desire to keep them [the settlers] loyal and contented, you should give them the prospect at the earliest possible period, of that representative form of government to which . . . they have become accustomed; and that if you desire a strong Government for the preservation of internal order, no Government we can make, without

the rule of armies, is so strong as that which the whole society is enlisted in securing respect to the laws which it has the privilege to enact, and has no motive to rebel against the authority in which it participates.[58]

Bulwer-Lytton's plan won wide support, although there were objections to the name "New Caledonia," and in the end of course it was changed to "British Columbia."[59] On July 19th, however, Gladstone raised a more serious objection, opposing the granting of quasi-dictatorial powers to the Colony's Governor and urging the immediate establishment of free institutions.[60] Bulwer-Lytton replied that the Ministry felt it had to "establish, as soon as possible, a Government for a district which was threatened with great danger, and which . . . had no legal Government at all."[61] Labouchere supported Bulwer-Lytton's view, on the grounds that it was essential to take a firm hand with the "shiftless" population moving into the Colony.[62] On August 2nd, the Bill passed essentially as Bulwer-Lytton had presented it.

Bulwer-Lytton took great pride in the new Colony and carefully supervised its development. He kept a wary eye on the activities of the Hudson's Bay Company, whose pursuit of profit he believed posed an obstacle to progress. In July, for example, he learned that Douglas had two months earlier issued a proclamation reaffirming the Company's monopoly of trade in the area and prohibiting American boats from entering the Fraser River with spirits, arms and ammunition; and that he had also entered into negotiations with a steamship company for service to the territory, stipulating that the ships would carry only goods belonging to the Company and only miners who had taken out licenses, and that the Company would receive two dollars "head money" for each miner carried. This news confirmed Bulwer-Lytton's suspicions; he immediately nullified both the proclamation and the proposed steamship arrangement, and reprimanded Douglas.[63]

Bulwer-Lytton recognized, nonetheless, that Douglas's ability and unrivaled experience in the area made him by far the best candidate to become the new colony's first Governor. Accordingly, he offered him the appointment, on condition that he resign as Chief Factor of the Hudson's Bay Company and divest himself of his holdings in the Puget's Sound Agricultural Company. To the surprise of some observers, Douglas agreed to these conditions. Bulwer-Lytton then proceeded to fill the Colony's other civil offices — including a judge, police, and customs officers — in all cases with men free of any connection with the Company.

He also sent out, with great fanfare, a detachment of Royal Engineers to plan a communications system, survey townsites, and supply military protection.[64] In an address given on shipboard as the Engineers were about to set sail for the Colony, Bulwer-Lytton expressed his own lofty hopes for British Columbia:

> The enterprise before you is indeed glorious. Ages hence industry and commerce will crowd the roads that you will have made; travelers from all nations will halt on the bridges you will have first flung over solitary rivers, and gaze on gardens and cornfields that you will have first carved from the wilderness . . . . You go not as the enemies, but as the benefactors of the land you visit, and children unborn will, I believe, bless the hour when Queen Victoria sent forth her sappers and miners to found a second England on the shores of the Pacific.[65]

At all events, Bulwer-Lytton had certainly made a great success in his first essay at Empire building. As a friendly contemporary rightly put it, Bulwer-Lytton had managed to call

> a new and gigantic Colony into existence with almost magical rapidity! A Colony, not alone sketched out in its superficial dimensions upon the map but elaborately organized in all its minute details and comprehensive systemization.[66]

It is no wonder that, on leaving office, Bulwer-Lytton remarked that he regarded the founding of British Columbia as the most important achievement of his tenure as Colonial Secretary.[67]

Some other problems were to prove less tractable. Among these was the controversy concerning Rupert's Land, the vast expanse between British Columbia and the Colony of Canada in the east. The Hudson's Bay Company, by charter right granted in 1670, governed Rupert's Land and, in addition, held a license (due to expire in 1859) for exclusive trading rights there. The Government of Canada had long sought to overturn the charter as invalid, so that Canadians might settle the fertile lands of the region. The Company, for its part, was willing to give up the charter, but only for substantial compensation. Labouchere, while still Colonial Secretary, tried to pressure the Company into allowing at least some settlements by threatening not to renew its license for exclusive trade. He was about to arrange a compromise under which the license would be renewed when the change of government removed him from office.[68]

Bulwer-Lytton, as we have seen, regarded the Company as an impediment to progress, and consequently, on his succession, undertook to terminate its control of Rupert's Land. He repudiated the arrangements Labouchere had made and stated he would not renew the license unless the Company agreed to litigate before the Privy Council the question of whether its charter was valid.[69] When the Company refused, Bulwer-Lytton, after consulting with the law officers, asked the Government of Canada to initiate such proceedings. Then, he waited. For months, despite Bulwer-Lytton's repeated prodding, Canada took no action. At last, in April 1859, Sir Edmund Head, Governor General of Canada, informed Bulwer-Lytton that Canada would not comply with his request, since it considered it Britain's responsibility to strip the Company of the charter. Bulwer-Lytton was exasperated, but by this time he was himself about to leave office and therefore had no further opportunity to bring this vexed question to a satisfactory solution. His sole consolation was to allow the Company's license to expire that spring.[70]

One further matter concerning Canada may be briefly mentioned. In Augusta 1858, Sir Edmund Head proposed the confederation of all the British North American Colonies. Bulwer-Lytton considered that such a step would-be premature; only one Canadian political party had endorsed the idea, and for the Imperial Government to advocate so far reaching a measure under such circumstances would, he believed, stir up much resentment in the Colonies.[71] Quite apart from the merits of the question itself, Bulwer-Lytton greatly deprecated Head's making so important a proposal without first consulting the Colonial Office. He was about to censure Head when he learned from Herman Merivale, the able permanent undersecretary, that the Governor had been justified in his action, as Bulwer-Lytton then explained to Lord Derby:

> I found that, though unauthorized in all public dispatches, Sir E. Head was warranted in the step he had taken by private conferences with Mr. Labouchere, and, to some extent, by a private correspondence with Lord Stanley. . . .
> The evil is great — each secretary of state thus carries away with him from the office the records of the policy he had suggested or sanctioned — and nothing remains to guide his successors but a series of dispatches cautiously framed so as to avoid all that could irritate Canadian parties or enlighten English ministers.[72]

In hopes of avoiding similar misunderstandings in the future, Bulwer-Lytton urged all the colonial governors to communicate with him as much as possible through official dispatches rather than private letters. The governors, however, persisted in their preference for treating sensitive matters privately.[73]

Colonial governors were difficult men to control. The great gulfs of time and distance that separated them from London made it impossible for the Imperial Government to subject them to close supervision. Nonetheless Bulwer-Lytton was determined to assert the authority of the Colonial Office. It was this determination that led to his becoming embroiled with Sir George Grey, the Governor of the Cape Colony and High Commissioner for South Africa, in a bitter controversy which has, more than any other incident during his tenure at the Colonial Office, brought down on Bulwer-Lytton the condemnation of historians. John W. Cell, to cite one example, has outlined the conflict between Grey and Bulwer-Lytton in these terms:

> There is Grey: headstrong, imaginative, and forceful; seeking through one bold stroke to solve his local problems and to build a great and lasting nation overseas. There is Lytton: timid and vacillatory; neglecting his work for months on end . . . ; trying to avoid problems instead of solving them; worrying most about how the correspondence would look in the parliamentary blue book; in effect, and perhaps in intention, setting a trap for Grey.[74]

At this point, certainly, it is appropriate to consider and re-evaluate this entire matter.

Grey had become Governor and High Commissioner at the end of 1854. Previously he had served as Governor of New Zealand, where he had earned a reputation for energy and enterprise, and "he had been allowed the most complete freedom to apply what measures he considered best suited to the problems of his administration."[75] Despite his undoubted ability — or perhaps because of it — he was ill suited for his new position. The mood in British governing circles favored a passive stance in South Africa. The precepts of liberalism then prevailing demanded reduction of expense and responsibility in the colonies. In accord with this policy, Britain in the early 1850's agreed to renounce all claim of sovereignty over the two Boer republics: the Orange Free State and the Transvaal. There was even an inclination to limit British influence to the Cape Colony, and only the fear that to do so would increase the danger of conflict between settlers and natives persuaded policy makers to maintain the two additional colonies of British Kaffraria and the Natal.[76] But the watchword in colonial policy remained above all economy.

Grey, in contrast, believed with missionary zeal in a policy of expansion. He envisioned a federation of all the states of South Africa, arguing that such a union would result in economic prosperity and amicable relations with the natives.[77] He pressed this policy on Labouchere as early as 1856, but without success.[78] On June 9, 1858, he similarly urged Lord Stanley to reverse British policy, stating that "nothing but a strong Federal Government which unites within itself all the European races in South Africa can permanently maintain peace in this country, and free Great Britain from constant anxiety for the peace of her possessions here."[79]

Whatever the merits of Grey's proposals, there was no reason to expect Bulwer-Lytton to regard them any more favorably than had his predecessors. For one thing, retrenchment was the motto of the Derby Ministry. The recent wars against Russia and China had saddled the Exchequer with a substantial debt, and Disraeli was pressuring all his colleagues to reduce the expenditures of their departments.[80] It was therefore not unnatural that Bulwer-Lytton sought to maintain British interests in South Africa at the least possible cost, and viewed skeptically Grey's potentially expensive plans to expand Imperial responsibilities.

This is not to say, however, that Bulwer-Lytton was wedded to the status quo. He agreed with Grey, for instance, that the conventions establishing the independence of the Boer republics had been unjust in that they permitted British sales of arms to the Boers but not to the natives. With regard to the conflict between the two groups, Bulwer-Lytton maintained, "neutrality is our present policy," and he even expressed the wish to "get rid" of the existing conventions with the Boer republics. In this regard, he observed, "confederation may be wise hereafter," but insisted that "now it seems to me that we should have much more to lose than to gain by it."[81] And whatever private thoughts he may have had about the future feasibility of confederation, Bulwer-Lytton made clear his absolute opposition to any such policy in his communications with Grey. For instance, when Grey asked for instructions as to how he should respond in case (as he anticipated) the Orange Free State should petition for unification with the Cape, Bulwer-Lytton's answer was unequivocal:

> It is . . . my duty to state that Her Majesty's Government continue thoroughly persuaded of the sound policy of maintaining the absolute

separation of the Orange Free State from the British Dominions. . . . It requires very little familiarity with past South African History to be certain that if the Territory were once more subjected to the Crown . . . a fresh and very heavy outlay would inevitably follow.[82]

Clearly, the only innovations Bulwer-Lytton favored were those that would reduce expenses. To this end, he conceived the idea of federating the three *British* entities into a single colony. Under existing arrangements, the British government had to bear the burden of defending the Crown Colony of British Kaffraria. Bulwer-Lytton hoped that under a federation the prosperous Cape Colony would assume a large share of this cost, perhaps even making possible a substantial withdrawal of British troops. Bulwer-Lytton was anxious to have Grey's expert opinion on this idea. Therefore, in a private communication accompanying the dispatch just quoted, he asked,

Do you think that the time has happily arrived when the military force, maintained by this country in South Africa may be substantially and permanently reduced? . . . Supposing you to be of opinion that the present force, or something approaching to it, must be maintained — Do you think it would be safe and expedient to unite British Kaffraria with the Cape Colony, placing it under the same Executive? Do you think it would be practicable to carry the extension further, so as to include Natal?[83]

It is important to reiterate that, in raising these questions, Bulwer-Lytton did not at all contemplate confederation with the independent Boer republics. Indeed, he referred to those republics in his dispatch only to ask Grey whether his "opinions in these subjects" were "modified by consideration of the policy to be adopted towards the free states"; and to ask what policy Grey would recommend toward the free states, "consistently always with the maintenance of public faith pledged by the existing treaties . . . ."[84]

Grey replied, however, by composing a powerful and comprehensive argument for federation of the British colonies with the Orange Free State and, in due course, with the Transvaal. Grey's statement[85] showed him to be far ahead of his time in his ideas on responsible government, and his presentation undoubtedly has more value as a historical document today than it did as a state paper at the time. Carnarvon was correct when he commented on it, in a minute to Bulwer-Lytton:

Sir G. Grey's dispatch is an answer to yours of the 6th Sept., but instead of replying to the questions asked there he enters at length upon a matter to which you never even alluded. . . . Your question relates exclusively to British Colonies; Sir G. Grey's answer is confined almost as exclusively to the reunion of the independent Dutch States with the Cape, Kaffraria, and Natal . . . . This from Sir G. Grey's own point of view may be a . . . ready mode of solving all the intricate questions which would arise in effecting an union of our Colonies as suggested in your dispatch, but I do not think that it is a practical measure which under present circumstances . . . any English Minister could propose to Parliament. It is not less than a proposal that we . . . resume a sovereignty from which we have recently with trouble and expense disembarrassed ourselves . . . . [86]

Bulwer-Lytton concurred with Carnarvon's analysis. He considered that federation with the independent republics would only result in Britain's being dragged into conflicts between the Boers and the natives. For that reason, on November 5th, he ordered Grey not to reply to any overtures for union that might come from the Orange Free State, except to say he would have to await instructions.[87] Not surprisingly, Bulwer-Lytton's only reply to Grey's dispatch was once again to rule out "the resumption of British sovereignty in any shape over the Orange Free State."[88]

Grey proceeded, however, to act in outright defiance of this policy. When the Volksraad of the Orange Free State passed a resolution favoring union or alliance with the Cape Colony, Grey promised to place the proposal before the Cape Parliament.[89] When this news reached him, Bulwer-Lytton wrote at once in an effort to save the Governor from his own folly. After reminding Grey of the earlier instructions not to reply to the Volksraad without approval from the British Government, he stated that

I am forced . . . to conclude that you thought proper to give the President [of the Orange Free State], not the answer which you were instructed to give . . . , but a different answer in accordance with your own views . . . . I can only hope that this may have reached you in time to prevent or modify that communication to the Cape Government which you had undertaken . . . to make . . . . It is always in your power to expound your own views when opposed to ours, and within reasonable limits, delay acting on instructions which you may deem inexpedient, but not leave them unnoticed and act in opposition to them.[90]

Grey undoubtedly had not received this dispatch when the Cape Parliament convened on March 17th; but it probably would have made no difference if he had. He proceeded not only to place the Orange Free State resolution before the Parliament, but to recommend in the warmest terms the formation of a federal union.[91] Two weeks later, he went so far as to state that the British Government had suggested it would favor such a union.[92] These curious remarks strongly suggest he was hoping to present the Government with a *fait accompli*. The matter went no further, however, for at the end of May Bulwer-Lytton learned what had transpired, and immediately fired Grey.[93]

The question of whether the policy Grey proposed would have served the long term interests of South Africa lies outside the scope of this biography. Here we are concerned with assessing Bulwer-Lytton's performance of his duties as Secretary of State. The evidence demonstrates neither that he vacillated nor, certainly, that he misled Grey. Throughout the dispute, Bulwer-Lytton held firmly to a clearly defined policy which, for better or worse, in the temper of those times was the only one he could have followed. The real significance of the clash between Bulwer-Lytton and Grey derives from the fact that it exemplified a problem that would constantly recur in the course of Imperial history: should policy be made by officials in the colonies, or by the responsible authorities at home? Grey himself, in defending his conduct after his recall, addressed this issue:

Can a man who, on a distant and exposed frontier, surrounded by difficulties, with invasions of Her Majesty's territories threatening on several points, assumes a responsibility which he, guided by many circumstances which he can neither record nor remember as they come hurrying on one after the other, be fairly judged . . . by those who, in the quiet of distant offices in London, know nothing of the anxieties or nature of the difficulties he had to encounter?[94]

This point of view, however appealing or romantic, if carried to its logical conclusion would inevitably have involved the British people in endless adventures and costly conflicts which their elected representatives would have been powerless to prevent. Bulwer-Lytton, in the dispatch containing his dismissal of Grey, put his finger on the problem when he took Grey to task for "incurring heavy liabilities . . . and leaving the Secretary of State to choose between the difficult alternatives of repudiating your proceedings, or supporting you in that which he could no longer prevent."[95]

If Grey was the most truculent of Bulwer-Lytton's subordinates, he was not the most difficult to manage nor, certainly, the most important. For, in November 1858, Bulwer-Lytton appointed William E. Gladstone as Lord High Commissioner Extraordinary for the Ionian Islands. The story of this curious episode may be briefly told.

The Treaty of Paris of 1815 had designated the Ionian Islands an independent state, but at the same time placed it under the protection of Great Britain. For over thirty years, British High Commissioners ruled the Islands with virtually dictatorial powers. A new constitution, introduced in 1849, gave the Islanders a considerable degree of self government, including their own legislature, but preserved the overall authority of the High Commissioner. This arrangement failed to satisfy the Islanders, who overwhelmingly favored ending the protectorate altogether and securing annexation to Greece. By the summer of 1858, Ionian agitation against British rule had reached a disturbing level, and Bulwer-Lytton undertook to conciliate the Islanders and to treat their grievances.

The first step to effect improvement, Bulwer-Lytton decided, would be to replace the incumbent High Commissioner, Sir John Young. In 1857, Young had sent the Colonial Office a dispatch advising that five of the seven Ionian Islands be transferred to Greece, and that the remaining two, Corfu and Paxo, be made a British Colony. Soon afterward, Young reversed himself completely, and urged that the Ionian constitution be scrapped in favor of absolute British rule over the Islands.[96] He even planned to entice the Ionian legislature into passing some rash condemnation of British rule, so that he might use this as an excuse to annul the constitution.[97] Bulwer-Lytton rejected these suggestions; he wrote to Derby that,

> It may be right to reform or annul the existing constitution. . . . But this Britain of *herself* has no *power* and no *right* to *do*--whatever the defects of the assembly she herself assisted to create.

Any such change, he continued, would require the "assent of the Great Powers in Congress" and the "assent of the Ionian Legislature itself."[98] Clearly, Young, whom Bulwer-Lytton described as "extremely unpopular"[99] in the Islands, was not the man to entrust with the task of reconciling the Ionians to the British protectorate. He should be replaced, Bulwer-Lytton concluded, by someone who "can thoroughly enter by taste, if not scholarship, into the Greek character," and who had "a *liking* for the Greeks, despite all their faults"; he should be, moreover, "a great gentleman," with "more superiority over petty piques, more popular ease in his dignity than the mere clever politician."[100] Bulwer-Lytton was to prove singularly successful in finding just such a man.

William Gladstone, at this stage in his career, was still nominally a Tory and, although he had declined an earnest offer from Disraeli to serve in Derby's Cabinet, appeared interested in taking on an overseas assignment.[101] Carnarvon, who had been told of this fact by Gladstone's friend Sir Robert Phillimore, suggested to Bulwer-Lytton that he offer to send Gladstone to the Ionian Islands.[102] Bulwer-Lytton then gleefully informed Disraeli that there might be a chance after all to attach this formidable figure to the Conservative Ministry:

It has struck me that I could in private conversation, very probably influence Gladstone to go. Of course for a special purpose, for a limited time and without the necessity of vacating his seat for Oxford.

I have received some information privately which makes me believe that he would listen more favorably to such a proposal than you might imagine at the first blush.

The peculiar position of the man at present, his scholarly tastes and associations, the prospective fame of saving the Constitution of a great people might be placed before him. . . .

As a party move for the government I think success here would be a master stroke in negotiation--and besides . . . , I believe he would suit the occasion better than any other man we could send.[103]

Disraeli, based on personal experience, believed Bulwer-Lytton's approach to Gladstone would result in nothing but "endless correspondence."[104] For a time it seemed this prediction might prove correct. For weeks Bulwer-Lytton and Gladstone conversed and corresponded constantly, without a decision being reached. Bulwer-Lytton described the purpose of this "Special Commission" as "to inquire into all grievances and to suggest remedies," intending particularly to reform the existing constitution in accordance with the principles of representative government.[105] But Gladstone felt disposed to favor "the ultimate incorporation of the islands except Corfu . . . and Paxo, with Greece."[106] Bulwer-Lytton disagreed, on the grounds that British withdrawal would serve to invite the Russians into the area. He explained that

> We had not only to determine whether these Islands are a desirable accessory to our maritime power, but whether it would be menacing to England and unsafe for Europe, that they should fall under the control of any other first rate nation.[107]

Bulwer-Lytton, however, was all the while anxious to smooth over disagreements, and simply urged Gladstone to adhere to a "policy of keeping out of any official report any opinions, should you form them, in favor of annexation."[108] At the end of October, Gladstone at last agreed to take on the assignment.[109]

Virtually all of Gladstone's political allies advised against and then regretted his acceptance of the appointment. Lord Aberdeen, for example, told him he "wondered Bulwer-Lytton had not asked . . . [Gladstone] to black his boots for him."[110] It was widely assumed that Bulwer-Lytton and the insidious Disraeli had played upon Gladstone's love of all things Greek in order to trick him into accepting a position at once subordinate and replete with a grave risk of failure. This suspicion seemed borne out when, shortly after Gladstone's departure, the secret dispatch Sir John Young had sent the Colonial Office in favor of annexing five of the Islands to Greece appeared in the *Daily News*. This revelation was disastrous, for it created the false impression, in the Islands and elsewhere, that Gladstone had been sent out to implement this policy, thus prejudicing the mission before it had fairly begun. Gladstone's friends were furious, and accused Bulwer-Lytton of giving the documents to the newspapers in order to sabotage Gladstone.[111]

In fact, the dispatches had been purloined, and Bulwer-Lytton reacted forcefully to this development. He at once wrote to Gladstone to assure him that the Government had had no complicity in the publication.[112] He then proceeded personally to investigate the theft. Based on his handling of this matter, it seems a pity that Bulwer-Lytton never wrote detective stories. He interrogated the editor of the *Daily News*, who refused to identify the person who had given him the papers, except to say he had a "peculiar" name.[113] Bulwer-Lytton, however, also observed in the newspaper office that the papers had been placed in an envelope of the sort used by the War Office, and that it bore the watermark "1854." He then returned to the Colonial Office, and asked the clerks if they had recently had any visitors who had served in the military at the time of the Crimean War. This query resulted in the identification of the culprit, one Wellington Guernsey, who was then, at Bulwer-Lytton's insistence, placed on trial for his action.[114]

Gladstone, meanwhile, had received a mixed reception in the Islands: enthusiasm from those who thought he would effect their union with Greece, and hostility from those who thought he would not.[115] In fact, Gladstone had come around to the belief that the Islands should remain under British protection. No doubt Bulwer-Lytton had considerably influenced this change of heart, for he had forwarded to Gladstone numerous reports from military and naval authorities emphasizing the Islands' strategic importance.[116] Thus at the end of December, Gladstone reported to the Queen that, in view of the unstable situation in eastern Europe, it would be "an act of criminal folly on the part of England" to encourage the unification of the Islands with Greece.[117]

At the same time, Gladstone was preparing a plan of liberal constitutional reforms, which he hoped would to some extent reconcile the Islanders to the continuance of the protectorate. Bulwer-Lytton tried to influence Gladstone's thinking on this subject as well. In January, for example, he wrote that

> Something, in making concessions on behalf of freedom, should be added in defense of the executive, and this for the value of freedom itself: for all I have ever seen or read of human affairs convinces me that whenever Freedom and Order come into collision, Order, in the long run, is sure some how or other to get the better.
>   Freedom is the crowning luxury of civilized states. Order their most vital necessity.[118]

Gladstone, however, took a more liberal view, just as he had earlier in the debate on British Columbia. He proposed to weaken the Ionian executive in favor of the legislature and to establish responsible government on the British model.[119] Bulwer-Lytton felt this Plan went too far, and asked Gladstone:

> If under responsible government the Legislature declare against the protectorate and for Greece and a ministry it will support becomes impossible to form, what then?[120]

But Gladstone was not deterred, and Bulwer-Lytton had no wish to antagonize this formidable figure. When Lord Derby objected to the plan, Bulwer-Lytton went so far as to ask Disraeli to intercede with the

Prime Minister, so that Gladstone would be allowed to do as he pleased. Disraeli agreed with Bulwer-Lytton, and wrote to Derby,

> If we decline Gladstone's proposal, it is clear to me that he will lose no time in bringing it forward in the House of Commons. There I am persuaded it will be carried, and Gladstone will be the master of the situation.
>
> If we accept his present offer, and he fails, the failure will be his: if he succeed, the credit will redound to the Government which selected him.[121]

Thus, Gladstone was given the authority to present his plan to the Ionian legislature.

The details of Gladstone's mission to the Islands belong to his biography, not Bulwer-Lytton's. Suffice it to say that the Ionian legislature was unwilling to accept any substitute for annexation to Greece, and rejected Gladstone's proposals for constitutional reform. Gladstone then returned to England. He had been unable affect the course of events in the Ionian Islands and the effort had become an ordeal. For that reason he particularly appreciated Bulwer-Lytton's reasonable and straightforward attitude in the matter. "Lytton's conduct throughout has been such that I could have expected no more from the oldest and most confiding friend," Gladstone commented as he neared the end of the mission.[122] And years later he described Bulwer-Lytton as "in many respects one of the best of Colonial Secretaries."[123]

Few histories today would agree with that assessment of Bulwer-Lytton. Yet he did undoubtedly have certain outstanding qualities: a willingness to take responsibility, to make decisions, and to stand by the policy he had decided on. He had, moreover, a clear idea of what the British Empire should be. He aimed to realize in practice the ideal he had conceived in *The Caxtons*, of the Empire as a new world of opportunity for the British people, an outlet for energy and enterprise, and a safety valve for an overcrowded Island. In this spirit he founded the new colony of British Columbia.

On the other hand, he had no visionary compulsion to paint the map red. As he showed in his dispute with Sir George Grey, he believed with most other mid-Victorians that the Empire must not become a financial burden. He had little interest in raising the flag in areas unsuitable for British settlement. Still, he was more sensitive than most of his contemporaries to the strategic considerations that so often militated in favor of retaining far-flung outposts. It was after all largely for the sake of maintaining a potentially valuable British naval base and of shielding the eastern Mediterranean from Russian intrusions that he advocated the preservation of the protectorate in the Ionian Islands.

An incident occurred in February 1859, that revealed much about Bulwer-Lytton's attitudes on such matters. It was at that time that Sir James Brooke, the remarkable adventurer who had become Raja of Sarawak in northern Borneo, attempted to persuade him to make that region a British protectorate in order to safeguard the interests of the Borneo Company Limited, which Brooke himself had established. Bulwer-Lytton was unmoved. He wrote a memorandum on the subject for the Foreign Office, pointing out that Sarawak was not a desirable possession because it would not be self-supporting, had little value as a naval base, and because

> you can never rest content with it. Your very civilization will compel you to encroach upon the . . . barbarous dominion that adjoins it — you will be involved in new annexations and conquests — you will have India again on a small scale — with little glory and great cost.[124]

Despite these objections, and despite his dislike of establishing protectorates ("where you have undefined rights you have small moral powers"),[125] Bulwer-Lytton refused to rule out the idea of making Sarawak a Crown Colony. The Dutch were establishing colonies in the area, and he believed it worthwhile to take over Sarawak simply to prevent another European power from doing so. While he thought it proper to allow the Foreign Office to make the final decision, his memorandum indicates that, had Bulwer-Lytton lived in the late nineteenth century, when many other nations were competing with Britain for colonies and for strategic and commercial advantage in the underdeveloped world, he would have been much more of an annexationist than he was in the relatively placid mid-Victorian period.[126]

Despite Bulwer-Lytton's many excellent qualities and accomplishments as Colonial Secretary, his tenure in office cannot be considered a success. In the fall of 1858, he suffered a physical breakdown, which made it impossible for him to perform his duties with diligence. While the strain of official work itself must have been a factor, it would be a mistake to attribute his breakdown solely to this, for his prodigious literary output proves he was no stranger to hard work. The notorious controversy with his wife, which coincided with the early months of his administration, certainly contributed to his collapse. Then, too, one suspects that he had grown temperamentally unsuited for public life. After all, if his occasional appearances in Parliament as a private Member had sometimes brought on bouts of hypochondria, it is no wonder that the sustained exertions involved in holding office took their toll on his nervous sensibility. At all events, within four months of his appointment, he began showing signs of strain. One clerk in the Colonial Office observed that "he puts letters in the wrong envelopes and sends secret and confidential documents to his clerks by mistake for official despatches."[127] He found it almost impossible to concentrate. One of his lungs, he said, was "affected" with consumption, and his pulse, normally 70, was up to 90, which he believed indicated "organic heart disease."[128] Thus, for reasons of health, he tendered his resignation to Lord Derby on December 16, 1858.[129]

From the standpoint of Derby and Disraeli, however, Bulwer-Lytton's resignation was a matter of serious inconvenience. They were then preparing a Parliamentary Reform Bill, and two of the more conservative members of the Cabinet had already threatened to resign in protest. For Bulwer-Lytton to resign as well would seriously undermine the prestige of the Ministry. Derby consequently urged Bulwer-Lytton to keep his intentions temporarily a secret;[130] and Disraeli, who suspected Bulwer-Lytton was not really ill but fearful of being subjected to further embarrassments by his wife,[131] wrote rather unkindly that

> It is quite impossible that a man more than fifty, who has accomplished such great work as you have done . . . can experience any real deficiency of nervous energy. It is not organic or natural, and must be the result of some quacking . . . .
> Whatever your illness may be, your secession will be a paralytic stroke to the Ministry.[132]

Bulwer-Lytton replied that his health would not permit him to remain in office even a few weeks longer, adding that "I do not think the reasons for my retirement can be received by the public with incredulity, in as much as the delicacy of my health is sufficiently stamped on my appearance. . . ."[133] After a meeting between the two men, however, Disraeli persuaded Bulwer-Lytton to remain in office, apparently on the understanding that he would be free to get as much rest as his health required. Disraeli promised to look after any difficult colonial problems that might arise.[134] On New Year's Day, therefore, Disraeli was able to report to Derby:

> I have had a long interview with Lytton: he remains. . . . He expects
> to die before Easter, but, if so, I have promised him a public funeral
> . . . .[135]

For the next five months, Bulwer-Lytton was Colonial Secretary in name only. He passed most of his time resting at Knebworth or taking the waters at Malvern. Carnarvon, meanwhile, managed the Colonial Office and forwarded to Bulwer-Lytton such important papers as required his attention.[136] Disraeli also helped; when, for example, notice was given that a question relating to the Ionian Islands would be asked in the House of Commons, Bulwer-Lytton wrote to Disraeli, "Will you give me a line to say what should be my exact answer."[137]

This arrangement was of course most unsatisfactory. Although Carnarvon and the permanent staff could handle all the routine matters that came before the Colonial Office, the lack of leadership left no possibility of enterprise or initiative. Bulwer-Lytton's habitual absence from the office, moreover, inevitably led to inconvenience and delays. And, to top it off, his health failed to improve. As he informed Derby in the spring, "In suspending attention to business, I do not suspend its responsibilities. . . ."[138] He remained anxious to escape these responsibilities.

At the end of March 1859, the Ministerial Reform Bill was defeated, and the Cabinet decided to dissolve Parliament. Bulwer-Lytton, who had privately urged his fellow Ministers to resign,[139] did not relish the prospect of facing another election. He could see but one chance of saving both his health and his political career, that Derby should grant him a peerage. He wrote at once to the Prime Minister to make the request, adding

> I believe my main and my strongest motive to be that of being enabled
> by the comparative rest of the upper house to render some little public
> and Parliamentary service.[140]

But Derby was not more willing to accede to this wish than he had been the year before. Bulwer-Lytton then renewed his resignation and added that he would not stand for re-election to the House of Commons. He reminded Derby that he had wished to resign in December, but that

> Your Lordship did me the honour to think that my retirement at that time when the Reform Bill was under the consideration of the Cabinet would be liable to misconstruction and might add to the difficulties of the government . . . . There can now be no misconception as to disagreement with my colleagues . . . [and] meanwhile my health has suffered more and more . . . .[141]

This time, Derby promised to "take an early opportunity" to submit the resignation to the Queen.[142]

Derby was nonetheless annoyed, apparently feeling that a Ministerial resignation on the eve of a general election could do their party no good. "What on earth is to be done with this fellow," he complained to Disraeli.[143] Disraeli thought it best to pull his old friend back into line, but he rather overdid it, striking at Bulwer-Lytton's most sensitive point, his sense of honor:

> I don't think [Disraeli wrote] you can, as a man of honour, take the step you so strangely contemplate — in every sense it must be a suicidal one.
>
> P.S. I can't call, as I really must keep my mind calm and my head cool.[144]

This rebuke provoked a very revealing, if hysterical, counterblast from Bulwer-Lytton. It began, without any prefix,

> The letter you have sent me I would fain regard as unwritten. . . . I allow no one the right to call in question my conduct as a "Man of Honour." . . . It is and while I live and retain intellect always will be, whether in Parliament or out of it, in my power to render aid to a government or to a party. No Government and no Party can make me lesser or greater than I am.[145]

Disraeli then hastened to arrange a meeting, and, although by his own admission later on, Bulwer-Lytton displayed "irritability" during the discussion,[146] the quarrel was largely patched up. Bulwer-Lytton agreed not to announce his resignation until after the election.

Disraeli hoped to persuade Bulwer-Lytton to stand for re-election, even promising to find him a seat where he would be unopposed. Bulwer-Lytton declined the offer, however, explaining that, if he wished to stand, he could[147] probably win at Hertfordshire without a contest. He then proceeded to the county, intending (he said) to bid farewell to his constituents. Instead, he yielded to their blandishments that he stand once again, and in the general election he was once more victorious.[148]

Soon after the elections, he wrote yet again to Derby, asking that his resignation — which the Queen had already accepted — be made public.[149] This turned out to be a moot point, for the Conservatives had failed to win a majority, and soon after the convening of the new Parliament, the Derby Ministry surrendered the seals of office.

In his brief tenure at the Colonial Office, Bulwer-Lytton showed he had the makings of an outstanding Secretary of State. Yet, he fell far short of his potential. The tragedy of his year in office — indeed the tragedy of his life — was that his flawed personality kept him from achieving all the success that his powerful intellect could easily have given him. The reappearance of Rosina, like a spectre of his past coming back to haunt him at what should have been his moment of triumph, aptly symbolized this tragedy, and foreshadowed his failure. Then too, nothing can gainsay the fact that when Bulwer-Lytton left office, he had not the slightest wish ever to return,[150] nor, one can be sure, did the leaders of his party intend to give him the chance again.

NOTES

1. Bulwer-Lytton to Forster, February 24, 1858, Lytton Papers, D/EK C27.

2. *Ibid.*

3. It is noteworthy that there was no other Conservative with a strong claim to this office. Sir John Pakington had held it in 1852, but his appointment then had provoked ridicule and, while he would serve in the 1858-9 Cabinet, he certainly had no priority claim on his former post. See Blake, *Disraeli*, 300-301.

4. See E. M. Wrong, *Charles Buller and Responsible Government* (Oxford: Clarendon Press, 1926), 14 and *passim*.

5. Edward Bulwer, Speech at Lincoln, Easter, 1838, Lytton Papers, D/EK W100.

6. Bulwer-Lytton, *The Caxtons*, 313.

7. T.H.S. Escott, *Society in the Country House* (Philadelphia: George W. Jacobs, 1907), 467.

8. Escott, *Edward Bulwer*, 276-277.

9. *Ibid.*, 273. To appreciate the importance of *The Caxtons*, it is not necessary to accept Escott's exaggerated estimate of its impact. Bulwer-Lytton wrote it at a time when enthusiasm for the Empire was at a low ebb. In his zealous appreciation of the importance of the colonies, he certainly anticipated the unabashed Imperialism that would flourish in a later generation. *The Caxtons* enjoyed an enormous popularity in its day, and Escott's statement evidences at least that Bulwer-Lytton was among those who sowed the seeds that would flower in the Imperial revival of the late nineteenth century.

10. Bulwer-Lytton, Speech at Hertford, June 8, 1858, Lytton Papers, D/EK W101. At that time, acceptance of Cabinet office required a member of Parliament to stand immediately for re-election.

11. *Ibid.*; Bulwer-Lytton to Disraeli, n.d., Hughenden Papers, Box 104, B/xx/ly; Lord Derby to Disraeli, February 25, 1858, in Buckle, *The life of Benjamin Disraeli*, IV, 118.

12. *Ibid.*

13. *Ibid.*

14. Disraeli to Lord Derby, February 25, 1858, in *Ibid.*

15. Earl of Malmesbury, *Memoirs of an Ex-Minister* (London: Longmans, Green, 1884), II, 101.

16. Bulwer-Lytton to Disraeli, n.d., Hughenden Papers, Box 104, B/xx/ly.

17. Malmesbury, *Memoirs of an Ex-Minister*, II, 101.

18. *Illustrated London News*, February 27, 1858, 203.

19. Bulwer-Lytton to Disraeli, n.d., Hughenden Papers, Box 104, B/xx/ly.

20. Bulwer-Lytton to Disraeli, n.d., *Ibid.*

21. Bulwer-Lytton to Disraeli, n.d., *Ibid.*

22. *Ibid.*

23. Cited in Sir Arthur Hardinge, *The Life of Henry Howard Molyneux, Fourth Earl of Carnarvon* (London: Humphrey Milford, 1925), I, 119-120.

24. On Ellenborough's resignation, see Blake, *Disraeli*, 366-367.

25. Lord Derby to Queen Victoria, May 23, 1858, in Arthur Benson and Viscount Esher, ed., *The Letters of Queen Victoria* (London: John Murray, 1908), III, 292.

26. See for example, Adolphus Murray to Bulwer-Lytton, June 3, 1858, Lytton Papers, D/EK 023.

27. Bulwer-Lytton, Speech at Hertford, June 8, 1858, Lytton Papers, D/EK W101.

28. Lady Lytton to Augusta Boys, June 11, 1858, in Devey, *Life of Rosina Lady Lytton*, 282.

29. Quoted by Sir William Fraser, *Hic Et Ubique* (London: Sampson, Low, 1893), 59-62.

30. *Ibid.*

31. Lady Lytton to Augusta Boys, June 11, 1858, in Devey, *Life of Rosina Lady Lytton*, 283.

32. Fraser, *Hic Et Ubique*, 59-62. Transportation to the Colonies had often been used as a punishment for crime.

33. *Ibid.*

34. Lady Lytton to Augusta Boys, June 11, 1858, in Devey, *Life of Rosina Lady Lytton*, 284-285.

35. Earl of Lytton, II, 262-267. Rosina referred to a lady-in-waiting who had died after being ostracized by the Queen because of a false report of immoral conduct.

36. Bulwer-Lytton to Forster, October 7, 1857, *Lytton Papers*, D/EK C27. Forster advised against having her placed in restraint. See Earl of Lytton, II, 326.

37. Charles Hyde to Rebecca Ryves, September 26, 1857, Huntington Library, Box II.

38. Earl of Lytton, II, 265.

39. Charles Hyde to Rebecca Ryves, September 26, 1857, Huntington Library, Box II.

40. Lady Lytton to Hale Thomson, June 12, 1858, in Earl of Lytton, II, 271.

41. Earl of Lytton, II, 271-272.

42. *Ibid.*

43. Her obsessive hatred of her husband and her delusions of persecution (which come out very strongly in her letters) certainly caused her to act in an abnormal manner. But she seems to have been quite capable of managing her own affairs and was evidently rational when involved with matters not concerning her husband. She seems to have been suffering from monomania, not insanity. See Devey, *Life of Rosina Lady Lytton, passim.*

186

44. Earl of Lytton, II, 274.

45. Quoted by Devey, *Life of Rosina Lady Lytton*, 318-321.

46. Earl of Lytton, II, 275-277. This trip ended, typically enough, in the estrangement of mother and son. Lady Lytton had wanted her son to be her champion against Bulwer-Lytton, and when Robert Lytton refused to take sides, she turned against him.

47. See Devey, *Life of Rosina Lady Lytton*, 308, 336.

48. *Ibid.*, 337-339.

49. Quoted by Earl of Lytton, II, 281.

50. Quoted by Henry L. Hall, *The Colonial Office* (London: Longmans, Green, 1937), 57.

51. Hardinge, *Fourth Earl of Carnarvon*, I, 121.

52. *Ibid.*, 120-121.

53. Margaret A. Ormsby, *British Columbia: A History* (Vancouver: Macmillan, 1959), 135-144.

54. *Ibid.*, 144-149.

55. Rochester, *The Derby Ministry*, 192.

56. Ormsby, *British Columbia*, 148-149.

57. *Hansard*, CLI, 1102-1103.

58. *Ibid.*

59. It was pointed out in Parliament that there was already a French colony "New Caledonia." One M.P. suggested therefore as an alternative name for the new colony, "Lytton Bulwer." See *Ibid.*; 1119. Queen Victoria herself suggested the name British Columbia. See Queen Victoria to Bulwer-Lytton, July 24, 1858, in Benson and Esher, *The Letters of Queen Victoria*, III, 296.

60. *Hansard*, CLI, 1762-1763.

61. *Ibid.*, 1767-1768.

62. *Ibid.*, 1764-1766.

63. Ormsby, *British Columbia*, 152-153; John S. Galbraith, *The Hudson's Bay Company As An Imperial Factor* (Berkeley: University of California, 1957), 304-305.

64. Ormsby, *British Columbia*, 153-157.

65. Quoted by Earl of Lytton, II, 291-293.

66. Rochester, *The Derby Ministry*, 144.

67. Bulwer-Lytton to Herman Merivale, June 18, 1859, Lytton Papers, D/EK 101.

68. Galbraith, *The Hudson's Bay Company*, 333-348.

69. The British Government could not itself initiate this litigation since it had itself originally granted the charter, and therefore could not legally call into question one of its own acts. If the validity of the charter was to be considered by the Privy Council, either the Hudson's Bay Company or the Government of Canada would have to initiate the proceeding. See *Ibid.*, 347.

70. *Ibid.*, 349-353. George F. G. Stanley, *The Birth of Western Canada* (Toronto: University of Toronto, 1961), 29-30.

71. John W. Cell, *British Colonial Administration in the Mid-Nineteenth Century* (New Haven: Yale University, 1970), 196-197.

72. Bulwer-Lytton to Lord Derby, September 18, 1858, Lytton Papers, D/EK C26.

73. See, for example, Sir William Denison to Bulwer-Lytton, September 6, 1858, Lytton Papers, D/EK 01.

74. Cell, *British Colonial Administration*, 199. For another condemnation of Bulwer-Lytton's handling of this matter, see W.P. Morrell, *British Colonial Policy in the Mid-Victorian Age* (Oxford: Clarendon Press, 1969), 23, 111-124; see also William Lees Rees and L. Rees, *The Life and Times of Sir George Grey* (London: Hutchinson, [1892]), 289.

75. Eric Walker, ed., *The Cambridge History of the British Empire*, VIII, *South Africa, Rhodesia And The High Commission Territories* (Cambridge: Cambridge University, 1963), 403.

76. *Ibid.*, 400-401.

77. Morrell, *British Colonial Policy*, 103-106.

78. *Ibid.*, 105-108.

79. Grey to Stanley, June 9, 1858, in *Ibid.*, 110.

80. Blake, *Disraeli*, 377-378.

81. Quoted by Morrell, *British Colonial Policy*, 111.

82. Bulwer-Lytton to Grey, September 6, 1858, *Ibid.*

83. *Ibid.*,111-112

84. *Ibid.*

85. It is reproduced in full in Kenneth N. Bell and W. P. Morrell, eds. *Select Documents on British Colonial Policy 1830-1860* (Oxford: Clarendon Press, 1928), 181-191.

86. *Ibid.*, 191-194

87. Morrell, *British Colonial Policy*, 113.

88. Bulwer-Lytton to Grey, February 11, 1859, *Ibid.*, 116.

89. *Ibid.*, 117.

90. Bulwer-Lytton to Grey, March 5, 1859, in Hardinge, *Fourth Earl of Carnarvon*, I, 128.

91. Morrell, *British Colonial Policy*, 117.

92. Hardinge, *Fourth Earl of Carnarvon*, I, 129.

93. Bulwer-Lytton to Grey, June 4, 1859, in Rees and Rees, *Sir George Grey*, 283-284. For an excellent account of Bulwer-Lytton's motives and actions during the crisis, see Walker, *South Africa*, 416-417. Grey returned to England after his dismissal, but was re-instated as Governor for a short time by Bulwer-Lytton's successor as Colonial Secretary, the Duke of Newcastle, on condition that he accept the continuing policy of the British Government against annexation of the Orange Free State. See Morrell, *British Colonial Policy*, 119.

94. Quoted by Cell, *British Colonial Administration*, 199.

95. Bulwer-Lytton to Grey, June 4, 1859, in Morrell, *British Colonial Policy*, 118.

96. Morley, *Life of Gladstone*, I, 601.

97. Bulwer-Lytton of Lord Derby, September 18, 1858, in Lytton Papers, D/EK C26.

98. *Ibid.*

99. *Ibid.*

100. *Ibid.*

101. Morley, *Life of Gladstone*, I, 594-595.

102. Hardinge, *Fourth Earl of Carnarvon*, I, 132.

103. Bulwer-Lytton to Disraeli, September 23, 1858, Hughenden Papers, Box 104, B/xx/ly.

104. Monypenny and Buckle, *The Life of Benjamin Disraeli*, IV, 162.

105. Bulwer-Lytton to Gladstone, October 5, 1858, Lytton Papers, D/EK 028/1.

106. See H.C.G. Matthew, ed., *The Gladstone Diaries* (Oxford: Clarendon Press, 1978), V, 329.

107. Bulwer-Lytton to Gladstone, October 9, 1858, Lytton Papers, D/EK 028/1.

108. Bulwer-Lytton to Gladstone, October 16, 1858, *Ibid.*

109. See Matthew, *The Gladstone Diaries*, V, 333.

110. Quoted in R. A. J. Walling, *The Diaries of John Bright* (London: Cassell, 1930), 235.

111. Hardinge, *Fourth Earl of Carnarvon*, I, 133.

112. Bulwer-Lytton to Gladstone, November 15, 1858, Lytton Papers, D/EK 028/2.

113. Sir Henry Drummond Wolff, *Rambling Recollections* (London: Macmillan, 1908), I, 284-285.

114. Bulwer-Lytton to Lord Derby, December 26, 1858, Lytton Papers, D/EK C26. Guernsey was acquitted, however, because the papers had no intrinsic value. See Drummond Wolff, *Rambling Recollections*, I, 284-285.

115. Morley, *Life of Gladstone*, I, 601-616.

116. Bulwer-Lytton to Lord Derby, December 26, 1858, Lytton Papers, D/EK C26.

117. Gladstone's report is published in Matthew, *The Gladstone Diaries*, V, 351-358.

118. Bulwer-Lytton to Gladstone, n.d., Lytton Papers, D/EK 028/2.

119. Matthew, *The Gladstone Diaries*, V, 355.

120. Bulwer-Lytton to Gladstone, February 1, 1859, Lytton Papers, D/EK 028/2.

121. Disraeli to Lord Derby, January 6, 1859, in Morley, *Life of Gladstone*, I, 617.

122. Gladstone to Sidney Herbert, February 17, 1859, in Morley, *Life of Gladstone*, I, 617.

123. Quoted in Arthur Berriedale Keith, ed., *Selected Speeches and Documents on British Colonial Policy 1763-1917* (London: Oxford University, [1918]), II, 27.

124. Bulwer-Lytton, "Memorandum on Sarawak," in Lytton Papers, D/EK 01.

125. *Ibid.*

126. *Ibid.*

127. Quoted in Blake, *Disraeli*, 382.

128. Bulwer-Lytton to Disraeli, December 22, 1858, *Ibid.*

129. Earl of Lytton, II, 295.

130. Lord Derby to Bulwer-Lytton, December 19, 1858, in *Ibid.*, 296-298

131. See Monypenny and Buckle, *The Life of Benjamin Disraeli*, IV, 190-192

132. Disraeli to Bulwer-Lytton, December 20, 1858, in Earl of Lytton, II, 298-299.

133. Bulwer-Lytton to Disraeli, December 22, 1858, in Hughenden Papers, Box 104,, B/xx/ly.

134. This can be inferred from a number of letters; for example, Bulwer-Lytton on one occasion wrote to Disraeli, "As you so kindly said you would see to any questions relative to my office — I enclose you minutes on the only matters affecting it which I see in the Paper for next week." n.d. [April, 1859], Hughenden Papers, Box 104, B/xx/ly.

135. Disraeli to Lord Derby, New Year's Day, 1859, in Monypenny and Buckle, *The Life of Benjamin Disraeli*, IV, 192.

136. Hardinge, *Fourth Earl of Carnarvon*, I, 136.

137. Bulwer-Lytton to Disraeli, n.d. [January, 1859], Hughenden Papers, Box 104, B/xx/ly.

138. Bulwer-Lytton to Lord Derby, May 7, 1859, Lytton Papers, D/EK C26.

139. Bulwer-Lytton to Lord Derby, n.d., *Ibid.*

140. Bulwer-Lytton to Lord Derby, April 1, 1859, *Ibid.*

141. Bulwer-Lytton to Lord Derby, April 4, 1859, *Ibid.*

142. Lord Derby to Bulwer-Lytton, April 5, 1859, *Ibid.*

143. Quoted in Blake, *Disraeli*, 385.

144. Disraeli to Bulwer-Lytton, n.d. [April 4, 1859], Lytton Papers, D/EK C26.

145. Bulwer-Lytton to Disraeli, April 4, 1859, *Ibid.*

146. Bulwer-Lytton to Disraeli, April 6, 1859, Hughenden Papers, Box 104, B/xx/ly.

147. *Ibid.*

148. Bulwer-Lytton to Lord Derby, April 8, 1859, Lytton Papers, D/EK C26; Charles Pearson to Bulwer-Lytton, April 5,1859, *Ibid.*, D/EK 023; Bulwer-Lytton to Lord Derby, May 2, 1859, *Ibid.*, D/EK C26.

149. *Ibid.*

150. Bulwer-Lytton to his son, n.d., in *Earl of Lytton*, II, 305.

CHAPTER EIGHT

A TOUCHSTONE OF HIS TIME

The Parliamentary Reform Bill which the Derby Ministry proposed in 1859 marked the Conservative party's first attempt to legislate on this question. In retrospect, the measure seems significant only because it helped prepare the way for more far-reaching efforts in the future. As Disraeli explained to T. E. Kebbel:

> I was determined to vindicate the right of the party to a free hand, and not allow them to be shut up in a cage formed by the Whigs and Radicals; confined within a certain magic circle which they were not to step out of at the peril of their lives.[1]

To many other Tories, however, Parliamentary Reform remained a question their party ought never propose but always oppose. The winter of 1858-9 saw deep dissension in the Derby Ministry, and two members of the Cabinet, J. W. Henley and Spencer Walpole, threatened to resign — and eventually did so — in protest against the Reform Bill.

Disraeli remained undaunted. In February, 1859, he presented to Parliament a Bill which represented months of study and haggling. It proposed to reduce the occupier franchise in the counties from £50 to £10 (*i.e.* equal to what it was in the boroughs); to require that urban freeholders vote in the borough instead of the county; and to institute a "lateral extension" of the franchise, by giving votes to those who had demonstrated their "fitness," even if they were not £10 householders: ministers, doctors, lawyers, certified school teachers, University graduates, or possessors of either £10 a year from the Funds, £60 in a savings bank, or a lodging in a £20 house.[2]

While Bulwer-Lytton did not play a significant part in drawing up the Bill,[3] he did join with Disraeli and Stanley in advocating a greater extension of the franchise than most of the Cabinet wanted.[4] He regarded the measure as it emerged with enthusiasm. To John Bright, who dismissed the Bill's special qualifications as "fancy franchises," he expostulated that the Bill "opened out important principles for future adoption — for the first time [it] abandoned property as a qualification for voters, giving the franchise to . . . intelligence when not connected with property."[5]

Bulwer-Lytton expanded on this theme in the House of Commons in a speech many Members regarded as one of the greatest they had ever heard in Parliament.[6] It was essentially an exposition of his belief that the survival of liberty depended upon the maintenance of social order. Radical reform, he warned, even if undertaken in the name of liberty, might destroy it by weakening social stability. He wished therefore to grant the franchise only to those committed not to upset the existing order. The virtue of the Conservative Reform Bill, he stated, was that it would

> Confirm and extend to the middle class the political power which, during the last twenty-seven years they have exercised, so as to render liberty progressive and institutions safe; but at the same time, to widen the franchise the middle class now enjoys, so that it may include all belonging to the class now without a vote; and, instead of bringing the middle class franchise down to the level of the workmen, lift into that franchise, the artisan who may have risen above the daily necessities of the manual labourer by the exercise of economy and forethought.[7]

He then expressed his strong disagreement with those Whigs and Radicals who wanted to enfranchise a larger proportion of the working class. In reference to Lord John Russell's motion that the House should not accept any Bill that failed to reduce the borough franchise, Bulwer-Lytton stated that,

> You in this House will determine whether . . . you really secure the title deeds of . . . commerce, and take solid guarantees for the safety of . . . old English freedom by . . . a pledge to the working class . . . which you can never redeem . . . until you have placed capital and knowledge at the command of impatient poverty and uninstructed numbers.[8]

Despite these apprehensions, Bulwer-Lytton denied that he harbored any hostility toward the working classes. Instead, he insisted, he admired both "the simple village peasant, with his homely virtues," and "that noble human being, the skilled mechanic of our manufacturing towns."[9]

But to give these uneducated masses political power, he told the House, would only pave the way for demagogues and tyrants:

> Freedom has no enemy so fatal as the [popular] favorite, who may push its advancement one inch beyond the boundaries of order . . . . [In the French Revolution] What killed liberty? The democracy of large towns, and the terror which that democracy itself had [caused as a result] of its own excesses. But democracy in France still exists — a democracy of universal suffrage and vote by ballot.[10] Pardon me if I prefer the freedom of which this House is still the guardian — a freedom safe because education controls and property does not fear it.[11]

Education, then, was to be a prime qualification for admission to the political nation. This was after all the rationale behind the "fancy franchises." Carrying this line of reasoning one step further, Bulwer-Lytton favored an even wider extension of the franchise than the Whigs proposed, if the necessary safeguards were respected:

> I would not object to the widest possible suffrage, if you can effect a contrivance by which intelligence shall still prevail over numbers. If that be impossible, then, I say, at least, the first step toward anything that approaches universal suffrage should be something that approaches to universal education.[12]

The question of how best to achieve universal education was one to which he had devoted considerable thought; his views had changed significantly since the 1830's, when he had called for a centrally directed system of national education.[13] In 1854, he expressed the hope that British education would never be "altogether paid for and regulated by the State." He preferred the American system of independent school districts, in which the local citizenry consented "to levy a rate upon themselves for education" and undertook to see to it that their children got "the education . . . of the best kind . . . and adapted not to some rigid and inflexible State machinery."[14]

His opposition to centralization no doubt derived in large measure from his fear that State-directed education would fail to emphasize moral instruction. Paradoxically, there was in Bulwer-Lytton a streak of anti-intellectualism, growing out of his fear that the dissemination of half-baked theories could have an unsettling effect on the poor; as he put it, "knowledge in itself is not friendly to content."[15] The purpose of education, he stated, should be "to elevate our . . . moral qualities. . . ."[16]

Centralized education on the continent had, he acknowledged, resulted in a higher literacy rate than obtained in Britain, but it had failed to produce "that moral good we might have anticipated." "What does it signify if a whole people can read and write," he asked, "if the books most thrown in their way only serve to stimulate the baser passions, to set class against class, to loosen the ties of hearth and home, of prosperity and order"?[17] A more worthy aim than merely to raise the literacy rate was to "elevate the masses in character":

> Of all instruction for a community, that which inculcates in early childhood a clear sense of moral obligations is the most valuable. That is, for the most part, acquired at home. Parents may be unable to read and write, but their lives may teach children to be honest and industrious, faithful to trust, and patient under trial. Honesty, industry, fidelity, fortitude — these are ideas that preserve a commonwealth and secure the superiority of races more than a general diffusion of the elements of abstract science.[18]

This is not to say that Bulwer-Lytton believed mass education should consist exclusively of moral homilies. While he considered it dangerous to teach students facts and ignore the moral framework, he did not propose to do the reverse. He endeavored rather to increase public awareness of the importance of intellectual education, and he spoke frequently on this subject at mechanics' institutes, hoping to foster a climate of opinion conducive to the establishment of rate-supported schools across the country. He believed, moreover, that the state should help stimulate voluntaryism. As he once put it, because

> free nations are governed either by the preponderance of numbers or by the ascendancy of cultivated intelligence, so a conservative policy, if it does not maintain itself in power by the first, must seek to conciliate and identify itself with the second. It should have no fear of the calm extension of knowledge; its real antagonist is in the passionate force of ignorance . . . . It should befriend and foster all the intellectual powers which enrich and adorn a state. . . . It should be the friend of commerce, of art, of science, of letters, and should carefully open up every vista by which merit can win its way to distinction. . . .[19]

At that time, indeed, there was little more that could be done. The Dissenting Churches still posed a formidable barrier to any plan for national education under which the Established Church might dominate religious instruction. The House of Commons, Bulwer-Lytton once complained, was "united as to the expediency of obtaining a good education for the people of the country," but it could not agree on the means to do so.[20] His proposal for voluntary action on the American model at least offered a way to break the deadlock, even if it also meant that universal education, however desirable, would remain a distant prospect.

That fact served to increase his anxiety over the prospect of universal suffrage, which he considered inevitable. "Democracy in England," he commented privately a few weeks after his speech on the Reform Bill of 1859, "is as sure as that we are in this room."[21] This foreboding indeed had been implicit in his speech, when he stated that the great merit of the Ministerial measure was that

> it meets some of the requirements of the day present, and does not give today what you may regret tomorrow that you cannot restore. Democracy is like the grave; it perpetually cries, "Give, give," and like the grave, it never returns what it has once taken. . . . Do not surrender to democracy, that which is not yet ripe for the grave.[22]

In the years ahead, therefore, Bulwer-Lytton was to oppose all proposals that in his estimation tended toward universal suffrage, hoping to forestall democracy until, through education, the nation had been prepared for it.

The issue of Parliamentary Reform again came to the fore, at least briefly, in 1860, when Lord John Russell, Foreign Secretary under Lord Palmerston, introduced a Bill to lower the franchise to £6 in the boroughs and £10 in the counties. Bulwer-Lytton felt this went too far, telling Forster that,

> I think few can be aware of how low it is. There is not a little town in this county [Hertfordshire] where the working man pays less than 2 [shillings] & 6 [pence] a week. . . . Therefore a 6£ franchise must be Household suffrage.[23]

Convinced that the proposed Reform would be a dangerous step towards democracy, Bulwer-Lytton determined to denounce it in the House. As matters turned out, however, he need not have worried. The majority of the Ministers had little enthusiasm for Russell's Bill; Palmerston, the one man who could have assured its passage, was almost ostentatiously indifferent. George Cornewall Lewis, then Home Secretary, was so unconvincing in his speech for the Bill that Bulwer-Lytton, when his turn came, was able to bring down "the laughter and cheers of both sides of the House" by describing Lewis as apparently having "come to bury Caesar, not praise him."[24]   Ultimately, Russell announced the Government had decided to withdraw the Bill.[25]

For five years thereafter, the question of Parliamentary Reform lay dormant. Lord Palmerston saw to that. "His primacy," as Donald Southgate put it, "really meant that . . . the administration had no domestic policy at all."[26] This was the calm, confident Indian Summer of the mid-Victorian era, and the octogenarian Prime Minister set the tone. His supremacy was undoubted; but so too was the mood: *apres moi, le deluge.*

These years saw Bulwer-Lytton's Parliamentary career at a virtual standstill. During the entire period of this second Palmerston Ministry (1859-1865), he spoke only twice in the House of Commons: in opposition, as we have seen, to Russell's abortive Reform Bill, and against the malt tax in 1865.[27] He rejected, on the grounds of ill health, a request from Disraeli that he speak in the debate over the Government's failure to defend Denmark against Prussia and Austria.[28]   More surprisingly, he did not wish to speak on the Ministry's cession of the Ionian Islands to Greece (though he disapproved of it) and agreed only with great reluctance to Disraeli's request that he take part in the debate. In the end, however, it did not prove necessary for him to deliver his speech, and he was glad of it: "The Ionian Question would have been a bad party fight for us," he had concluded, believing the public apathetic on the matter.[29]

Inactive as he was, he had not given up on politics. The compulsion to pursue an active career apart from literature remained central to his personality. He even dreamed of holding office again. The fact that he was nearing sixty, far from deterring, spurred his ambition. The approach of old age unsettled him; he was, as Disraeli said, "always mourning over his lost youth." He tried therefore to persuade himself that life had not passed him by, and in this context he found the prospect of future political activity most encouraging. Disraeli recalled that:

> Bulwer said to me one day, in his sort of confidential, pompous style — perhaps, instead of pompous, I would rather say oracular — "One of the advantages of public life is that it renews youth. A Cabinet Minister at fifty may not absolutely be a young man, but he is a young Cabinet Minister."

This remark was particularly appropriate during the years of Palmerston's supremacy. Disraeli noted an occasion in 1860 when Bulwer-Lytton was

> sitting next to me in the House of Commons . . . and watching Palmerston at 76 making a speech . . . . There was noise, gaiety, health [in Palmerston]. Bulwer looked fascinated. "That man," he whispered to me in his Delphic tones, "is a Future."[30]

This resurgence of ambition met a serious check in 1864, when Lady Lytton renewed her irrational efforts to embarrass her husband. Bulwer-Lytton, who insisted he had not failed to pay her allowance,[31] gave the following account of the situation

> This morning I received a letter from Disraeli, which conveyed the thunderbolt that L[ady] L[ytton] has resumed attacks — written he says, to my colleagues and friends, making horrible and nameless accusations. I can conceive how annoying and humiliating these letters would be, especially if to Derby and others of that class . . . . This horrible calamity weighs on me . . . . Of course, it will prevent office. I cannot go through such public scandals again as an official character. I have heard nothing from her myself . . . . But this thing effectively damps the ardor I was beginning to have for politics.[32]

His fear that Lady Lytton might commit "more violent actions of some kind at the next general election, or should I ever again take office"[33] no doubt influenced his decision to inform his constituency, when Parliament was dissolved in the summer of 1865, that he would not stand for reelection. His supporters in Hertfordshire, however, earnestly entreated him to reconsider, just as they had in 1859, assuring him that his withdrawal would result in the election of a Liberal to one of the seats.[34] No doubt he found their attitude a comfort. He agreed to stand and proceeded to win what was to prove his last Parliamentary election.

October 1865 saw the death of Lord Palmerston. Bulwer-Lytton sincerely regretted the loss of this erstwhile antagonist whom he had grown to admire. "I felt a strange shock at Pam's death," he told his son. "Something has gone out of the world that one had looked upon as part and parcel of it."[35] Palmerston's death removed the great bulwark against the forces of change. His successors, Lord Russell as Prime Minister and Gladstone as Leader of the House of Commons, would certainly revive the long dormant question of Parliamentary Reform.

On March 12, 1866, Gladstone introduced the expected Reform Bill. It turned out to be a relatively moderate measure, proposing to reduce the franchise to £7 in the boroughs and £14 in the counties. It nonetheless encountered heavy opposition. Disraeli, of course, was determined to defeat his rival's proposals; he was satisfied, however, to play a relatively inconspicuous part in the debates, leaving a clique of right wing Liberals, spearheaded by Robert Lowe, to deliver the most stinging denunciations of democracy. This state of affairs led Disraeli to remark that he was pleased to be "not unable, but unwilling to speak."[36]

Bulwer-Lytton, for his part, was willing to speak, and he proceeded to deliver what was probably the outstanding speech from the Opposition front bench in this debate.[37] He repeated, to a large extent, the arguments he had used in his speeches in 1859 and 1860. He emphasized the idea that no single class, whether aristocrats, scholars, or working men, should control the destinies of the nation. Parliament, rather, should represent "the common sense of the common interest." For this reason, he argued, the middle class should remain "on the whole, largely predominant," for it

> most faithfully represents all the interests and opinions which constitute the mind and welfare of a nation, and the most felicitously reconciles the securities of order with the demands of freedom.[38]

His emphasis on the necessity of Parliament's continuing to represent various "interests" and not merely population led up to the one new idea he presented in this speech. Realizing that the working-class could not be permanently excluded from a greater shares of political power, he proposed a plan whereby their "interest" could be given a greater voice in public affairs, without allowing their vast numbers to overwhelm the other "interests." Instead of instituting, as Gladstone had proposed, "an uniform abasement of the franchise applied equally to all boroughs," Parliament should, Bulwer-Lytton suggested, designate a specific number of boroughs to represent the working class. He further argued that

> having decided how many boroughs should be devoted to majorities of the working class, then select those constituencies in which the prevalence of skilled labor tends to create a superior class of artisans, and in which their numbers alone would be some safeguard against the bribes of a candidate; and giving there such a suffrage as would amply secure your object, decline to apply the same low rate of franchise to

those . . . boroughs in which the skilled artisans are too few to become a fair representation of the intelligence and integrity of their class . . . .[39]

In this speech, he did not state how many seats he would give the working class "interest." Some years earlier, however, he had privately outlined a similar plan in greater detail:

The only safe and fair plan would be to divide boroughs into 2 classes. Take 50 of the largest, give them 3 members each—let 2 members be chosen by household suffrage—that would give the working class 100 members and property 50—consider that the other boroughs are for the middle class, and only enlarge the 10£ franchise further by a few fancy franchises . . . . Pass a law like the American that the constitution thus settled cannot be amended say for ten years without consent of 2/3 of the House of Commons. Thus you might have some fair self denial.[40]

These proposals, if impractical, were characteristic of Bulwer-Lytton. He sensed that public opinion would begin to demand increasing installments of democracy, and he hoped to forestall this trend by timely concessions to the "spirit of the age." His speech was exactly opposite to that of Robert Lowe, who opposed any extension of the suffrage and did not hesitate to express his contempt for the working class. "Thank heaven Lowe's speech was not made by one of us," Bulwer-Lytton commented to a fellow Tory. "I have never heard a speech more clever or more unwise. . . . Such a speech from our side would have damaged the party for years to come."[41]

Despite this difference in approach, Bulwer-Lytton's own fear of democracy quite equaled Lowe's. He perhaps did not realize how offensive his own speech might have seemed to the working class. He warned, for example, that

if there be a country in the world in which democracy would be a ruinous experiment, it is surely a country like England . . . , with a commerce so based upon credit and national prestige, that it would perish forever if by any neglect of democratic economy, or what is more probable, any adventure of democratic rashness, our naval power were destroyed; and with differences of religious sects so serious that we should find it impossible to precede democracy by that universal and generous system of education without which it would be madness to make the working class the sovereign constituency of the Legislative Assembly.[42]

Ironically, such denunciations of democracy by Bulwer-Lytton and Lowe, clashing in the 1866 debates with the vindications of working class rights enunciated by Gladstone and Bright, only fired up popular demand for Parliamentary Reform. Bulwer-Lytton recognized, after the defeat of the Reform Bill of 1866 had forced Russell to resign in favor of Derby and the Conservatives, that the new Government "must bring in a reform bill since People want a Reform." He hoped that a Conservative Reform Bill, which he assumed would be a moderate measure, might serve to "extinguish" Bright and his demands for democracy. But he wondered whether there was not a risk that such a Bill might prove, not an extinguisher, but a "bellows?"[43]

When Derby took office, Bulwer-Lytton hoped to play an active part in the new Ministry. Although it was rumored at the time that he would return to the Colonial Office,[44] there was never, one imagines, any likelihood that Derby and Disraeli would have wanted him back in their cabinet. Instead, they sought to satisfy him with the peerage he had so long craved. Thus, in July 1866, Bulwer-Lytton became the First Baron Lytton of Knebworth.

This was the fulfillment of a lifelong ambition. "My first thought," Lytton remarked shortly after receiving the honor, "was of my poor mother, and I said as if she were living still on this earth, or wherever she be, caring for such matters: 'How it will please her'"[45] Yet, despite the pleasure he took in his new position, he experienced "a strange mixture of feeling." He feared the peerage would hurt his political career. "I know of no instance," he observed, "in which a man passing from the Commons to the Lords without office at the time has ever done anything in the Lords."[46] Despite this drawback, he had by no means given up on politics. Being in the Lords certainly had advantages as well. He would never again have to face an election, for example, which meant he could take office without fearing a repetition of Lady Lytton's appearance at the hustings. Possibly this consideration was on his mind when he told Forster that "my present idea is that I may be more alive there [in the Lords] than in the Commons — and could possibly have, if I desire, a . . . less obstructed career." For the sake of that career, he was determined to dispel the idea that he had gone to the Lords instead of taking office as a result of ill health. Paradoxically enough, in view of the number of times he had excused himself from Parliamentary activity on the grounds of illness, he complained to Forster that the agents of the present government . . . seek to prevent my not taking office being thought a loss and therefore exaggerate what the Pall Mall Gazette calls my "infirmities"—viz. I suppose Distress and delicate health. I do not think either of those misfortunes sufficient to shelve me for ever in the world, and perhaps if any occasion occurs in the Examiner, put a hint that if I might not be strong enough for the commons I might be strong enough for the lords—where I suppose Hercules is a rare god—I should be much obliged.[47]

Clearly Lytton did not realize it, but, as matters were to turn out, his political career had already ended. He was soon to find himself out of step with events. Rapid changes and startling reforms dominated the period 1866-1873, and Lytton, who believed progress should be cautious and stability assured, could have scant sympathy with the contending forces. Even had he remained in the House of Commons, he would undoubtedly have receded completely into the background. His removal to the Lords, along with infirmity and age, made his isolation complete.

The first manifestation of this acceleration of change came in March 1867, when Disraeli, after several false starts, introduced his new Reform Bill in the House of Commons. Instead of merely lowering the borough franchise, as the Whigs had tried to do, he proposed a kind of household suffrage, checked, however, by requirements for personal payment of rates (taxes) and a two-year residency, and balanced by a system of dual voting for the middle class. Even with these "safeguards," the Bill was far more radical than the one Disraeli had opposed when Gladstone introduced it the previous year. Cranborne, Carnarvon, and Jonathan Peel resigned from the Cabinet in protest against Disraeli's proposals.[48] Lytton, the erstwhile Radical, found himself in sympathy with the right-wing rump of the Conservative party. He believed the Government was "floundering," and told a friend "I could never defend this bill or their management of it in Parliament."[49] But worse was to come.

Disraeli was determined to carry his Reform Bill—to win in the great political game—and it seemed hardly to matter what form the Bill finally took. To achieve his objective, he reached an understanding with the independent Radicals, and thus maintained a majority in the House of Commons against the Liberal opposition. During the course of the session, in order to preserve this majority, he accepted a series of amendments proposed by these Radicals, sweeping away all the safeguards his original Bill had placed on household suffrage. But he opposed and defeated the amendments offered by the Liberal leadership, completely outmaneuvering his great rival Gladstone, who admitted he had suffered "a smash, perhaps, without example." Still more remarkably, Disraeli demonstrated his genius for political management by keeping his party together (with very few exceptions) in support of a Bill which only months before they would have considered revolutionary. And that it was; the electorate was doubled, and working class voters were to be the majority in the towns.[50]

Obviously, Lord Lytton could not have welcomed a Bill whose provisions he had long opposed. Yet, when the Bill came before the House of Lords, he composed a speech in support of it. One could argue that this draft did not reflect his true feelings, that he intended it only as a display of party loyalty; and that at all events he never actually delivered the speech. However, it would appear that this draft on the whole accurately reflected Lytton's attitude toward the 1867 Reform Bill.

To begin with, he frankly acknowledged that "I consent, or rather submit to" the Reform Bill "with greatest reluctance." He even reiterated his preference for a Bill based on that the Tories had proposed in 1859. The failure of that measure, he continued, had resulted from the refusal of the ten-pound householders — the middle-class electors in the boroughs — to support the Conservative party. "Is it not too much to expect," he asked, "that of all political parties the Conservatives should make themselves the thankless martyrs in the cause of these 10£ householders, who have been as a body the least conservative part of the constituency. . . ?"[51] Certainly the Conservatives, for two decades the minority in the House of Commons, might hope to gain by scrapping the existing arrangements.

This point ties in with one of the larger controversies concerning the significance of the Reform Bill of 1867: the idea Robert Blake described as a "Conservative myth," that

> Disraeli, infinitely more discerning than the dull squires who followed him, had long perceived that household suffrage would enfranchise a class basically more Conservative than the electorate created in 1832; that he aimed throughout at this objective, carrying Derby with him and educating the rest of his party in the process . . . . [52]

Blake rejects this theory on evidence that Disraeli expected the urban working class to support the Liberals and that he acted as he did out of purely tactical considerations.[53] Be that as it may, it is clear that Lord Lytton, for his part, did anticipate the emergence of the Conservative working man. In the 1850's, he had in his novels described Tory as well as radical artisans.[54] Despite his oft expressed concern that demagogues might incite the uneducated poor to revolution, he also wrote that the upper classes could effectively counter incendiary propaganda by fulfilling the obligation of their station to aid the impoverished.[55] It was therefore by no means a new departure for him to write that the electorate the Reform Bill of 1867 created might prove surprisingly conservative: "I do not think that experience shows that a very popular suffrage at least in ancient communities is necessarily of a democratic spirit in the worst sense of the word democracy." As evidence he cited the old scot and lot boroughs which, he said, had been more conservative than the constituencies the Reform Act of 1832 established in their place, on the basis of the more exclusive ten-pound householder franchise.[56]

Carrying his argument further, Lytton wrote that the Reform Bill of 1867 would itself help to reconcile the working class to the existing order, and thereby secure the stability of the state. In view of the agitation on the question that had begun in the wake of the defeat of Gladstone's Reform Bill in 1866, to continue to exclude the working class would constitute

> in their eyes one of those affronts . . . which none of us . . . can desire to inflict upon that class from whose industry the state demands its revenues, and on whose contentment it founds its safety.

The particular merit of the Reform Bill therefore was its finality. It checked "the angry passions and all the wild speculative theories" which the agitation on the question had set loose. A statesman, he observed, should know "when to yield as well as when to resist. . . . "[57] It would seem reasonable to conclude, then, that Lytton had really reconciled himself to the Reform Bill. He viewed the measure with "deep anxiety," to be sure, but he refused to share "in those fears which have been expressed here and elsewhere with that eloquence which is never more imposing than when it assumes the attributes of superstition and peoples the dark with spectres."[58]

At the same time, however, Lytton remained unreconciled to Disraeli's management of the Bill. Despite Lytton's comments in his draft about "statesmanlike yielding," evidently he considered Disraeli guilty of placing expediency above principle. Perhaps Lytton was expressing his true feelings about Disraeli in his novel *Kenelm Chillingly* (1873) when he described the character "Chillingly Gordon," an exemplar of ruthless ambition, who says of himself:

> I am no fanatic in politics. There is much to be said on all
> sides — *coeteribus paribus*, I prefer the winning side to the losing;
> nothing succeeds like success.

That could well have been Disraeli's motto in the Reform Bill crisis.
Lytton indicated his own attitude through another character, who
described "Chillingly Gordon" as

> a coming man . . . , thoroughly in the pursuit of one object, — the
> advancement of Chillingly Gordon. If he get into the House of Commons,
> and succeed there, I hope he will never become my leader; for if he
> thought Christianity in the way of his promotion, he would bring in a
> bill for its abolition.[59]

In the aftermath of the Reform Act, Lytton was Disraeli's supporter
in name only. When, as a result of Lord Derby's becoming seriously ill,
Disraeli's accession as Prime Minister appeared imminent, Lytton
commented privately that Derby's loss would be "irreparable," and that
Disraeli could not "long command the confidence of the country."[60]
Soon after Disraeli became Prime Minister, Lytton remarked that "there
is great coldness between me and Dis . . . ,"[61] and, in the same vein,
wrote to his son after meeting Disraeli at a party:

> Disraeli was there and wonderfully cordial to me. He talked of old
> days and kept pressing my hand, which is not his wont. However, I
> feel steely to him and his Government.[62]

Lytton even welcomed the Liberals' election victory at the end of
1868. "I feel as if the change of government relieved me from an
incubus and somewhat restores my jaded interest in politics," he
commented.[63] He predicted that Gladstone, the new Prime Minister,
would have a long tenure unless a war broke out: "I don't think the
country has faith in him as a war minister." As for Disraeli, who had
"smashed the numerical strength of his party," Lytton felt he would never
become Prime Minister again. "The chance of the party rests with
Stanley or Salisbury," he added.[64]

It should not be thought, however, that Lytton had become a
Gladstonian. He considered the Prime Minister weak when it came to
asserting Britain's influence as a world power, a serious matter in view
of the emergence of Prussian dominated Germany in 1870. Rearmament
was essential, if Britain were to reassert "that influence on the civilized

world which she has of late years abnegated—and which she cannot maintain if she stands unarmed among armed nations."[65] Instead, the Prime Minister continued to believe in retrenchment. Lytton was particularly concerned about British naval strength. "I venture to doubt," he told one correspondent, "whether two or three years hence our navy will be in the high state of preparedness you assume—under the auspices of the present Government."[66]

Lytton also opposed a number of Gladstone's domestic reforms such as the Ballot Act of 1871 (he acquiesced, however, as did many other Conservatives, to the disestablishment of the Irish Church), [67] but he never resumed an active career in politics. "I cannot say that I at all like the aspect of political affairs," he remarked at the time of the passage of Irish disestablishment, "But I think the worst calamity that could happen would be another weak Conservative government with a hostile House of Commons."[68] The events of 1867 clearly had lasting effect on his thinking.

Although he prepared several speeches, Lytton never spoke in the House of Lords. He was content, instead, to express his views on public affairs in a more general way in his novels, notably in his utopian satire *The Coming Race* (1871). In the opening of that work, for example, the central character relates his background in a passage that neatly encapsulated Lytton's sardonic view of democracy:

> I am a native of _____, in the United States of America. My ancestors migrated from England in the reign of Charles II; and my grandfather was not undistinguished in the War of Independence. My family, therefore, enjoyed a somewhat high social position in right of birth; and being also opulent, they were considered disqualified for the public service. My father once ran for Congress, but was signally defeated by his tailor.[69]

From this auspicious beginning, Lytton went on in *The Coming Race* to satirize the socialistic and egalitarian ideals fashionable among *avant garde* philosophers. The hero of the novel discovers a subterranean civilization in which those ideals have been realized. The inhabitants of this netherworld live in perfect harmony and equality (women are not only liberated but superior), thanks to the fact that they have harnessed the power of "vril," a force that must be regarded today as an extraordinary precognition of nuclear energy and the guided missile. As the narrator put it, this people have invented certain tubes by which the vril fluid can be conducted toward the object it is meant to destroy, throughout a distance almost indefinite; at least, I put it modestly when I say from 500 to 600 miles. And their mathematical science as applied to such purpose is so nicely accurate that . . . any member of the vril department can . . . reduce to ashes, within a space of time too short for me to venture to specify it, a capital twice as vast as London.[70]

Since any member of the community could easily use "vril" to destroy any other, conflict is pointless, and the "coming race" enjoys perfect peace. But the narrator observes significant flaws in this theoretically ideal state of affairs. For example, he discovers that the "coming race" produces virtually no literature, apart from scientific tracts. One of them thus explains to him the reasons for this:

Do you not perceive that a literature such as you mean would be wholly incompatible with that perfection of social or political felicity at which you do us the honor to think we have arrived? We have at last, after centuries of struggle, settled into a form of government with which we are content, and in which, as we allow no differences of rank, and no honors are paid to administrators distinguishing them from others, there is no stimulus given to individual ambition . . . . We have no events to chronicle. What more of us can be said than that "they were born, they were happy, they died"?[71]

Thus Lytton suggested that the destruction of individualism implicit in egalitarianism would stifle enterprise and creativity, and the realization of the fine sounding theories of socialistic philosophers would culminate in a world of unbearable blandness. As the narrator of *The Coming Race* concludes:

It would be . . . utterly impossible to deny that the state of existence among the Vril-ya is thus, as a whole, immeasurably more felicitous than that of superterrestrial races, and, realizing the dreams of our most sanguine philanthropists, almost approaches to a poet's conception of some angelical order. And yet, if you would take a thousand of the best and most philosophical of human beings you can find in London, Paris, Berlin, New York, or even Boston, and place them as citizens in this beatified community, my belief is that in less than a year they would either die of *ennui*, or attempt some revolution by which they would militate against the good of the community, and be burned into cinders at the request of the Tur [chief magistrate].[72]

It is clear from *The Coming Race*, as well as from other novels, that Lytton continued to the end of his days to take an acute interest in public affairs and in the tides of opinion then prevailing. Yet, he no longer sought to play an active part in public life. The restless energy that had so long compelled him to participate in politics had at last run its course. He had his peerage, and there remained no other object for his ambition. He himself nicely summed up his attitude during his last years with respect to politics when, on arriving one day in London, he wrote his son:

> I came to town meditating all sorts of political action, but the cold and gloom of the weather have stricken me into inertia, and I am longing to get back to Torquay. . . . In youth one says, "What would I do were I in the position time gives to some senior." One gains the position and then says: "Ah, what would I do now, if I were but young."[73]

These last years were the most tranquil of Lytton's life. He had become calmer, more at ease, and not so sensitive as he had been. A fellow author, who visited him during this period, aptly described him as

> a "charming man," tranquil, almost Eastern, in manner, talking in a dreamy way. . . . His grave, deliberate, "finished" manner made a deep impression on me. His air and dress, the tones of his voice, seemed to favor this association with the East, which, perhaps, he sought to suggest.[74]

If Lytton had grown more serene, he apparently had not stopped trying to make an impression. His affected manner, in fact, frequently offended admirers of his writings who met him. For example, Wilkie Collins, for whom Lytton had been a boyhood idol, found him rather ridiculous in person, and mocked his "usual lofty gesture of throwing out his arm and lowering his voice."[75] Charles Reade, similarly, thought Lytton's manner "the height of transparent artifice" and "comic beyond the power of the pen to describe."[76] It was no wonder that Lytton's vanity became proverbial. Disraeli's comment on this subject is well known: when asked why he had not read Greville's *Memoirs*, he explained, "Greville was the vainest being . . . that I ever knew, and I have read Cicero and was intimate with Lytton Bulwer."[77]

Lytton liked to act the Great Author. But it should be remembered that that was how most of his contemporaries saw him. Despite his frequent complaints about hostile reviews, Lytton had many admirers. Edgar Allan Poe, for example, wrote:

> Who is there uniting in one person the imagination, the passion, the humor, the energy, the knowledge of the heart, the artist-like eye . . . of Edward Lytton Bulwer? In a vivid wit—in profundity and a Gothic massiveness of thought—in style—in a calm certainty . . . of purpose—in industry—and, above all, in the power of controlling and regulating, by volition, his illimitable faculties of mind, he is unequaled—he is unapproached.[78]

A preponderance of the public apparently agreed. "The giants of popular fiction," Edmund Gosse wrote, "did, indeed, enjoy larger single successes than Bulwer-Lytton did, but none of them, not Dickens himself, was so uniformly successful."[79]

Dickens was one of very few writers whose reputation, in their own day, surpassed Lytton's. The two men were good friends and admirers of each other's works, even if, as Disraeli believed, Lytton was "dying of jealousy and envy" of Dickens' superior stature.[80] It would seem however more likely that Lytton—who once described himself as "too vain to be jealous of any person"[81]—resented not so much Dickens' success as his borrowing from Lytton's works. The famous climax of *A Tale of Two Cities*, to cite one example, was obviously taken from *Zanoni*. But this by no means diminished the cordiality between the two men, and through the years each benefited from the counsel of the other. In the most famous incident of their relationship, however, it is open to question whether the result can be described as "beneficial." It was on Lytton's advice that Dickens altered *Great Expectations* to have it end happily with "Pip" getting married, a conclusion critics have ever since deplored as inappropriate to the story.[82]

Lytton's advice to Dickens on *Great Expectations*, "Don't leave Pip a lonely man," may have been a literary blunder but it was very revealing of the man.[83] He knew enough of loneliness in his own life, and longed for the "peace and happiness. . . [which], despite my own experiences I know. . . are best found—at the warm household hearth."[84] More valuable than success, he said, were "Health, Home, affections, tranquillity of mind—the esteem of the few *we* esteem. . . ."[85] These were the things he would never have. He had, to be sure, romantic relationships with other women after his separation from his wife;[86] but he could not remarry and thus he remained, unlike "Pip," a lonely man.

In his later years, especially, he seemed a melancholy figure. S. C. Hall, who knew him in youth, thus described him in old age:

His once handsome face had assumed the desolation without the dignity of age. His locks—once brown inclining to auburn—were shaggy and grizzled; his mouth, seldom smiling even in youth, was close shut; his whole aspect had something in it at once painful and unpleasant.[87]

Sir William Fraser, that great hero worshipper of the Victorian age, formed a similar if more sympathetic impression:

I have heard that in youth he was handsome: many men with good features retain a beautiful outline in age: there was nothing of this in Lord Lytton: a worn-out face, of extreme melancholy; a thin, aquiline nose; hair of a nondescript tint bordering on red; a rather high, but somewhat narrow forehead. I have never seen two more unhappy faces in repose than Lytton's and Disraeli's. Lord Lytton's figure was slim: he was active in his movements; and certainly had none of the languor of age in his gestures, nor mode of speaking . . . . [88]

Lytton indeed remained active to the end of his days and no doubt he found hard work a consolation. He was extremely methodical, and once observed significantly that "monotony, even under circumstances least favorable to the usual elements of happiness, becomes a happiness in itself. . . ."[89] His invariable habit was to write for four hours each morning, then go out at midday, and resume work after supper, continuing into the early hours of the morning.[90] To adhere to so severe a regimen, he found it necessary to soothe his nerves by using laudanum[91] and, more often, tobacco. He smoked eight to ten ounces of Latakia tobacco a week, employing a pipe seven feet long. In addition, his valet reported,

I always place seven cigars on the little table beside Sir Edward's bed, and when I go into his room at eight o'clock in the morning . . . , if I see two cigars left I awake him, and take his orders; if I find that he has smoked them all, I let him lie another hour.[92]

His methodical working habits account for his remarkable literary output, of which there was no let up, even in his last years. In the months preceding his death, he was hard at work on two novels simultaneously: *The Parisians*, which, though well advanced, was to remain unfinished; and *Kenelm Chillingly*, which he completed only days before his death, on January 18th, 1873, and which on its appearance became a sensational best-seller.[93]

Perhaps, as he worked furiously to finish *Kenelm Chillingly*, Lytton suspected he had not long to live. At all events, a letter he wrote to a confidante a month before his death gives us a clear idea of his state of mind at the time:

> The completion of my book naturally weighs much upon my mind and is attended with extreme bitterness of thought — in the certainty that nothing I do will ever be fairly estimated by an English Public influenced by English reviewers. I scarcely ever see a literary journal without seeing myself either insulted or ignored.[94]

Even on the threshold of death he fretted about the future, and feared the critics would deprive him of his rightful place in Letters. He had always placed great stress on posthumous reputation; there was some truth to Disraeli's remark that Lytton "never wrote an invitation to dinner without an eye to posterity."[95] Now he hoped that at least later generations would do him justice, as his own contemporaries had not. He expressed this hope rather pathetically in 1870 when he reissued his long poem *King Arthur*. This work had flopped when it first appeared in 1848; critics considered it an uninspired imitation of Pope. Yet Lytton always regarded it as the greatest of all his works and "immeasurably above the *Idylls of the King*."[96] In a preface to the 1870 edition, he thus explained the reason for its reappearance:

> A new generation has . . . grown up around me, to whose notice the present edition of the poem is offered . . . ; not without the hope of a wider audience among the generations that succeed. Such a hope is natural to every writer who has done his best to insure the elements of durability to his work; and if it be often an erroneous, it is never an ignoble one.

Those unfamiliar with the work, he added, should judge it "uninfluenced by the reports of those who would rather condemn without reading than read without condemning."[97]

The irony of these words is obvious. His plea to posterity fell on deaf ears, and within a generation after his death Lord Lytton was listed, if at all, among the minor authors. The acclaim he received from his contemporaries, which he thought inadequate, seems today far beyond his deserts. So precipitously did his reputation sink that it is now difficult to realize that he was truly, as Michael Sadleir put it, an individual who might have been one of the dominant figures of his age, had he but possessed the two or three special qualities which in England make for dominance; who might conversely, have ended in disaster but for his stubborn gallantry of mind. For Bulwer conquered without a sense of victory, failed where he thought to have achieved; and has become a legend half impressive, half absurd, to a posterity which can see his faults and read the satire of his enemies, but cannot appreciate wherein lay his power over his age, or understand why, if he was the great man he must have been, he was not greater still.[98]

This comment applies equally to his political as to his literary career. In youth, he set out to conquer the political world, armed with an exceptional intellect, enviable powers of expression, and thoughtful opinions on how to solve the problems of the age. While he never lived up to his early promise, he did over the course of his long career prove that he possessed real, practical ability. Though not a natural orator, by dint of hard work and determination he made himself a notable Parliamentary debater. Even during his brief, unhappy tenure at the Colonial Office, he showed flashes of constructive energy and vision that strongly suggest he had at least the makings of a statesman. All this being said, however, one can do no more than echo Sadleir: with such great gifts, why was he not greater still?

Bulwer-Lytton failed as a politician in large measure because he never learned to deal with other people. Aloof and high-strung, he could not play the hail-fellow-well-met. Disraeli, whose personality in so many ways resembled Bulwer-Lytton's, overcame this problem, and thus succeeded as Bulwer-Lytton never did. In one of his early novels, Disraeli wrote that,

> Yes we must mix with the herd; we must enter into their feelings; we must humor their weaknesses; we must sympathize with the sorrows we do not feel; and share the merriment of fools. Oh yes! to *rule* men we must be men. . . . Mankind then is my great game.[99]

Bulwer-Lytton never learned to play this game. Raised in isolation from other children by an adoring mother, he was by the age of eight "overcome by the sense of his own identity."[100] His subsequent experiences at school, where he found the mores of the other boys distasteful, only intensified his egocentrism; he became convinced, not unreasonably, of his intellectual superiority. Unfortunately, he acted ever after the part of an Olympian among mortals.

Inability to "mix with the herd" would prove his undoing in politics. Early in his career, he often bemoaned his exclusion from the inner councils of the Whigs; yet it is also true he could get along with only a handful of his fellow Radicals. Even after he had joined the Conservative party and become a front bencher, he remained on the periphery. Certainly Derby did not confide in him. Lord Henry Lennox observed in 1857 that during a three-day visit to a country house, Bulwer-Lytton was "in despair" because, "Not a word could he extract from Derby about Public affairs: nothing but the odds and tricks . . . ; he fell back on me; but of course I only told him as much as was good for him."[101] Such was Bulwer-Lytton's lot throughout his career.

His personality was even less suited to dealing with the electorate. It required a considerable effort of will for him to force himself to appear before the public, and though once having taken the icy plunge he could be effective on the hustings, he could never completely conceal his distaste for such endeavors. S. C. Hall commented that Bulwer-Lytton

> was thoroughly an aristocrat . . . ; although he sought, and thought, to connect himself with the hard-handed men of the working classes. I could fancy him scrupulously washing his hands after a meeting with his constituents.[102]

The repugnance with which Bulwer-Lytton regarded the vulgarity of politics did his career irreparable harm. The loss of his seat in Lincoln in 1841 was due in large measure to his failure to cultivate the constituency.[103] He was thirty-eight years old when he lost his seat, and did not return to Parliament until he was forty-nine. The prime years of manhood were thus, politically speaking, wasted. The years of his absence, moreover, saw great upheavals in the political world. Had he been in the House in 1846 at the time of the debate on the repeal of the Corn Laws, he might have become a central figure in the Protectionist party. When at last he took his place in that party, he showed himself able, especially during the Crimean War, to hold his own against the foremost Parliamentarians of the day. He did just well enough to make one wonder whether, had he not frittered away eleven years outside of politics, he might have done a great deal more.

In the end, however, he failed in his quest to achieve greatness as a statesman, just as he failed — in the judgment of posterity — to achieve greatness as an author. Yet, though he failed, he left his mark. Ironically, the contrast between the enviable literary reputation he enjoyed

215

in his own day and the obscurity into which he has descended since underscores his importance as a spokesman for the Victorian age. Whatever readers of today may think of his writings, they ought not forget that once he was read and admired by a vast public. Flawed as he was, Bulwer-Lytton understood his age and spoke to it, and it listened with satisfaction. As G. K. Chesterton put it:

> You could not have the Victorian age without him. . . . There was something in his half aristocratic swagger as poet and politician that made him . . . a real touchstone of his time.[104]

He reflected his age particularly in his political career. What could have been more "Victorian" than the emphasis he placed all his life on the importance of exercising a moral influence? The morality he advocated was not a force for repression, however, but a guarantor of the liberty of the individual. The security of personal liberty was as central to his thought as any other element. His famed vanity and aristocratic swagger, after all, reflected in fact an overdeveloped sense of individuality. As he once wrote,

> I am, and, as long as I live, I believe I shall be, a passionate lover of freedom. Individually, freedom is the vital necessity of my being. I can not endure to cripple my personal freedom for anything less than my obligation to duty. What I, as a man, thus prize for myself, I assume that each community of men should no less ardently prize.

Moral strictures, he continued, ought not be considered destructive of liberty, for,

> If I desire and will do that which I ought to do . . . and will not do that which I ought not to do, my freedom and my duty are practically one . . . . If, for instance, the principle of honor has become part and parcel of my mind, I can not pick pockets – the law against picking pockets is no restraint on me. If the law permitted me to do so, I still should not and could not pick a pocket.

The same principle, he added, applied to the state as well as to the individual: "that state will be the best in which liberty and order so . . . fuse into each other, that the conditions prescribed by order are not felt as restraints on liberty."[105]

This message has particular poignancy today. We equate "Victorian Morality" with repression. But the reaction against Victorianism has not fostered freedom. Merely shedding restraints does not mean gaining liberty.

Untrammeled greed and uninhibited license are far graver threats to freedom than any of the excesses of Victorian censorship. Only ethical and spiritual elevation make an individual or a society truly free. The apotheosis of liberty and morality appears each time an individual foregoes ephemeral advantage, restrained only by the dictates of his own conscience.

It was when he spoke in this cause that Bulwer-Lytton spoke to the ages.

NOTES

1. T. E. Kebbel, *Lord Beaconsfield and Other Tory Memories*, 16-17.

2. Monypenny and Buckle, *The Life of Benjamin Disraeli*, IV, 200-201.

3. Disraeli would seem to have been the author of the Bill. See Blake, *Disraeli*, 383.

4. Malmesbury, *Memoirs of an Ex-Minister*, II, 145.

5. Walling, *Diaries of John Bright*, 236.

6. This was the opinion of Palmerston and of Disraeli. See Earl of Lytton, II, 302; and Disraeli to Queen Victoria, March 22, 1859, in Monypenny and Buckle, *The Life of Benjamin Disraeli*, IV, 206.

7. *Hansard*, CLIII, 558.

8. *Ibid.*, 559.

9. *Ibid.*, 555.

10. Bulwer-Lytton had supported the Secret Ballot in the 1830's, but had become an opponent of the idea by the time he returned to Parliament in 1852, arguing that the Ballot had failed to prevent bribery and intimidation in America and France. Bulwer-Lytton, Speech at Hitchin, June 22, 1852, Lytton Papers, D/EK W98.

11. *Hansard*, CLIII, 554-555.

12. *Ibid.*, 556-557.

13. See Bulwer, *England and the English*, I, 233-243.

14. Quoted in Earl of Lytton, II, 200.

15. Bulwer-Lytton, *My Novel,* (New York: J. F. Taylor, 1896), I, 256.

16. Quoted in Earl of Lytton, ed., *Speeches of Edward Lord Lytton* (Edinburgh: Wm. Blackwood, 1874), I, 179.

17. *Ibid.*, 182.

18. *Ibid.*, cii.

19. Bulwer-Lytton, *Caxtoniana*, 441.

20. Bulwer-Lytton, Speech at Bishop Stortford School, July, 1856, in Lytton Papers, D/EK W99.

21. Bulwer-Lytton to Henry Drummond Wolff, April 1, 1859, in Earl of Lytton, II, 308.

22. *Hansard*, CLIII, 558.

23. Bulwer-Lytton to Forster, April 19, 1860, Lytton Papers, D/EK C27.

24. McCarthy, *History of Our Own Times*, II, 173.

25. Bulwer-Lytton's arguments in this speech were essentially those he used in his 1859 address supporting the Conservative Reform Bill. See *Hansard*, CLVIII, 143-166.

26. Donald Southgate, *The Passing of the Whigs* (London: Macmillan, 1962), 293.

27. Bulwer-Lytton, as we have seen, had long opposed the malt tax. In this instance, he supported a motion brought forward by Fitzroy Kelly against Disraeli's wishes. See Monypenny and Buckle, *The Life of Benjamin Disraeli*, IV, 406.

28. Bulwer-Lytton to Disraeli, n.d., Hughenden Papers, Box 104, B/11/ly.

29. Bulwer-Lytton to Disraeli, February 4, 1863, *Ibid*; Bulwer-Lytton to Henry Drummond Wolff, February 3, 1863, and same to same, February 12, 1863, in Drummond Wolff, *Rambling Recollections*, I, 394-395.

30. Benjamin Disraeli, "Biographical Reminiscences," Hughenden Papers, Box 26, parts 26, 39.

31. Bulwer-Lytton to Disraeli, January 20, 1864, *Ibid.*, Box 104, B/xx/ly.

32. Bulwer-Lytton to Robert Lytton, January 20, 1864, Earl of Lytton, II, 356.

33. Bulwer-Lytton to Forster, January 20, 1864, Lytton Papers, D/EK C27.

34. Bulwer-Lytton to R. W. Gaussen, June 6, 1865, *Ibid.*, D/EK C26.

35. Bulwer-Lytton to Robert Lytton, October 18, 1865, Earl of Lytton, II, 362.

36. Quoted in Monypenny and Buckle, *The Life of Benjamin Disraeli*, IV, 432.

37. See *Ibid.*

38. *Hansard*, CLXXXII, 1247.

39. *Ibid.*, 1241.

40. Bulwer-Lytton to Forster, April 19, 1860, Lytton Papers, D/EK C27.

41. Bulwer-Lytton to William Kent, April 28, 1866, Boston Public Library.

42. *Hansard*, CLXXXII, 1244.

43. Lytton to William Kent, January 27, 1867, Boston Public Library.

44. See Charles Lever to John Blackwood, July 2, 1866, in Edmund Downey, *Charles Lever* (Edinburgh: Wm. Blackwood, 1906), II, 159-160.

45. Lytton to Robert Lytton, July 31, 1866, Earl of Lytton, II, 369.

46. *Ibid.*

47. Lytton to Forster, n.d., Lytton Papers, D/EK C27.

48. See Blake, *Disraeli*, 438-444.

49. Lytton to William Kent, March 24, 1867, Boston Public Library.

50. Blake, *Disraeli*, 444-459.

51. Lytton, Speech For House of Lords On Reform Bill, Lytton Papers, D/EK W99.

52. Blake, *Disraeli*, 457.

53. *Ibid.*, 458-459.

54. See for example, Bulwer-Lytton, *What Will He Do With It?* (Boston: Aldine, n.d.), 5-6.

55. Bulwer-Lytton, *My Novel*, I, 338-341.

56. Lytton, Speech For House of Lord on Reform Bill, Lytton Papers, D/EK W99.

57. *Ibid.*

58. *Ibid.*

59. Bulwer-Lytton, *Kenelm Chillingly* (Boston: Little Brown, 1893), I, 348, 384.

60. Lytton to William Kent, February 20, 1868, Boston Public Library.

61. Same to same, May 11, 1868, Parrish Collection, Princeton University.

62. Lytton to Robert Lytton, 1868, Earl of Lytton, II, 448.

63. Lytton to Forster, December 12, 1868, Lytton Papers, D/EK C27.

64. Lytton to W. Meynell, November 29, 1868, *Ibid.*, D/EK C26.

65. Lytton to F. W. Farrar, August 4, 1870, *Ibid.*

66. Lytton to Abraham Hayward, June 30, 1871, in Carlisle, *Correspondence of Abraham Hayward*, II, 230.

67. Lytton to Derby, June 6, 1869, Lytton Papers, D/EK C26.

68. Lytton to Benjamin Hall Kennedy, October 12, 1869, *Ibid.*

69. Bulwer-Lytton, *The Coming Race* (New York: F. M. Lupton), 5.

70. *Ibid.*, 55. On the comparison between the "vril" and nuclear energy, see Christensen, *Edward Bulwer-Lytton*, 178-180.

71. Bulwer-Lytton, *The Coming Race*, 66.

72. *Ibid.*, 113.

73. Lytton to Robert Lytton, February 14, 1870, Earl of Lytton, II, 459.

74. Percy Fitzgerald, *Memoirs of an Author* (London: Richard Bentley, 1895), I, 131-132.

75. Quoted in Nuel Pharr Davis, *The Life of Wilkie Collins* (Urbana: University of Illinois, 1956), 231.

76. Reade also described Lytton as "wonderfully like Mephistopheles, as drawn by German artists," and he quoted Lytton saying he had *"photographs* of *maniacs* in different postures. . . ." See Charles L. Reade and Rev. Compton Reade, *Charles Reade* (New York: Harper, 1887), 263-266. It should be noted, however, that Reade was a friend of Lady Lytton's. See Wayne Burns, *Charles Reade - A Study in Victorian Authorship* (New York: Bookman, 1961), 233.

77. Disraeli to Lady Chesterfield, October 26, 1874, in Marquis of Zetland, ed., *The Letters of Disraeli to Lady Chesterfield and Lady Bradford* (New York: D. Appleton, 1929), I, 209.

78. Edgar Allan Poe, *The Works of Edgar Allan Poe*, ed. by Edmund Clarence Stedman (Chicago: Stone & Kimball, 1895), VII, 277.

79. Edmund Gosse, *Some Diversions of a Man of Letters*, 128.

80. Disraeli, "Biographical Reminiscences," Hughenden Papers, Box 26, part 36.

81. Bulwer to Mrs. Cunningham, October 15, 1826, Lytton Papers, D/EK C26.

82. On this point, and other aspects of the relationship between Dickens and Bulwer-Lytton, see Jack Lindsay, *Charles Dickens* (London: Andrew Dakers, 1950), 114, 196-198, 345-364, and *passim.* One should also note that Dickens named one of his sons Edward Bulwer Lytton Dickens.

83. On this point, see Richard Renton, *John Forster and His Friendships* (London: Chapman & Hall, 1912), 151.

84. Bulwer-Lytton to William Kent, June 13, 1853, Boston Public Library.

85. Bulwer-Lytton to Mrs. Gascoyne, September 21, 1853, Parrish Collection, Princeton University.

86. See Earl of Lytton, II, 503-504.

87. S. C. Hall, *Retrospect of a Long Life* (New York: D. Appleton, 1883), 155.

88. Fraser, *Hic Et Ubique*, 55.

89. Bulwer-Lytton, "On Monotony in Occupation as a Source of Happiness," in *Caxtoniana*, 31-32.

90. See Earl of Lytton, II, 18.

91. Davis, *The Life of Wilkie Collins*, 231.

92. Quoted in Earl of Lytton, II, 19.

93. *Ibid.*, 16, 480-484, 500.

94. Lytton to Lady Sherborne, December, 1872, Lytton Papers, D/EK C26.

95. Disraeli, "Biographical Reminiscences," Hughenden Papers, Box 26, part 34.

96. Lytton to Forster, July 9, 1870, Lytton Papers, D/EK C26. On *King Arthur*, See Earl of Lytton, II, 469-473.

97. Lytton, *King Arthur* (New York: Harper Brothers, 1871), v.

98. Sadleir, *Bulwer: A Panorama*, v.

99. Quoted by Blake, *Disraeli*, 23.

100. Earl of Lytton, I, 36.

101. Lord Henry Lennox to Disraeli, January 7, 1857, in *Ibid.*, 354.

102. Hall, *Retrospect of a Long Life*, 155.

103. See above, Chapter Four.

104. G. K. Chesterton, *The Victorian Age in Literature* (New York: Henry Holt, 1913), 136-137.

105. Bulwer-Lytton, *Caxtoniana*, 432-433.

BIBLIOGRAPHY

The leading biography of Bulwer-Lytton remains that written by his grandson, the Second Earl of Lytton. An accomplished author and statesman in his own right, Victor, Lord Lytton wrote with a degree of skill and objectivity seldom found in official biographies written by relatives. His work superseded that of his own father, Robert, the First Earl of Lytton, who had attempted to write the official life of Bulwer-Lytton, but only covered the period up to the early 1830's. Later, Michael Sadleir wrote an outstanding study of Bulwer-Lytton's early years, from 1803 to 1836. The older biography by T.H.S. Escott is of relatively little value.

· The present work is based primarily on research in the Lytton Papers in the Hertfordshire County Record Office. These papers were collected in connnection with the preparation of the official biographies by Bulwer-Lytton's son and grandson. The papers are well organized and provide a mine of information about Bulwer-Lytton and his era.

MANUSCRIPT COLLECTIONS

Boston Public Library, Boston, Massachusetts

Firestone Library, Princeton, New Jersey
    Parrish Collection

Hertfordshire County Record Office, Hertford
    Lytton Papers

Hughenden, High Wycombe
    Hughenden Papers

Huntington Library, San Marino, California

University of Nottingham Library, Nottingham

A SELECTION OF WRITINGS BY EDWARD BULWER-LYTTON

Books:

Alice (1838). Rpt. Philadelphia: J.B. Lippincott, 1881.

Caxtoniana (1863). Rpt. New York: Harper & Brothers, 1864.

The Caxtons (1849). Rpt. London: George Routledge, 1880.

The Coming Race (1871). Rpt, New York: J.F. Taylor, 1897.

England and the English. Two Volumes. New York: J.J. Harper, 1833.

King Arthur. New York: Harper Brothers, 1871.

The Last Days of Pompeii (1834). Rpt. New York: J.F. Taylor, 1898.

Letters of the late Edward Bulwer, Lord Lytton to His Wife.
  Edited by Louisa Devey. New York: G. W. Dillingham, 1889.

Letters to John Bull. London: Chapman & Hall, 1851.

My Novel. Four Volumes (1853). Rpt. New York: J.F. Taylor, 1897.

Paul Clifford (1830). Rpt. New York: Hurst, 1880.

Pelham (1828). Rpt. New York: Popular Library, 1974.

Rienzi - The Last of the Roman Tribunes (1835). Rpt. New York: Charles
  Scribner, 1905.

Speeches of Edward Lord Lytton. Edited by the Earl of Lytton. Two
  Volumes. Edinburgh: Wm. Blackwood, 1874.

What Will He Do With It? (1858). Rpt. Boston: Aldine, n.d.

Zanoni (1842). Rpt. Boston: Little, Brown, 1893.

Articles:

"Arrest of the Five Members by Charles the First." *Quarterly Review*, 108 (October, 1860), 499-547.

"Defense of the Whigs." *Edinburgh Review* 70 (October, 1839), 245-281.

"England and Her Institutions." *Quarterly Review*, 120 (October, 1866), 536-560.

"The People's Charter." *Monthly Chronicle* (October, 1838), 297-302.

"Pitt and Fox." *Quarterly Review*, 97 (September, 1855), 513-590.

"Present State and Conduct of Parties." *Edinburgh Review*, 71 (April, 1840), 275-314.

"The Reign of Terror: Its Causes and Results." *Foreign Quarterly Review*, 58 (July, 1842), 275-309.

SECONDARY WORKS

Alison, Sir Archibald. *My Life and Writings*. Two Volumes. Edinburgh: Wm. Blackwood, 1883.

Bell, Kenneth N. and Morrell, W.P., eds. *Select Documents on British Colonial Policy 1830-1860*. Oxford: Clarendon Press, 1928.

Benson, Arthur C. and Esher, Viscount. *The Letters of Queen Victoria*. Three Volumes. London: John Murray, 1908.

Besant, Walter. *Fifty Years Ago*. New York: Harper & Bros., 1890.

Blain, Virginia. "Rosina Bulwer-Lytton and the Rage of the Unheard." *Huntington Library Quarterly*, 53 (Summer 1990), 211-236.

Blake, Robert. *Disraeli*. New York: Anchor Books, 1968.

Briggs, Asa. *The Making of Modern Engalnd* 1783-1867. New York: Harper & Row, 1965.

Briggs, Asa. *Victorian People*. Chicago: University of Chicago Press, 1970.

Broughton, Lord. *Recollections of a Long Life*. Edited by Charlotte Hobhouse Carleton. Six Volumes. London: John Murray, 1911.

Burns, Wayne. *Charles Reade - A Study in Victorian Authorship*. New York: Bookman Associates, 1961.

Cell, John W. *British Colonial Administration in the Mid-Nineteenth Century*. New Haven: Yale University, 1970.

Chesterton, G.K. *The Victorian Age in Literature*. New York: Henry Holt, 1913.

Christensen, Allen C. *Edward Bulwer-Lytton*. Athens: University of Georgia, 1976.

Davis, Nuel Pharr. *The Life of Wilkie Collins*. Urbana: University of Illinois, 1956.

Devey, Louisa. *Life of Rosina, Lady Lytton*. London: Swan Sonnenschein, Lowrey, 1887.

Dod, Charles R. *Electoral Facts from 1832-1853*. Brighton: Harvester Press, 1972.

Downey, Edmund. *Charles Lever*. Two Volumes. Edinburgh: Wm. Blackwood, 1906.

Duncombe, Thomas H. ed. *The Life and Correspondence of Thomas Slingsby Duncombe*. Two Volumes. London: Hurst and Blackett, 1868.

Edsall, Nicholas. *Richard Cobden-Independent Radical*. Cambridge: Harvard University Press, 1986.

Escott, T.H.S. *Edward Bulwer, First Baron Lytton of Knebworth*. London: George Routledge, 1911.

Escott, T.H.S. *Society in the Country House*. Philadelphia: George W. Jacobs, 1907.

Feiling, Sir Keith. *Sketches in Nineteenth Century Biography*. London: Longmans, Green, 1930.

Fitzgerald, Percy. *Memoirs of an Author*. Two Volumes. London: Richard Bentley, 1895.

Flower, Sibylla Jane. *Bulwer-Lytton*. Aylesbury: Shire Publications Ltd., 1973.

Fraser, Sir William. *Hic Et Ubique*. London: Sampson, Low, 1893.

Frost, Alfred William. *Bulwer-Lytton*. London: Lynwood, 1913.

Galbraith, John S. *The Hudson's Bay Company As An Imperial Factor*. Berkeley: University of California, 1957.

Gosse, Edmund. *Some Diversions of a Man of Letters*. London: William Hunemann, 1919.

Grote, Harriet. *The Philosophical Radicals of 1832*. New York: Burt Franklin, 1970.

Hall, Henry L. *The Colonial Office*. London: Longmans, Green, 1937.

Hall, S. C. *Retrospect of a Long Life*. New York: D. Appleton, 1883.

Hardinge, Sir Arthur. *The Life and Correspondence of Henry Howard Molyneux Herbert, Fourth Earl of Carnarvon*. Three Volumes. London: Humphrey Milford, 1925.

Hollingsworth, Keith. *The Newgate Novel 1830-1847*. Detroit: Wayne State, 1963.

Holloway, John. *The Victorian Sage*. New York: W.W. Norton, 1965.

Houghton, Walter. *The Victorian Frame of Mind.* New Haven: Yale University, 1972.

Jones, Wilbur. *Lord Derby and Victorian Conservatism.* Athens: University of Georgia, 1956.

Kebbel, T.E. *Lord Beaconsfield and Other Tory Memories.* New York: Mitchell Kennerly, 1907.

Keith, Arthur Berriedale, ed. *Selected Speeches and Documents on British Colonial Policy, 1763-1917.* Two Volumes. London: Oxford University, 1918.

Lindsay, Jack. *Charles Dickens.* London: Andrew Dakers, 1950.

Longford, Elizabeth. *Queen Victoria-Born to Succeed.* New York: Harper & Row, 1965.

List of the Poll . . . For the City of Lincoln. Lincoln: John Stanton, 1847.

Lutyens, Emily. *The Birth of Rowland.* London: Rupert Hart Davis, 1956.

Lytton, Robert, First Earl of. *The Life, Letters and Literary Remains of Edward Bulwer, Lord Lytton.* New York: Harper & Brothers, 1884.

Lytton, Victor, Earl of. *Bulwer Lytton,* London: Horn and Van Thal, 1948.

Lytton, Victor, Earl of. *The Life of Edward Bulwer,* First Lord Lytton. Two Volumes. London: Macmillan, 1913.

Malmesbury, Earl of. *Memoirs of an Ex-Minister.* Two Volumes. London: Longmans, Green, 1884.

Matthew, H.C.G. *The Gladstone Diaries.* Six Volumes. Oxford: Clarendon Press, 1978.

McCarthy, Justin. *A History of Our Own Times.* Two Volumes. New York: Harper & Brothers, 1881.

Mineka, Francis E., ed. *The Earlier Letters of John Stuart Mill.* Toronto: University of Toronto, 1963.

Monypenny, W.F. and Buckle, G.E. *The Life of Benjamin Disraeli.* Six Volumes. New York: Macmillan, 1910-1920.

Morley, John. *The Life of William Ewart Gladstone.* Three Volumes. New York: Macmillan, 1903.

Morrell, W.P. *British Colonial Policy in the Mid-Victorian Age.* Oxford: Clarendon Press, 1969.

Nicholson, Watson. *The Struggle For A Free Stage in London.* New York: Benjamin Bloom, 1966.

Ormsby, Margaret A. *British Columbia: A History.* Vancouver: Macmillan, 1959.

Prest, John. *Lord John Russell.* London: Macmillan, 1972.

Rathburn, Robert C. and Steinmann, Martin, eds. *Jane Austen to Joseph Conrad.* Minneapolis: University of Minnesota, 1958.

Raymond, E. Neill. *Victorian Viceroy-The Life of Robert, The First Earl of Lytton.* London: Regency Press, 1980.

Reade, Charles L. and Rev. Compton Reade. *Charles Reade.* New York: Harper, 1887.

Rees, William Lees and Rees, L. *The Life and Times of Sir George Grey.* London: Hutchinson, [1892].

Renton, Richard. *John Forster and His Friendships.* London: Chapman & Hall, 1912.

Ridley, Jasper. *Lord Palmerston.* New York: E.P. Dutton, 1971.

Sadleir, Michael. *Bulwer: A Panorama.* Boston: Little, Brown, 1931.

230

Sadleir, Michael. *The Strange Life of Lady Blessington*. Boston: Little, Brown, 1933.

Stanley, George F. G. *The Birth of Western Canada*. Toronto: University of Toronto, 1961.

Walker, Eric, ed. *The Cambridge History of the British Empire, VIII, South Africa, Rhodesia and the High Commission Territories*. Cambridge: Cambridge University, 1963.

Walling, R.A.J., ed. *The Diaries of John Bright*. London: Cassell, 1930.

Webb, R. K. *Modern England*. New York: Dodd, Mead & Company, 1969.

Whibley, Charles. *Lord John Manners and His Friends*. Two Volumes. Edinburgh: William Blackwood and Sons, 1925.

Wilkinson, William J. *Tory Democracy*. New York: Columbia University, 1925.

Wolff, Sir Henry Drummond. *Rambling Recollections*. Two Volumes. London: Macmillan, 1908.

Wrong, E.M. *Charles Buller and Responsible Government*. Oxford: Clarendon Press, 1926.

Zetland, Marquis of, ed. *The Letters of Disraeli To Lady Chesterfield and Lady Bradford*. Two Volumes. New York: D. Appleton, 1929.

NEWSPAPERS

Hereford Times
Hertford Mercury
Illustrated London News
The Standard
The Times (London)